SEX
SLAVES

SEX SLAVES

The Trafficking of Women in Asia

LOUISE BROWN

Half of the author's profits from the sale of this book will be
divided equally between Sanlaap, Calcutta,
and The Cambodian Women's Crisis Center, Phnom Penh

A *Virago* Book

First published by Virago Press 2000
This edition published by Virago Press 2001
Reprinted 2001

A CIP catalogue record for this book
is available from the British Library.

ISBN 1 86049 903 1

Typeset in Minion by M Rules
Printed and bound in Great Britain by
Clays Ltd, St Ives plc

Virago
A Division of
Little, Brown and Company (UK)
Brettenham House
Lancaster Place
London WC2E 7EN

For 'Dolly'

CONTENTS

CONTENTS

PREFACE

This book would have been impossible to write without the help of many individuals and organisations working on the problems associated with prostitution and trafficking in Asia. These included non-governmental organisations, governmental bodies, international agencies, human rights groups, political activists, journalists, lawyers and medics. Far too many people helped me with their time, experience and contacts for me to list them all here and it would be very unfair to name only a few. Many, for political or professional reasons, or for reasons of personal safety, also wanted to remain anonymous. I would like to take this opportunity to convey my thanks to every one because, as any author knows, a book is never the work of a single individual. So many people have made such a substantial contribution to my work that this book is as much a reflection of their experiences and effort as it is mine.

Prostitution is not a subject that is easily tackled using traditional research methodology. Standard research techniques were particularly useless when the issues to be investigated were trafficking and sexual slavery, as the slave owners were understandably sensitive about an outsider interviewing the slaves. Close observation of the girls' time with their clients was also out of the question, and approaching clients directly proved to be personally risky.

Practising sex workers were one of my principal sources of information. Interviews with a large proportion of these women were short. At times this was because they had to get back to work and sometimes it was because they were under the control of a pimp or a brothel keeper. Many of the sex workers who had achieved a degree of independence welcomed me into their homes with a generosity of time and a warmth of spirit. They were not obliged to do this and I am eternally grateful for their kindness in helping me to understand the shape of their lives and what had brought them into prostitution. Some of the most rewarding hours of my life were spent in the company of these women. My thanks for this can never be adequate enough.

Girls and very young women who have survived the trauma of sexual slavery provided the most detailed and the most harrowing information. In general, these were girls who had escaped from brothels and who were staying in shelter homes. They told their stories in painful detail and I am indebted to them for their courage and for their willingness to relive such traumatic events. Their bravery provides the substance upon which this book is built.

The resilience of these young women has taught me a great deal about the stereotypical weakness and subservience of Asian women. This stereotype is a myth. Poor Asian women may be vulnerable, and many may be subject to terrible abuse, but they are not weak. There is a world of difference between these two descriptions. I have been privileged to witness remarkable reserves of psychological strength in young women who have suffered immense physical and emotional tortures. I have learned a humbling respect and an enormous admiration for the girls and young women who, after being treated as sub-human and sold like livestock, have then managed to rebuild their lives. These girls and women are the greatest contributors to this account of trafficking and sexual slavery. In order to preserve their anonymity and privacy I promised to remove their real names from print whilst keeping the substance of their stories intact. Wherever possible I have told the stories in the words of the girls and the women themselves. I hope I have kept their faith and I pray that I have done them justice.

I would like to express my gratitude to the Nuffield Foundation, which funded my research in South Asia. My thanks also need to be extended to the University of Birmingham, which granted me a sabbatical to undertake some of the necessary travel. My parents, Julie and Peter Brown, deserve an extra special mention in any list of acknowledgements, as they took such loving care of my three young children during the long months while I was away from home. And I cannot forget to thank my assistants, Rosie, Lorna and Joseph, who endured a preoccupied mother while I wrote about a subject they could not even begin to understand.

I am sure that some of the most important contributors to this record and interpretation of sexual slavery and the trafficking of women will disagree with its perspective. The views I express are not those of any organisation with which I am professionally associated. The conclusions, as well as the failings, of the book are entirely my own responsibility.

Birmingham, England
January 2000

Chapter One

THE MARKET

I met Sahana when she was nineteen years old. She was an illiterate Nepali woman who possessed two valuable qualities: she was young and she was pretty. Her face earned her family the equivalent of fifty pounds when she was sold, aged twelve, to a brothel in India. It also earned her ten customers a day and HIV. She no longer works as a prostitute. This is not because she has been rescued from prostitution, or because she has found a happier livelihood, but because she is going to die. She was ejected from her caged brothel in Mumbai because she had become too thin to attract the clients, and the brothel owner thought she was a bad advertisement for business.

Stories like Sahana's have become clichés. But, staggeringly, even clichés like these can still be true. All over the world women are sold, tricked, forced or lured into prostitution. They are incarcerated in brothels and girls who are little more than children are compelled to service innumerable clients. They are unable to refuse the customers and unable to escape from brothels that are nothing but prisons. These tales are not myths or figments in the imagination of journalists looking for new angles on an old story. They are ancient horror stories, and they are contemporary ones too, shared by hundreds of thousands of girls and young women.

These women are modern-day sex slaves – and Asia, in particular, has far more than its fair share of them. Perhaps this is only to be expected. It should come as no surprise that societies that practise female infanticide, that have millions of 'missing' women, that have 'dying rooms' in orphanages for unwanted daughters, and that systematically discriminate against females should also sell girls and young women for sex. The question that produces far more surprising answers is: who is buying them?

Research on the trafficking of women and systems of sexual slavery in Asia is a revelation because it gives a stark insight into the real workings of a society. The view from the barred window of a closed brothel is very different from the sunny picture of happily regulated sexuality that is commonly described by the spokespersons of Asian societies.

At the beginning of the 1990s I lived with my family in Nepal. During the two years I spent in the beautiful Kathmandu Valley I had some vague awareness of the migration and export of Nepali girls to north Indian brothels. It was one of Nepal's many dreadful social problems and was considered a by-product of the country's appalling poverty. Like most other people in the circles in which I mixed, I thought it was a relatively minor issue. In hindsight, these views must have been coloured by the fact that the girls and women involved were poor, rural, powerless and silent. They were ignored because they were unimportant in the busy world of Kathmandu's political elites. Eight years on, and after interviewing dozens of Nepali women involved in sex work, I have changed my mind about the significance and the importance of these women's lives.

Back in England I began to teach Japanese history and politics at the University of Birmingham. Despite the vast differences between the levels of economic development in Nepal and Japan, I gradually became aware that the two countries shared some similar but discreet patterns. In particular, Japan has an image of an impeccably clean and ordered society. So why were there reports, tucked away in the press, of Thai and Filipina women who had suffered grievous harm at the hands of the Japanese sex industry? And why did their stories bear such striking similarity to the stories of Nepali women in Indian brothels? Eventually it made a kind of sense. The stories were the same because trafficking and prostitution are part of a vast and global industry. And in Asia this industry is just about as vigorous – and as hidden – as you can possibly find.

Commercial sex is widespread in Asia. In fact, it is probably even more common than in the West. The difference is that it is a very, very quiet business. The West has highly visible sex industries. Female sexuality is used to sell virtually all products, and sex is bought on the streets, in brothels, in massage parlours, in clubs and through advertisements. Asia has a similar phenomenon, but you have to be an Asian man to know where to look for it. That is why it is hard to write about the sale of sex in the region. It is also why it is important for the rest of the world to listen to the experiences of women who sell sex, and to the experiences of women who are sold for sexual recreation in Asia. It is especially important when the consumers of these young women and girls are men who are supposed to be too morally upstanding to be buying the product in the first instance.

The people who endure the grossest forms of commercial sexual abuse throughout the world are those who are at the bottom of lots of different, and very complicated, hierarchies. They are female, they are from poor families in poor communities, and they belong to despised racial and ethnic minorities. They are abused and exploited, and a proportion are locked into sexual slavery precisely, and simply, because they *can* be: they are society's most vulnerable people. In Asia there is plenty of opportunity for the creation and maintenance of systems of sexual slavery because there are such massive differences between the rich and the poor and because Asia is the grim home to some of the worst gender discrimination on earth.

The trafficking of women for prostitution is a global phenomenon and so it might appear unfair to single out Asia for specific criticism. Research on prostitution in the former Soviet Union, in Eastern Europe and in Latin America would probably yield broadly similar results. Female sexual slavery is found everywhere. Asia, however, is worthy of special attention because it is here that the industry and trafficking networks are most sophisticated and well developed. Ironically – and astonishingly – it is also a part of the world in which the local men are thought not to buy sex.

In addition, Asia, along with South and Central America, is a region in which the scandal of child prostitution is acute. And this cannot simply be because Western paedophiles visit Asian countries to buy sex with children. There are so many child prostitutes in Asia that the demand for their services must also be coming from another, far more important quarter.

Evidence from organisations working with prostitutes indicates that the average age of sex workers in Asia has been falling in the past decade. In large parts of the region prostitutes begin selling sex when they are children. The sex industry likes cheap and compliant staff and the customers prefer disease-free teenagers. The most disturbing aspect of the sex business that I encountered, and the hardest to accept, was the fact that when Asian men buy sex they seem to prefer to buy girls and not women. The premium age for prostitutes in Asia is between thirteen and sixteen. Virgin girls are in greatest demand and the price that the customers are willing to pay for them is very, very high. As I interviewed former child prostitutes in South Asia, I was acutely aware that these girls had begun work at around, or even before, the age of puberty.

Asia-bashing has become something of a sport in the West in the past three or four years. The 1997 Asian economic crisis provided

Western critics with an antidote to the wearisome and worrying success of Asian economies, and more than a few observers were smug that Asia's economic invincibility and the superiority of its economic models had proved to be myths. Asian economies are recovering well from the financial crisis but there are other, even greater, myths about Asia which need to be challenged.

Asia is commonly portrayed as the home of wholesome family values and conservative sexual morality. This would be hilarious if its impact upon women, and particularly prostituted women, was not so devastating. A fashionable debate emerged a few years ago about the importance of 'Asian values' in the success of South-East and East Asian economies. Although this debate was never wholly convincing, especially as Asia is so diverse, a core set of values was identified as 'Asian'. These included the attachment of an individual to his or her family; respect for authority; the importance of education and thrift; deference to established social structures; and adherence to conservative social and sexual codes. While studying the Asian sex industry I began to think that some important things might have been missing from this list. Perhaps we also need to add hypocrisy and men's contempt for women.

I do not wish to depict the West as a great model of social and sexual morality. Analysis of Asian men's prostitute use is not intended to glorify Western sexual and social ethics. All societies have their problems and European and North American societies have just as many, if not more, than anywhere else. But the violence, the social decay and the inescapable world of commercial sex in Western societies are on show for the entire world to see. They can be criticised and damned. Asian societies, however, hide their problems away. In fact they are not even acknowledged as problems. I have sat through too many work-related meetings and attended too many social functions in which educated Asian men have flatly denied that there is any incidence of prostitution in their own societies. They should be more honest. Vice, we are told, is the preserve of the decadent West and Asia has a superior moral and sexual code. This message should be sent to the sex slaves of Asia's closed brothels to debate. Unfortunately no one is likely to let them out in order for them to receive it. That, precisely, is the point.

All societies moralise. And we should be aware by now that what is portrayed in public discourse as normal sexual conduct is often very different from what people actually do in private. From a Western perspective there seems to be a vast gulf between Asian societies' emphasis upon the family and the reality of men's sexual practices. This gulf between theory and practice can be explained, in part, by the fact that we are not comparing the same thing. The rather vague concept of 'family values' will inevitably vary within different cultural contexts. In Western societies there is an assumption that fidelity is a requirement of marriage. Most classes within most Asian societies, on the other hand, do not make this assumption – at least not in practice. In this respect there is no hypocrisy in the Asian family values system. Men hold family values very dearly but in an Asian setting family values mean stability of the family unit. They mean that the family sticks together and that divorces are frowned upon. Yet the size of the sex industry suggests that those same values do not necessarily require that a husband must be faithful to his wife. In this case the only hypocrisy lies in the farcical assertion that Asian men uniformly adhere to a conservative sexual code that stresses fidelity and virtue.

In most Asian societies sex and the family are two almost wholly separate facets of a man's life. Marriage, reproduction and the family are economic and social contracts. Sex is an obligation within this contract but it is not something that necessarily has to be good, or to be enjoyed, or to be consistently practised – although, of course, it helps. Sex is a recreation, a sport which men – and only men – can legitimately pursue outside the confines of the marriage bed. Adventures with mistresses and frequent tumbles with prostitutes are accommodated within this framework firstly because wives are not really threatened by their husband's dalliances. After all, sex is not what their marriage is all about. Secondly, there is absolutely nothing a wife can do if she objects to her husband's behaviour. In other words men can buy sex because they can get away with it. Finally, there is a pool of women to indulge these men in their sexual sports. Some of these women are willing and, if there are not enough young women who are willing to sell their bodies, then the sex industry can be guaranteed to furnish some unwilling ones too. For most of the customers the difference is unnoticed and sometimes unappreciated. For some it is a positive stimulant.

The prostitutes that these men enjoy are stigmatised women. This is especially true in South Asia. Time after time sex workers refer to themselves as being 'outside society'. And they are right – they are despised outcastes. Yet, paradoxically, far from being outside society they are at its very core. They are not peripheral to the social system because they are vital to its functioning. We can learn a lot about the structure of a society from analysing prostitution. In the Asian case, we might have good cause to think that family values and prostitution are just opposite sides of exactly the same coin.

Today's Asian sex industry has been built on some solid and very nasty foundations. Women have traditionally been a commodity to be exchanged, and in the nineteenth century the commodity acquired a market value in rapidly commercialising Asian economies. The first large-scale commercial trafficking involved Chinese women who were sold to brothels in Malaya, Singapore and modern-day Thailand in order to provide sexual services to single or unaccompanied Chinese male migrant labourers. Women were also sent as far as the United States for the same purpose. In the 1880s impoverished Japanese girls known as *karayuki-san* were exported to South-east Asia to provide sexual services. Now it is the second largest economy in the world, Japan does not need to export its women. Instead, it has reversed the flow and imports poor women from other countries.

The most well-publicised antecedent of modern-day sexual slavery in the region is Japan's forced recruitment of over 100,000 girls
and women during the Second World War. These girls, most of
whom were Korean, are known euphemistically as the 'Comfort
Women' and they were rounded up for use as prostitutes in military
brothels.[1] Most were teenagers and young women when they were
recruited. Many never made it into full adulthood. They served up
to seventy soldiers a day who stood in lines outside the girls' rooms.
The demand was so great that some of the girls did not even have a
chance to move off their beds. Unsurprisingly, many died, committed suicide or were killed by the Japanese when it was apparent that
they would lose the war. Those that survived were too traumatised
and shamed by their experiences to even mention this war crime
until a handful of elderly survivors gathered the courage to speak
out over forty years after the event. Perhaps most significantly of all,
this vile episode was condoned, and even orchestrated, by the
Japanese Imperial Army.

Asia's sex industry went from strength to strength after the war.
Three things were absolutely crucial to its development. First, and
most important, was the region's economic development. Mass
prostitution did not really exist in traditional Asia. The region was
rural, feudal and poor. Women were chattels and were sexually
exploited but this usually took the form of concubinage or the land-
lords' sexual access to local peasant girls. This began to change
during the colonial period and, after the Second World War, it
altered more dramatically. Parts of the region, particularly in East
and South-east Asia, became more affluent. The pace of urbanisa-
tion and industrialisation increased and large numbers of people left
their villages and migrated to the cities. A few women began to earn
money in growth industries – but a greater number of men earned
far more. A significant proportion of these relatively affluent men
spent their money on the purchase of sex. The sexual access to
women that had previously been enjoyed by the powerful now came

within the reach of large numbers of men, and they took maximum advantage of this new and exciting opportunity.

The second spur to the industry was the expansion of military prostitution. Prostitutes have commonly been available to service troops and their officers. They accompanied armies when they went to war and red light areas thrived outside the walls of virtually every major garrison and fort in traditional Asia. Many of these brothel quarters linger on even today. But what gave military prostitution in Asia a real boost was the arrival of high-spending American troops during the Korean and especially Vietnam Wars. During the 1960s and early 1970s United States servicemen posted to Vietnam travelled to Thailand for R&R, or Rest and Recreation. More accurately, this was referred to as I&I, or Intercourse and Intoxication. A vast and lucrative sector of the sex industry thrived by providing sexual services to military personnel. Similar industries developed wherever US troops were based. In Korea brothel towns sprang up next to bases. The same happened in the Philippines, where thousands of women provided sexual recreation to men stationed in US military bases and to sailors from the visiting US naval fleet.[2]

When the US pulled out of Vietnam the Thai sex industry faced a worrying cut in profits. A rescue package was, nevertheless, close at hand. The sex business, in unofficial partnership with the tourist industry and the government, decided to diversify and to attract a new type of client. Tourists would replace military personnel. Consumers were sought from the developed nations of the West, and also from Japan. These consumers provided the third stimulus to the industry. They listened to the message and they liked what they heard: young, beautiful, submissive, sexy and cheap Thai girls were desperate to cater to the unfulfilled needs of men who deserved better treatment than that meted out by aggressive, demanding and unfeminine Western women. The advertising worked and the customers arrived in their millions.[3]

*

The Western media fasten upon sex tourism as if it is only inadequate and perverted Western men who are responsible for the sexual exploitation of Asian women. Certainly Western men flock in their millions to purchase Thai and Filipina sex workers. I spent an educational few weeks observing my fellow countrymen and their Western peers at play in the sex tourist destinations of Thailand and the Philippines. Contrary to the image of the sex tourist as a middle-aged or elderly pervert, the men escorting beautiful young women in Pattaya, Bangkok and Angeles were drawn from a whole spectrum of Western males. These men are our fathers, husbands, brothers and sons.

Western sex tourism is very different from the domestic Asian sex market. It is also different from Japanese sex tourism. Western sex consumers like to think there is choice in the sex for money transaction. They like to see the product – and plenty of it – before they buy. They like to pretend that a pretty nineteen-year-old girl really did 'connect' with them. They like to imagine that she did not do it 'just for the money'; that she enjoyed their time together; that they had something special, which trivial things like a vast age gap and large income differentials simply could not spoil.

In order for the customers to believe that there is choice in the deal, and that there is an element of mutual attraction in addition to the cash, the whole business has to appear open and informal and bags of fun. Western sex tourism is therefore outrageously visible. Tourists stroll arm-in-arm with teenagers around the streets of what, in effect, are giant open-air brothels. They visit clubs with subtle names like 'The Pussy Bar' or 'The Hot Girl Club'. Pattaya in Thailand is crammed with hundreds of bars and clubs in which Western men can buy young women. The sex business is incredibly blatant. Virtually everyone tries to sell you sex. Men who do not want to buy sex, and who are clearly with partners, are propositioned dozens of times every evening. Even the minibars in the hotel rooms are supplied with drinks, snacks and a selection of condoms.

The happy holidaymakers drool over erotic dancers in bars. They can be found having oral sex in the darkened corners of clubs; they give detailed gynaecological examinations to the women who provide floor shows; and they can be seen emerging from hotel rooms with girls young enough to be their granddaughters. One evening in a club in Angeles in the Philippines, I watched three men inspect half a dozen very nervous, teenage sex workers as if they were cattle at an auction. They gave the girls a manual check to assess the size of their breasts. They then paid the club owner for the girls' services and departed with their merchandise. A few hours later I saw them, riotously and unpleasantly drunk, in another bar where they were tutoring their purchases in coarse football anthems and racist chants that were clearly directed at the girls themselves.

You will rarely – if ever – see a local Asian man participating in this kind of commercial sex market. The visibility of the Western men's preferred form of purchased sexual encounter, however, is distorting because the sex tourists monopolise our field of vision and attract all of our condemnation. What this does is to obscure other, even more crucial, consumers from view. There is a vast amount of money to be made from Western sex tourism but the major demand for commercial sex in Asia comes from the domestic market. Most Asian prostitutes sell sex to Asian men. By comparison, the number of Western clients pales into insignificance, although these men are important because, on average, they pay far more. The sex tourism business grew from, and now grows alongside, the indigenous sex trade.

The Asian version of commercial sex is very different from the Western sex tourist scene. So an observer who looks for local Asian men crowding into go-go bars and the kind of Thai club that offers banana, 'smoking pussy', ping pong and razor blade shows will look long and hard – and without success. Asian men buy sex in a different kind of setting and in a different location. Often it is in areas catering specifically – and exclusively – to Asian men, and sometimes it is behind closed doors. Those people who have been looking for evidence of a local Asian sex market have been looking in the wrong place.

Sex tourism is inescapable in the Philippines. And so is the commercial sex market patronised by local men – providing you know where to go. Manila and Angeles are crowded with sex clubs catering to foreigners. They have neon lights, loud music and semi-naked women hanging around the doorway. It is much harder to see where Filipino men buy sex. In Manila, I visited a club catering to lower-middle-class and better-off working-class men. The clients were drivers, clerks and small-scale businessmen. From the outside the club looked completely innocuous. There were no indications that sex was sold inside this establishment – at least none that was clearly visible to a Western woman, even one who was fairly clued up on the commercial sex scene. From the external appearance of this club it looked remarkably like a large Mediterranean holiday-style disco. We paid our entrance fee to a couple of confused youths and entered a barn-like room that was filled with rows of tables and chairs. A small and incompetent band played to an audience of three extremely bored spectators who clapped whenever they were prompted.

We were ushered through a side door and walked down a long, narrow and poorly lit corridor. Then, to my surprise, we entered a large room that was so crowded that the waiter struggled to find us a table. The contrast with the empty, and very public, front of the club could not have been more dramatic. In the middle of this busy room was a small stage about three feet off the ground and surrounded by tables. At ten-minute intervals a couple of girls walked through the throng of men and danced on the stage. The braver ones undressed and the others performed a stiff and unconvincingly erotic shuffle while holding onto as many items of clothing as they could possibly manage. The vast majority of men ignored these shufflings and concentrated on talking to their friends while drinking copious quantities of beer. Every now and again one of the customers would get up, leave the table and follow the women to the dressing rooms. They did not return. Later a stream of men could be seen driving away from the dark car park at the back of the building with the young dancers in their cars.

This club is a Western-style venue for the local men but there is another even more authentically local variety of sex establishment. It is called a *casa* and it is a closed brothel. In other words the women cannot escape. Identifying *casas* is troublesome because they are hidden. They do not have signs, and new customers are introduced by regular clients. Gaining entry to some of these places is rather like gaining membership to an exclusive club.

Taxi drivers everywhere have a wealth of information about brothels, and Filipino taxi drivers are experts on *casas*. One particularly well-informed driver took me to a house in Manila that he insisted was a *casa* catering to rich men. It was a large, modern, multi-storey building in its own grounds and was surrounded by fences. Its windows were of darkened glass and it had no apparent purpose. It was the most unlikely brothel. The driver was so insistent that it was a *casa* – and I was so disbelieving – that I agreed to observe the building at night. Sure enough, he was right. Every evening men arrived in expensive cars and parked in an underground car park. They then stayed for a couple of hours and left as quietly as they had arrived. In contrast to the constant movement of men, I never saw any young women enter or leave the building.

Prostitution is illegal in the Philippines and we find the same kind of dissembling happening in other countries in which sex for sale is prohibited. Japanese brothels are not advertised as brothels but all the locals know what they are. Men talk about them and they visit them. Women know about them, but do not mention their existence. The subject is not one that is officially recognised. Commercial sex is both a joke among men and a subject that is not fit for discussion in polite society. Signs on the clubs in Tokyo that entertain Japanese men make the message quite clear. They say 'NO FOREIGNERS'. Clearly, Japan has a reputation to protect.

A similar phenomenon is found in Pakistan's sex sector. Brothels are not brothels. Instead they are 'dancing schools' or they are apartments and houses in respectable suburbs. Few people will tell you otherwise because there is a conspiracy of silence. New customers are introduced by trusted, existing clients. These men are guaranteed not to give the game away. And wives can also be guaranteed not to complain. They have no option. A very large proportion of rich Pakistani men keep mistresses – sometimes several of them – and they also visit prostitutes. Their wives have no choice other than to accept this behaviour because the only alternative is a socially and financially disastrous divorce. A husband irritated by a nagging wife may even decide to bring yet another wife home. Less affluent men may not be able to afford mistresses but they still might visit sex workers. The bitter unhappiness of the wives of poorer men, however, will not be tempered by gifts of jewellery and beautiful clothes.

In sexually repressive societies the most unlikely places become the venue for selling sex. In Pakistan, for example, favourite spots include the waiting rooms of hospitals because these are places where women can legitimately visit. Or they are particular stretches of road – especially the ones with traffic lights to stop the cars and a few bushes for the sake of discretion. It is impossible for the uninitiated to identify a Pakistani brothel. They look like ordinary houses in ordinary streets. I was taken round and round residential districts in Islamabad, Lahore and Karachi that were filled with brothels. Yet, until I was told, I could not identify which buildings were brothels and which were family homes. Many guest houses and small hotels are brothels – but you have to be told this to know about it, and you have to be part of a local, inner circle in order to enjoy the services offered. The girls and young women inside these places cannot speak about what happens within their walls because some cannot get out. And those who can leave will not speak about selling sex because to do so would amount to social and, in some cases, physical suicide.

India is a little more relaxed about commercial sex but, even so, the sex sector is still nowhere near as apparent as in the West. This does not mean, however, that it is smaller in size or importance than its Western counterpart. Quite the reverse. A visitor to India will not see an extensive sex sector if they look for pornography among the magazines and newspapers that are sold in the street and in the shops. Indian women dress with discretion and Indian cinema is unhealthily chaste. But a visit to places like Sonagachi in Calcutta, Kamatipura in Mumbai (Bombay) and GB Road in Delhi will quickly demolish the amusing proposition that Indian men do not buy sex. There are not many sex tourists in places like these.

Today India's traditional red light areas cater to ordinary men – just as they have done for centuries. A traditional urban brothel in India, and also in Bangladesh, is not a single building but a whole sub-sector of the city in which there are many sex establishments. Brothels in old urban centres are a warren of dark, often unpaved, winding lanes and alleys in which hundreds and sometimes thousands of women sell sex. There are usually many large, multi-storeyed and decrepit buildings each divided into separate, and competing, brothels. In turn, these brothels are divided into lots of tiny cramped rooms in which two, three or more prostitutes work. There is nothing glamorous about these places. There is little that can be described as erotic in the rat-infested, overcrowded and unsanitary rooms in which the women work. Places like these are the home to a large proportion of Asia's sex slaves.

Sex for sale is big business. In Asia, just like everywhere else in the world, it is an expanding and frequently violent business. It is also very hard to monitor because it is often illegal, linked to organised crime and constantly changing in form. It has many, and varied, faces. Like other industries the business of selling sex is highly stratified and there are innumerable sub-sectors. A similar basic product is packaged and costed to appeal to different types of consumers, and the transaction takes place in different types of venue.

At the top end of the Asian market is the high-class prostitution of call girls, who work in expensive hotels, luxurious apartments and who service wealthy men. Inevitably, this sector is most active in affluent Asia but it also exists on a small scale even in the poorest societies. There are executive clubs catering to businessmen who visit for sessions of corporate bonding and sexual recreation. Then there are bars, nightclubs, massage parlours, health clubs, restaurants and karaoke clubs that offer sex as well as other forms of entertainment and services. In less-developed Asia there are noodleshops, teashops, roadside cafes and truck stops that operate a lucrative trade in girls. Sometimes these girls are displayed when they serve meals and drinks. At other times they are kept in a back room, especially if they are very young. Down at the lowest end of the scale there is brothel and street prostitution. At the budget end of this already cheap sub-sector are child street prostitutes and the oldest women working in squalid surroundings.

Physical conditions within the brothels vary according to a country's level of economic development. So even a dreadful brothel in Japan will at least appear to be hygienic. It is a different story in poverty-stricken Asia. The women who work in cheap brothels in Cambodia, Bangladesh and India, for instance, endure living conditions that are comparable to those of other impoverished people. Women service their clients in overcrowded rooms or tiny cubicles. Sanitary conditions are minimal and, in some cases, they do not even have access to running water.

There is no stereotypical 'Asian prostitute', just as there is no single type of sex industry establishment. In order to make some sense of a very complicated industry, however, we can divide prostitutes in the region – as elsewhere – into various categories. For a start there are part-timers and full-timers. Some women will engage in prostitution for a short spell and some for many years. Some women repeatedly join and then leave the trade according to their financial needs.

The prostitution hierarchy is shaped like a pyramid. At the top are a small number of elite prostitutes, the majority of whom have chosen their work because they can earn substantial sums in a very short time by selling sex. These women have a select clientele and service a limited number of men. They are usually exceptionally beautiful, relatively well educated and with a good command of English. They tend to be from middle-class and well-off families and they are not selling sex simply because they are poor and have no other way to make a living. Short stays in top hotels in major cities and resorts throughout Asia were enough to convince me that many of these highly polished young women are doing very well financially from servicing wealthy tourists and businessmen. Yet, these women are not typical prostitutes and they do not represent the majority of women in prostitution.

In the middle section of the pyramid are a much larger number of prostitutes who cater to less affluent clients. Many of the women in this category have not made a positive choice to sell their bodies. Many have entered the profession because they have limited options and are forced to sell sex because of economic hardship. The further you descend in the prostitution hierarchy the less real and the less meaningful the element of choice actually becomes. At the base of the pyramid are the girls and women belonging to the mass market. These women constitute the largest number of prostitutes and they service society's poorer men. Very few of these girls and women have freely elected to become prostitutes. Most will have been forced into sex work by acute poverty and enormously restricted life chances. Some will have been physically coerced and some simply sold into the trade.

Attitudes to the sale of sex vary throughout Asia. In parts of the region prostitution is metamorphosing from an underground activity into a fully fledged industry that is accepted by society – even though this fact is never recognised in official statements. In some affluent parts of the region, and in other areas where prostitution is well entrenched, sex work is rapidly becoming just another business. A phenomenon known as *endo kosa* has emerged in Japan during the past few years and is a good illustration of this trend in the sex market. Girls, who are middle class, well educated and often still in high school, arrange 'dates' with middle-aged businessmen through telephone clubs or informal networks. The dates turn into sexual liaisons and the girls are rewarded with gifts and cash. Some say that it is not prostitution but is only a bit of fun. The girls are not poor and no one forces them: they need the money to buy the latest cute designer handbag and to keep up with their friends in a frenetic fashion competition. It is not a phenomenon that is restricted to a tiny minority but is a widespread activity among teenage girls. It may reflect a vacuous kind of existence constructed out of the pressures of an intensely materialistic society, but it is the girls' very own choice. Perhaps these girls really are the 'happy hookers' of legend.[4]

A lot of nonsense has been written about prostitution and has been portrayed in films. This nonsense links sex work with a romantic image of the successful courtesan who provided genteel and intellectually stimulating entertainment (as well as discreet and presumably artistically refined sex) to powerful and charming men. Perpetuating myths like this is irresponsible. Only a few elite women ever became highly accomplished *geishas* or bejewelled and fragrant courtesans patronised by leading men. What is more, even their power rarely lasted longer than their beauty, and the conduct of the leading men could be just as charmless as that of their brothers in the lower social orders. Most prostitution was, as it is today, just plain sad and rather sordid. A lot of it is also horribly brutal.

The world of the average sex worker lies very far from the world of elite prostitution. And it is the widespread abuses in the industry's mass market that this book concentrates upon. It tells the story of girls who are raised to be prostitutes, the story of girls who are sold into the trade and the experiences of those who are tricked and lured into the profession. It purposely avoids recounting some of the worst examples of abuse. We have all heard of teenagers who are burned to death while chained to their beds in Thai brothels, and of children who die from the internal damage caused by their sale to adult men. However, it is unfair to judge an industry and the business of selling sex by focussing exclusively on horrendous but relatively unusual tragedies. I have tried instead to reflect broader patterns and to screen out the most ugly and shocking stories. In this way I hope to avoid sensationalising both the women's experiences and the industry in which they are involved. Sadly, the reality is so shocking that it does not need to be sensationalised in order for it to be almost unbelievable.

The trafficking of women and the use of women in prostitution is the focus of this book because females form the overwhelming majority of sex workers. Male prostitution exists in Asia but it is not on such a wide scale and it has little in common with female prostitution. One exception to this rule may be Pakistan where the prostitution of boys appears just as rife – and perhaps more so – than the prostitution of girl children.[5] Boys of between ten and fourteen are in great demand with clients. In part this is because the movement of females is so highly restricted in Pakistani society. These boys do not work in brothels but as 'assistants' in garages, on buses, at truck stops, in small restaurants and in bathhouses. Their function within these establishments is not so much to 'assist' the proprietors as it is to attract the clients.

The recruitment system for male sex workers is not highly developed and the boys are not sold into prostitution and locked inside brothels. Recruitment is often achieved by more informal mechanisms. In less-developed Asia boys migrate to the towns and cities and some then become involved in sex work. They respond to peer pressure and to the pressure of poverty. They realise that they can earn substantially more by selling sex to men than by begging, running errands or working in a factory or shop. Like the girls in prostitution their options are limited but their range of choices is actually far greater than that of female sex workers. Overt homosexuality may be despised in large parts of Asia, and its existence may even be denied, but a gay sex worker will not be as roundly scorned as a female prostitute. There is nothing in male prostitution that is really comparable to the trafficked girl forced into selling sex in a closed brothel.

Some girls are sold directly into prostitution but, in terms of sheer numbers, the most common path to sexual slavery is that walked by girls who are searching for an escape from poverty. Ironically, these girls are frequently highly entrepreneurial and ambitious to improve upon their humble beginnings. Typically a girl or young woman is offered a job in some distant place, perhaps in a city or in another country. Yet once she gets there she finds that the job is very different from the one she was initially promised. In poorer parts of the region she might have thought that she would work as a domestic help in a rich person's house. In reality she is forced instead to provide sexual services to fifteen men a day. In more affluent Asia some women are offered lucrative jobs as hostesses or singers entertaining a few select and wealthy gentlemen in a luxurious club. In fact the select gentlemen turn out to be sadistic bullies, the girls do not get paid and the luxurious club is a terrifying prison. If this happened to one girl it would be bad enough, but it happens to thousands every day.

One of the difficulties in writing about the sex industry is that it is hard to find accurate statistics. Prostitution is illegal in large parts of Asia, as is the trafficking of people. Estimating the numbers involved in the business of selling sex, or the numbers who are trafficked, is fraught with difficulties, and anyone who engages in guesswork runs the risk of losing their credibility. Many of the figures that are bandied around have been pulled out of a hat, and exaggeration is so commonplace that it only creates disbelief and, ultimately, diverts attention from a genuine problem. Governments do not have adequate data on the scale of trafficking or sexual slavery. Either they are not capable of producing it or, in some cases, they do not want reliable data on the grounds that they would then be obliged to do something about it. Undoubtedly, however, the numbers involved are very large. Millions of females sell sex in Asia. Some of these are children. Some of the women have not consented to being put on the open sex market. And some of them are locked into a contemporary form of slavery. It is a scandal of appalling proportions.

The trafficking of women and sexual slavery are two separate issues. They are, however, interrelated because trafficked women are the easiest targets for the sex industry and form its most reliable supply of sex slaves. The trafficking of human beings is a complicated subject. It is much more complicated than the trafficking of drugs or arms. Part of the difficulty is the confusing overlap between migration and trafficking and the muddled debate that has surfaced over definitions. Migrant labourers, and especially illegal migrant labourers, frequently find themselves forced into exploitative working conditions. In this sense they are just like the victims of trafficking. But migrant labourers have not necessarily been tricked or deceived during the migration process. Trafficking, on the other hand, refers to the transportation of people within countries or across international borders using force, trickery or the abuse of power.[6]

People – men, women and children – are trafficked in order to channel them into exploitative forms of labour. There is a massive trade in these people because they are relatively poor to start with and they will accept lower wages and tolerate worse working conditions than local labourers. In the poorest parts of Asia they may expect little more than food, clothes and a roof over their heads. By transporting people from their homes, and often out of their original countries, traffickers make these vulnerable people even more vulnerable. They remove them from their social support networks and they place them in an environment in which the language, customs and work patterns may all be unfamiliar. Trafficked people are easy to manipulate and exploit because they are made to be dependent upon others. Until they can acclimatise themselves to their new surroundings they lose a large element of control over their own lives. This is why the sex industry likes trafficked girls. Sometimes trafficking victims are employed in sweatshops or on building sites. Sometimes they are trafficked to work as domestic servants, as beggars and sometimes as prostitutes. Certainly, not all women who have been trafficked are prostitutes. And not all women who are forced into prostitution have been trafficked. A trafficked woman who is prostituted, however, will almost invariably find herself in the very worst of exploitative situations.

The trafficking of women has been given media coverage both in Asia and the West for well over a decade. The issue has also exercised humanitarian agencies and human rights groups, and mountains of reports have been written on the subject. Unfortunately, this has done little more than to push trafficking and sexual slavery further underground and to encourage the sex industry to conceal its most gruesome aspects. The fate of trafficked girls is just about the most unsavoury aspect of this ugly business because trafficked girls staff the lowest tiers of the sex industry. They are recruited because they are available, cheap and powerless. Tragically it is a recruitment strategy that the Asian sex industry has fine-tuned to perfection.

Trafficking patterns are simple. Girls and young women are taken from poor countries, and from poor regions, to more prosperous ones. When girls are trafficked for prostitution they then become commodities that can be purchased by the more affluent societies' men. Great attention has been given to international trafficking by a host of non-governmental organisations and, more recently, by international agencies. It has become something of a *cause célèbre* in these circles and is the subject of frequent seminars and report writing. Yet, it appears as if domestic trafficking – that is from poor regions to more prosperous regions within a single country – is every bit as important as cross-border trafficking. The results for the women, moreover, can be just as devastating.

An international trafficking hierarchy parallels Asia's economic pecking order. At the bottom are the poorest nations. These are the 'sending' countries that export their women. They are typified by Bangladesh, Vietnam and Nepal. These countries do not import women because there is no one else poor enough to consider it financially worthwhile to sell sex in these desperately poor societies. At the top of the pecking order are 'receiving' countries: those rich societies that host sex workers from the poorer sending countries. The best example of a receiving country is Japan, which imports women from just about everywhere.

In the middle of the international trafficking networks are countries that have multiple functions: they are transit countries acting as brokers in the trafficking process and they can also be both receiving and sending countries. India and Thailand are the prime examples and both run an incredibly busy trade in women. To give just a few examples of the way the trafficking networks operate, there are thought to be well over a hundred thousand Nepali prostitutes in India, hundreds of thousands of Burmese women in Thai brothels and over a hundred thousand Thais and Filipinas in Japan.[7] The existence of 'Little Bangkoks' and 'Little Manilas' in Japan is well known. And now there are also 'Little Colombias,' 'Little Russias' and 'Little Romanias' too. The list goes on. Name a country with economic problems, limited opportunities for females and a flourishing criminal underworld and you can guarantee that at least some of its women will be recruited for Japan's vast and very demanding sex industry.

So many Japanese men wish to buy sex that the country has

resorted to the wholesale importing of women for use in the commercial sex sector. Naturally, not all the women who go to work in Japan are trafficked and forced into prostitution. Some migrate to work as prostitutes in Japan because they can earn comparatively high wages while they are there. Even so, there are many other women who are trafficked to Japan and who are forced to prostitute themselves. The majority of Filipina women who travel to Japan to work as entertainers, and who are known as 'Japayuki', do not know that they will be sold for sex. Or, if they are aware of the nature of their work, they have a seriously mistaken impression of the kind of prostitution they will be involved in and the conditions under which they will have to sell their bodies.[8]

One of the most puzzling things about the sex industry is how often the customers disappear from the debate. Of course poor and vulnerable women will form a ready supply of recruits to the industry. There are no surprises here. But there has been little analysis of the demand as opposed to the supply side of this industry. Who are these invisible customers who buy the bodies of so many children and young women? My guess, at least in large parts of Asia, is most men. This includes men from all social classes, religions and ethnic backgrounds.

There is an assumption in many Asian societies that men must inevitably want to buy sex: that it is a kind of natural function. This assumption is shared by both men and women. Good women – the kind who are socially respectable and whom men marry and provide with economic security – do not like sex. Sexual partners who are not a man's own faithful wife are, by definition, whores who can be purchased by all those legions of sex consumers frustrated by passive spouses and unavailable, or chaste, girlfriends.

Not every Asian man will buy sex and some would never dream of doing so. To claim that all Asian men are prostitute-users is as ludicrous and unbalanced as claiming that Asian males follow strict and morally determined sexual codes. We need to be far more accurate about these codes and their claim to virtue. There are, in fact, two types of code. The first type is the public code and the type held up to the world as a great model of social and sexual propriety. And then there is the second type: the unofficial code which tells men that they can have a string of mistresses and that they can buy sex on the open market. The only caveat is that it is best if the men do not get caught in the act.

Significantly, the extent of prostitution, trafficking and abuse within the sex trade is inseparable from the level of sexual repression within a society and the degree of control that is exercised over women. It is no accident that life for poor Pakistani prostitutes is abysmal because it is also pretty tough for most Pakistani women. There is a beautifully neat symmetry: strict sexual codes and rigorously male-dominated societies are mirrored by widespread systems of sexual slavery and a regular supply of trafficked women to the sex trade. When these unhappy factors are added to poverty and to wide income disparities the results are catastrophic for the most vulnerable women.

Sex workers' organisations and parts of the feminist movement become irritated when attention is concentrated upon trafficking and forced prostitution. They claim that an emphasis upon the grisly aspects of the industry discredits all of it when, in fact, some parts of the business are potentially just fine. Trafficking stories are victim stories and they give an incomplete and distorted picture.[9] Certainly, not all sex workers are victims and not all are forced to sell their bodies. Some of the women like their work – but not many – and we can question which proportion would choose prostitution as an occupation if society had offered them any other reasonable option.

For lots of women – especially in impoverished Asia – prostitution is all about survival. Even a lousy brothel is good for some poor and dispossessed women because it gives them the means to eat. The heavily made-up and brightly dressed girls and women lining the streets of India's red light areas, for instance, have rarely chosen sex work as a career. In Pakistan, I spent an evening at the home of a prostitute who is anything but a sex slave. She has her own house in the traditional red light district of Heera Mandi in Lahore and entertains a number of middle-class businessmen on a regular basis. She is not well-off but she makes an adequate living. She has few qualms about her trade. It is, she said, her choice to sell sex, and I believe that she told me the truth. She seems contented and at peace – at least most of the time. She began to teach me some of the dances of a courtesan and how to jangle dozens of bracelets in just the right way and at just the right moment. She also taught me how to drink half a litre of vodka without passing out and how she had begun to sell sex when she was abandoned by her husband and left destitute with two babies to feed. This woman is in her mid-thirties. She is beautiful, but you can see the traces of wear on her face. She knows she is getting older. Some of her clients are not as attentive and as generous as they were and her income is beginning to decline. I asked her what she was going to do in the future and, as I did so, her two daughters ran into the room. One was about thirteen and a little plain and very quiet. The other was about eight and as pretty and as vivacious as her mother. This child will be her mother's future and, within a few years, prostitution will be her trade. She is being groomed to sell sex. Even as a child she is dressed like an adult sex worker. What kind of choice, I thought, did this mother and her young daughter really have?

The sex industry has arranged a happy and profitable marriage with the neo-liberal economic theories that have enamoured the world for the past couple of decades. According to this economic agenda everything has a price, and a free and unfettered marketplace must determine that price. For a large number of the poor, and especially for poor women, the magic of the market has yet to work its wonders. It has, however, given a new impetus to the sex industry. It has increased the number of women and clients involved in the trade and, in more affluent societies, the industry has acquired the veneer of a serious and legitimate business. It is controlled and regulated by managers worthy of an MBA and it is protected and promoted by an astonishingly effective public relations effort.

Economic liberalisation policies have meant that a lot of people in Asia have become poorer while some have become a lot richer. People are moving more easily from one country to another as border controls have been relaxed and as people migrate in search of a livelihood. The trafficking of women, in a sense, is part of a much larger pattern of migration and social change. More people are increasingly desperate; more people are on the move; more women are mobile because they have greater opportunities; and more men have the finance to buy sex.

In an increasingly materialistic and unequal world it is largely inevitable that more women will end up in prostitution and that more men will buy their services. Asia's traditional cultures are rapidly being overlain by modern consumer cultures. This is a massive bonus for the sex industry because women's customary low status in Asian societies permits vulnerable women to be more easily manipulated for men's pleasure and for the sex trade's profit. Prostitution is giving some disadvantaged women the ability to improve their financial lot in life and to achieve a degree of social and economic mobility that otherwise would be out of their reach. But, although this is true, our first question should be the morality of a power structure that makes the provision of sexual services the only realistic path a young woman can follow if she wants economic security and the chance to lift herself and her family out of poverty.

Prostitution is a quick financial fix in places where inequitable patterns of economic growth have excluded the poor from the excitements of the consumer boom. Selling sex – or being sold for sex – is a form of work that the poor and badly educated can easily enter. The only necessary qualifications are youth and an element of physical charm. Prostitution is also a form of work that will continue to ensure that the poor, apart from a lucky few, remain poor and badly educated. It is, nevertheless, an employment trend, or a survival mechanism, that is fast becoming acceptable in large parts of Asia. It is acceptable to countries like Thailand and the Philippines, which see the sale of their women as a development strategy. It is acceptable to some families who will sell their children into prostitution. It is acceptable to girls who are raised and educated for little else, and acceptable to those women who see it as a lucrative career option.

Nepali women figure prominently in this record of the sex slaves of Asia's brothels. And so do Indian, Bangladeshi, Thai, Burmese, Pakistani, Cambodian and Filipina women. The stories come from women who are both the victims and the survivors of sexual abuse. Many of these women have had little say in the narrow options that have determined their fate. Some have had absolutely no choice. A few of the accounts tell of irredeemably shattered lives. Most stories, however, are a testimony to the capacity of individual women to cope with exploitation and to survive it with an inspiring dignity.

I have written this book after hearing a similar, appalling story from girls and women all over Asia. It is a story that tells something about the depths to which humanity can sink. More accurately it tells of the depths to which some men can sink and how women often abet them in the process. I hope it will convey something of the rank hypocrisy of societies that preach about sexual morality, and make a fetish out of virtuous womanhood, but simultaneously utilise the youngest and most vulnerable females for sexual pleasure and as the living material upon which men can exercise the thrills of domination. Neither those people who promote prostitution as work nor those who are implacably hostile to it will like this book. Many Asian men – and substantial number of women – will hate it. That is all the more reason to write it.

Chapter Two

THE COMMODITY

Prostitution pays. It profits many people – but not necessarily the girls and women whose bodies are sold. For some of Asia's poorest families, sending a daughter into prostitution makes the difference between absolute poverty and having just enough money to survive on a tiny and increasingly less fertile patch of land. For some women prostitution is the only way to survive in a world of limited options. Sex work has few competitors in terms of earning power for the badly educated and the unskilled. Some women choose to become prostitutes because of these financial rewards, but most women have no option. They are reared in poverty, socialised amid discrimination and conditioned to accept narrow choices. They are not exercising their right to 'choice' in entering sex work. They are vulnerable, and this vulnerability, together with their sexuality, is commodified and commercialised so that they can be traded on the sex market.

The link between poverty, prostitution and the trafficking of females is complicated. I want to be very clear: prostitution is not just a product of poverty. In more developed countries like Thailand poverty is no longer the driving force in the entrance of young women to prostitution. In northern Thailand prostitution is a career option for many young girls. If they are successful they will be able to buy a house and consumer goods and the respect of their family and neighbours. Many prostitutes are poor but their poverty is relative and not absolute. If prostitution was simply about poverty we could have expected a contraction of the sex industries in countries with fast-developing economies. But during the 1980s and 1990s the sex industry in countries like Thailand, the Philippines, Malaysia and Indonesia expanded as the standard of living of large sections of the population improved. There are many poor communities and families who would never send a child into sex work. I am afraid, however, that there are an increasing number who encourage and sometimes force daughters into prostitution. In some rural parts of Asia the breeding of girls for prostitution has become a kind of lucrative cottage industry.[1]

All women in Asia are discriminated against relative to men within their own social and economic classes. But this does not mean that all women are equally burdened by the weight of discrimination. The girls who find themselves trapped in the worst kind of prostitution are not from privileged families, nor are they from middle-class families. They come, almost invariably, from the poorest communities and they are often from ethnic minorities. In South Asia they are from untouchable castes and scheduled tribes and, almost without exception, they are very badly educated. They are exploited in the worst forms of prostitution for the simple reason that it is easy to exploit them. They are the poorest and most vulnerable members of largely powerless communities.

Both traditional and modern Asian societies are highly gender biased. This is changing in economically advanced Asia but even here the improvement in women's status is won at a price and, like in the West, old forms of discrimination are being reformulated to

preserve the sexual privileges of men. In many parts of contemporary Asia women are seen as the property of men. A woman finds a
role in society and is validated by her relationship with a male: first
with her father, then with her husband and later with her son. A
complex mix of religion, cultural practices and economics discriminate against women. In most parts of poverty-stricken South Asia
the birth of a daughter is unwelcome because a female is considered
to be an economic liability. The evil of dowry is fundamental to
this: families pay for girls to be married and the status of the match
is intimately related to the size of the dowry. In countries like
Bangladesh where dowry was not traditionally common, the practice is now spreading rapidly.[2] And in societies in which it is
customary, dowry prices are escalating. The financial problems of
giving birth to a girl child are therefore being magnified.

Payment of dowry is a duty that cannot be shirked if a daughter
is to make a respectable marriage and thereby to add to the prestige
of the family. Upon her marriage the girl then becomes the property
of her husband's family. So not only does a girl's family have to feed
and raise her but they also have to pay a substantial sum to marry
her off. Just at the time that she becomes a useful economic addition
to the family, she is transferred to another household, and her husband's family then own and profit from her labour. It is with good
reason that a girl in South Asia is often described as a 'guest in her
father's house'.

Not all communities in Asia pay dowry. Some pay brideprice –
which is a payment made by the bridegroom's family to the parents
of the girl. In theory this sounds like an improvement upon the
dowry system and, in some ways, it is. At least it acknowledges that
a female has some value and it has some impact upon the way that
girls are treated. Brideprice, for example, is paid in tribal areas of
Pakistan. Here a girl is seen as a financial asset and it is in her
family's interests to take care of her and feed her well until she marries.[3] No prospective husband will pay handsomely for a thin,

overworked and unhealthy wife. Yet, at the same time, this practice is only the lesser of two evils because brideprice implicitly recognises that a female is a commodity to be traded.

For those who cannot pay dowry the options are a marriage with an unpromising husband or no marriage at all. A sixteen-year-old prostitute in a Calcutta brothel explained how she had arrived in the city from an impoverished Bangladeshi village the year before.

> My mother died three years ago and my father married again soon after. My new mother didn't want me ... especially when she had a new son. And my aunts and uncles didn't want me either because no one wanted to have the expense of marrying me. So I was sent to the city to find work. That way they said that they wouldn't have the cost of feeding me either.

Millions of women are 'missing' from India's census because they were either aborted, killed at birth or because they died from neglect as children. In South Asia as a whole it is estimated that seventy-four million women are 'missing'.[4] In China too the sex ratio is unbalanced. In 1979 the Chinese government instituted a 'One Child Policy' in an attempt to control the country's demographic explosion. The policy was extremely successful but it had an unintended side effect: if couples were allowed to have only one child they wanted a son, who was considered far more valuable in the eyes of society than a daughter. Ten years after the policy was implemented 114 boys were born – and registered – for every 100 girls.[5] Female infanticide has a long-honoured tradition in China and the One Child Policy has done little to eradicate it.

In all parts of Asia girls are less highly valued by society. The situation is most acute in the poorer, least developed parts of the region. South Asia has some of the worst gender development indictors in the world and here girls are discriminated against from the moment of their birth.[6] They are given less care, less love, less food and less medical attention than their brothers are. Middle Eastern countries are usually assumed to perpetrate the worst abuses on women, but a glance at gender-related statistics indicate that it is Pakistan that wins the award for the most extremely women-hostile society. Its female literacy rate is only 23% compared with 49% for men. Among children aged between one and four, the female mortality rate is 12% higher than male mortality. Women's share of paid economic activities, their access to senior administrative and managerial positions, and their representation in the national parliament are all minimal.[7] To be a woman in South Asia is to be, in the words of a respected Pakistani economist and social commentator, 'a nonperson'.[8]

Children and women are considered to be the possessions of the traditional Asian family. In many countries legal frameworks have enshrined the rights of ethnic minorities, low castes and women, but the enactment of laws has not altered deeply seated cultural prejudices. The example of China is instructive. After the triumph of the communists in 1949 China attempted to remove sexual discrimination, polygamy, prostitution and the sale of women. On paper this looked like a magnificent and successful effort, but old practices persisted despite the propaganda. And, once the control that the Communist Party exercised over the economy was relaxed a little in the late 1970s, those ingrained behaviours returned. China buys and sells its women and girls today in much the same way as it did a century ago. Only now it does so in the name of the free market.

Women and girls are treated as property because they are dependent upon men economically and socially, and because they have very few opportunities to build a life outside the confines of the family. Girls are socialised to accept their second-class status and to look for validation from a man. Many take this to be entirely natural. Marriage for most women in Asia is the principal means to a livelihood and social status. In some parts of less-developed Asia, like in Nepal, women are denied basic property and inheritance rights, and they are excluded from jobs that can pay a living wage. This is changing in the developed countries of the region as women gain access to well-paid employment outside the home. And even in the poorest countries it is also changing – but it is doing so slowly.

In Thailand daughters are cast in the role of caretakers of the family. As in the rest of South-East Asia girls are expected to pay back their 'breast milk money'. In the Philippines girls are obliged – at least psychologically – to pay their *utang na loob* (debt of gratitude) to their parents. Children of Chinese families are in their parents' debt for giving them life.[9] Feelings of duty and the desire to look after parents are fundamental to a caring society. But for some families, driven mostly by poverty but sometimes by greed, there is no limit to what these obligations can entail. In areas where prostitution of girls is well established, families may expect pretty daughters to enter prostitution. In areas of Taiwan there is a tolerant attitude to women supporting parents through prostitution.[10] Exactly the same holds true for prostitute-recruiting grounds in Nepal, Indonesia, the Philippines, Thailand, India and southern China.

Families provide protection but they can also be a prison in which the worst abuses take place. This is a universal truth. But for the abused and exploited child in Asia there are few avenues for escape precisely because the family is accepted as the ultimate protector of women and children. The counterpoint to this is that girls become easy prey when families fail. The family is the protector of a woman's virtue. There is no protection for the girls whose families fail them. There is no economic security and no social status. When they do not belong to one man they belong, by default, to all. Women like these constitute a large proportion of the prostitutes of Asia.

It is a myth that the Asian family always looks after its own. Red light areas in South Asia are filled with a large proportion of women who have been widowed, divorced, deserted and left with young children to feed and clothe. These women have not received support from their own or their husband's families and so they have been doomed to a life of prostitution. Likewise in South-East Asia a significant number of prostituted women are unmarried or divorced mothers who have no other means of maintaining themselves and their children.

Women may be second-class citizens but paradoxically they are also vitally important. This importance goes beyond sustaining the family and giving birth to, and raising, a new generation. Women are signifiers of community and of hierarchy. All societies are hierarchical, and Asian societies are deeply hierarchical in a very formal sense. One of the principal means by which men denote these hierarchies is in the control of and access to women.

Women are exchanged in marriage. This means that marriage signifies the binding of two families rather than simply two people. It is an economic and social contract. Of course women can benefit from this. At the best of times they gain economic security and social status. But they can also suffer terribly because they are part of a transaction. They are commodities, and to be valuable commodities in the marriage market they must have had no previous owners.

Virginity and chastity are central to the dominant strands in Asia's value systems. A Korean proverb which says that 'chastity for a woman is more precious than life'[11] sums this up perfectly. The typical model is remarkably similar to that of middle-class Victorian England in which there were 'good' women and 'bad' women. It is another version of the whore/Madonna divide so central to Christian thought. This distinction between women has almost universal applicability because it is universally useful as a means of controlling women by granting men the right to label them as 'decent' or as 'whores'. First, there are the good women. These are the women whom men marry: they are good wives and dutiful daughters; they are the females a family can exchange to enhance its social status. Then there are the bad women. These are the prostitutes: the ones seemingly outside the family system. They are not owned by an individual family, or by an individual man. In this way they can be used by all. The existence of this group of women means that men can be assured of having sex with multiple partners even in a society in which women's sexuality is rigorously policed. And all this is achieved without having to disrupt the harmony of their own tightly structured families or those of other men.

A girl who has lost her virginity is irredeemably altered. Within marriage, defloration is a symbol of a husband's possession of his wife. It is a travesty for a woman to lose her virginity outside marriage. In the context of the moral codes of large parts of Asian societies a woman is thereby considered to be 'damaged goods'. A thirty-year-old prostitute in a big brothel in Delhi's GB Road explained the disgrace that had brought her to sex work.

I came from a large family and when I was thirteen I fell in love with a boy from my town. He promised that he would marry me so I started to have sex with him because I thought it was safe and that he would be my husband soon. Then I got pregnant. My boyfriend said we must run away and get married. So I ran away with him and he brought me to Delhi. Then he sold me to this brothel. I had to stay here. I was spoiled. My family wouldn't have accepted me and no man would marry me because I was pregnant. I've been in this place for seventeen years.

The obsession with virginity is closely bound up with concepts of honour and position within male power hierarchies. A woman's conduct, her family's capacity to 'protect' her, and her ability to make a respectable marriage are important markers defining the status of families and the power of men. Crucially, this form of male competition is not so much about power over women as it is about power over other men. In Pakistan, for instance, the *izzat* (honour) of men and their families has to be constantly reaffirmed – most significantly through their control of females. Generally, the higher the status of the family – whether it be in South, South-East or East Asia – the tighter are the controls that a family will impose upon its women. Logically, as the honour of families rests upon their women, higher status families have more to lose if their females transgress established codes. Most privileged women do not transgress these limits because they would not wish to jeopardise their social and economic privileges, even if those privileges lead them to live circumscribed lives. For some the costs of stepping outside the boundaries set by their families are awesome. In Pakistan, for instance, it is not uncommon for girls to be killed by their own brothers, cousins or fathers if they are suspected, even on the flimsiest and most ridiculous grounds, of having an illicit relationship. In a three-month period in 1996, sixty-six cases of *karo kari* (honour killings) were reported in the papers of Sindh province alone.[12] From the perspective of the murderous relatives these killings were honourable because they were interpreted as acts designed to preserve the reputation of the family.

The life stories of sex workers often have similar distinguishing marks. One of the common patterns, which was repeated in countries as far apart as the Philippines, Bangladesh and Cambodia, was rape as an entry ticket into prostitution. In societies in which there is little social interaction between men and women and little or no opportunity to form relationships outside marriage, virginity is highly valued as a symbol of inaccessible femininity. These are also societies in which there is a high demand for prostitution and in which the purchase of a girl's virginity and her 'freshness' carries a premium.[13] The other side of the coin is that once a girl has been deflowered she is then considered 'spoiled'. Even a victim of rape would be deemed a 'fallen' woman in these societies. An appalling example of this is the treatment meted out to victims of rape in Bangladesh. In the country's War of Liberation from Pakistan in the early 1970s Pakistani soldiers raped over 30,000 Bangladeshi women and girls.[14] Rape was used as an instrument of war. It was an attack upon the core of Bangladeshi society because the women were seen as the symbols of its honour and of the status of its men. After the war the women were called *birangona* and they were designated as war heroines in official discourse. But, in private, society marked them as impure. Whole families turned their backs upon their raped daughters, sisters, wives and mothers. There was no place for them at home because families could not bear the ignominy and shame of an unchaste woman in their midst.

Almost thirty years later attitudes remain the same. Sex workers on the streets of Dhaka tell of how they were raped before becoming prostitutes. I met one of them, a woman in her early twenties who services her clients while standing by an open sewer. She explained that she had come to the city as a child.

> I don't know how old I was but my breasts had not begun to
> grow and I was very small. I came here because there was no
> one to care for me at home and a woman who knew my
> uncle said she could get me a domestic job. I got work in a
> nice house cleaning and helping to look after the little chil-
> dren. But after a while the master would not leave me alone.
> He raped me and when his wife found out I was beaten and
> thrown out of the house. What could I do then because I was
> broken? I had no place to live and no food. So I went with a
> lady to a brothel and she sold me there. I have been in the
> business ever since that time.

Girls and women like this street prostitute have internalised the good woman–bad woman image. A very similar phenomenon can be found in the Philippines, despite its higher levels of economic development. Legitimate sexuality, at least for women, is found only within marriage. The 'home, hearth and heaven' myth is very strong in Filipino Catholicism and so is the cult of virginity. A girl who is raped, or who has a pre-marital relationship that turns sour, will frequently be burdened with the shame of no longer being a virgin. For some of these girls it is a shame that leaves them no option other than to become a prostitute because they honestly believe that they are no longer worthy enough to become the wife of a decent man.

In the most sexually and gender-repressive societies in Asia rape is an initiation into prostitution. A raped girl is unable to marry because she is no longer a virgin. Such women resort to sex work because it is the only form of work available to them and because they cannot survive as single women. Ironically the trauma of the rape and the devastating consequences that flow from it can sometimes bind the girl to her rapist. The perpetrator of the crime then becomes her trafficker and her pimp.[15] In other words he creates the prostitute and then he profits from her.

There is a horrible kind of circular logic in the attitudes to women in those societies that are the most repressive. Women have to be guarded from predatory males, or they have to be secluded so that the power of their sexuality does not tempt men. In Bangladesh this is sometimes cited as a justification for child marriage.[16] It is portrayed as a kind of preventative measure against child abuse on the grounds that a young unmarried girl, by the simple fact of her existence, is a sufficient reason to incite a man to rape. Women are kept in their place by fear. If they try to step out of traditional roles they are considered fair game. Yet at the same time, while they remain in their traditional spheres, the system that oppresses them continues to be validated and confirmed.

All of the world's major religions and ideologies discriminate against women – in practice if not always in theory. Asia's principal religious traditions reflect and perpetuate gender discrimination. In doing so they help to perpetuate institutions such as prostitution even if most do not explicitly encourage the sale of sex. In some instances, however, they actually encourage prostitution.

Buddhist texts would have you believe that women are just as capable as men are of achieving spiritual perfection. Unfortunately, social practice does not marry with this gender-sensitive viewpoint and women are seen as less spiritually refined because they are attached to the very unspiritual, material world by their basic reproductive functions. A woman is thought to have been born as a woman because of bad *karma*. In order to overcome this disadvantage a woman has to make more religious merit than men. According to the Theravada Buddhist tradition of Thailand and Burma, a son may make merit by becoming a monk for a few months. But for a daughter there is no similar option. Instead she is encouraged to make merit by caring for her parents. If she does this well, and earns money for her family, she can, conceivably, be reborn as a man in her next life. This desire to help their families has been identified as a powerful factor pushing young women into prostitution in Thailand.[17]

Hinduism stresses the importance of women's purity and chastity. A woman is thought to have a dual nature: there is the divine, nurturing and creative aspect of femaleness, and there is her dangerous, evil and carnal side. A man is essential in order to control and subdue her. Only a man can harness the positive aspects of her nature and repress the negative. Women are therefore simultaneously devalued and worshipped. They are caring, devoted and maternal or they are destructive, anarchic and intensely sexual beings. They are wives and mothers or they are voracious whores.

It is not a paradox but an inevitability that Hinduism makes provision for institutionalised prostitution. This form of prostitution is dressed up in religious garb in order to give it a gloss of respectability. The South Indian *devadasi* system is the best example of this.[18] Even though it is technically illegal, the practice of dedicating prepubescent girls to a deity continues today. This is how the system works: a rich patron buys a girl from an impoverished family and then oversees her marriage to a god and her dedication to a temple.

He does this in the alleged hope of amassing religious points for himself and his family. From then on the girl is prohibited from marrying and, when she approaches puberty, her virginity is auctioned off to the highest bidder – usually a leading local figure and sometimes, unsurprisingly, the very patron who dedicated her to the temple in the first place. As the *devadasi* cannot marry and seek the comfort and economic security of a family she is tied to a life of religious prostitution. And, in turn, her daughters will follow in her footsteps by becoming *devadasis* themselves.

The Hindu caste system incorporates prostitute castes. In Western Nepal the *Badis* are an untouchable caste of around 7,000 people.[19] Traditionally they were entertainers who offered their patrons cultural shows as well as sex. Now their functions are more basic. The daughters follow their mothers to become sex workers and the sons become pimps. In this caste the traditional South Asian lament at the birth of a daughter and the celebration at the birth of a son is reversed. A pretty daughter is no longer a liability – by selling sex she has become an asset. At one time this reversing of accepted attitudes applied only to small sections of Asia's poor but today it is changing. Increased poverty, higher material expectations, and greater knowledge of economic opportunities mean that whole impoverished communities in less-developed Asia see their girls as a way to survive and sometimes simply as a way to comfortable living.

Christianity did not make much headway in Asia. But where it proselytised well – like in the Philippines – it did so with great zeal. The Philippines has all the repressive qualities of traditional Catholicism mixed with a good measure of Asia's group mentality. The mixture is a very troubled one for Filipina women.[20] Sex is equated with sin, at least for women, and the only legitimate form of female sexuality must be found within the bonds of marriage. A girl's reputation in the Philippines depends upon her *ignorance* of sex and her sexual behaviour (which should be non-existent). She should not even ask about the subject in case she should be suspected of having impure thoughts. Even *knowing* about AIDS and how it is transmitted may pose a risk to her social standing.

Apologists for Islam's abysmal treatment of women point to the fact that Islam does not hold women to be ideologically or biologically inferior to men. The spirit of the Qur'an speaks of the complementarity of the sexes and the ultimate equality of men and women. Tragically this is not the way many Muslim women must experience their relationships with men.

Muslim societies take it as axiomatic that men are the dominant and superior sex. Societies are structured to express this, so men in countries like Bangladesh and Pakistan marry women who are significantly younger than they are, and who are frequently little more than adolescents. Men justify this by their superiority but, in fact, it also creates that superiority too by generating relationships that have wildly unbalanced power dynamics.[21]

Islam sees women as destructive. Females are suffused with *fitna* – inordinate sexual powers that have to be contained so that they do not disturb the harmony of society and lead to chaos. Men have to be protected from this sexual power so that they are not provoked and drawn away from a righteous path. Men, in this sense, are always seen as the victims of female sexuality.[22] In the words of one of the leading feminist scholars on the Muslim world, 'the whole Muslim social structure can be seen as an attack on, and a defence against, the disruptive power of female sexuality.'[23] Remedies are found in the monitoring of women and in the separation of the sexes. The rich place their women in seclusion (*purdah*) when they become nubile. Others who are conservative, but unable to afford the luxury of *purdah*, are veiled whenever they leave the confines of the home.

China, Korea and Japan share a common Confucian heritage that is built around the concepts of order, harmony and hierarchy. In pre-modern East Asia individuals had a specific place within this hierarchy: children were obedient and showed respect to their parents; the people owed allegiance to the emperor; and women showed deference to their husbands. To have questioned these articles of faith would have been to challenge the entire social system.

Viewing women as a commodity has a long pedigree in China. Rich men had many wives and concubines, and daughters were seen as property of the family: they were possessions to be disposed of as their father wished. In contrast, sons were important. They belonged to the family of their birth and it was only through the male line that a family's descent could be traced. Women were peripheral. Their bodies were simply the vehicle by which the patriarchal family perpetuated itself.

Children – especially girls – from poor families were sold as domestic servants when times were hard.[24] The pretty girls became prostitutes. When harvests failed and famine threatened, the market was flooded with children from desperate families and the going rate for a child would plummet. By the early twentieth century the selling of daughters had changed subtlely. They were not usually sold outright but were pawned and parents or guardians received a 'loan' upon which the girl acted as collateral.[25] This system operates in large parts of Asia today when families in Thailand and Nepal, for instance, take an 'advance' on their daughters' earnings in the sex trade.

In 1950 the newly victorious Chinese Communist Party enacted the Marriage Law. This law removed abuses like polygamy, concubinage and forced marriage. At least it did on paper. The Chinese state clamped down on prostitution. But in reality these evils were never fully eradicated and the old practices made a public comeback in the 1970s. In particular, trafficking in women reappeared in poor and remote mountain provinces. Many women from these regions had migrated and had married men in richer provinces in an attempt to build a better life. Unfortunately, the men left back at home were obliged by tradition to remain with their parents and to continue the family line in the family farm. However perpetuation of the bloodline was proving difficult in the absence of women to marry and mate with. The women who remained could command a hefty brideprice as a result of their scarcity and few families were willing to foot such a substantial bill. An answer to the problems of these eager bridegrooms was found in the marketplace. A supply of brides was brokered by traffickers who delivered a wife for a quarter of the amount necessary for brideprice.

Some of these brides were from even poorer communities and they were willing to be married to an unknown man in the hope that he would provide them with improved economic security. Many, however, were tricked and forced into the match. The phenomenon of the purchased wife is common in the remoter regions of China. Buying a wife is not considered to be a reprehensible practice in these communities because it builds on customary behaviour. Matchmakers and go-betweens were familiar characters in the arranged marriages of traditional China. Today's traffickers and sellers of women have a socially legitimate ancestry and those who buy their women do not believe that they are doing anything wrong in using the services of an agent specialising in human beings.[26]

Sexual access to females is both a privilege of male power and a symbol of that power. So rulers and local elites in Asian societies, as elsewhere, displayed and enjoyed their power by possessing and controlling women's bodies. A few had harems, many had multiple wives, a lot had concubines and most helped themselves to the local village girls and poor urban women. Things have not changed much.

In nineteenth-century Nepal thousands of girls from hill tribes in the Himalayas were taken to Kathmandu to become sexual partners of men from the ruling Rana family. In feudal Indonesia the king's power was measured, in large part, by the number of concubines he kept at court.[27] Women were a commodity and a kind of currency. This provided a firm and extensive foundation for the modern-day commercialised sex industry. Capitalism has added its own inequities and injustices to traditional aspects of gender exploitation so that customary forms of subservience and exploitation have been repackaged. If anything this has served only to entrench traditional structures of privilege.

The inescapable forces of globalisation and economic liberalisation have pushed more and more poor girls into prostitution throughout the world. The unrestrained capitalism that is emerging in large parts of Asia makes no allowances for the vulnerable and for the dispossessed. In that sense it harmonises perfectly with traditional Asia's hierarchical contempt for the lower orders. Capitalism's rawest and most rapacious forms – including the sex industry – seek to profit from that vulnerability. In Vietnam, to take one example, there has been an increase in trafficking and prostitution. In part this can be explained by the re-emergence of traditional attitudes to women, as the ideals of the Vietnamese revolution have atrophied under the twin pressures of a failing command economy and the reach of global capitalism. Intimately associated with this, and fundamental to the re-emergence of large-scale prostitution, are the growing disparities between the rich and the poor and the disintegration of the structure of the family under the impact of economic liberalisation.[28] A similar trend can be seen in Cambodia, where the institution of a free market economy in the early 1990s led not only to the enjoyment of pleasant economic freedoms but also to the freedom to trade girls on the open market. Today there is *nothing* in Cambodia that you cannot buy.

The bulk of prostituted women in Asia come from poor communities, tribal groups, low castes and ethnic minorities. Their origins are almost as despised as their occupation. In the less-developed parts of the region most sex workers were born and raised in poor rural areas. Two thirds of the girls and women who enter prostitution in India come from areas that are drought prone.[29] Throughout the whole of less-developed Asia the majority of girls who sell sex are poor and often illiterate and the sex industry likes them because their youth and lack of education makes them easy to manipulate and control. They also possess another important selling point: because they come from remote regions, and because they are young, clients are reassured that they are free of sexually transmitted diseases and HIV. Some customers, particularly Japanese men, are so insistent about this disease-free requirement that they visit villages in Thailand purely to buy sex with a girl who is guaranteed to be fresh and safe as well as cheap.[30]

In India the vast majority of prostituted women are from *dalit* – or untouchable – castes and also from the tribal groups.[31] These women suffer a triple burden of exploitation: they are poor, they are untouchable and they are female. For some, the intersection of these dreadful disadvantages can be devastating. I met a young prostitute in a Calcutta brothel who was from an untouchable caste. She looked about fifteen but she claimed that she was nineteen. She was a wretched, thin child wearing an ill-fitting Western-style dress and she carried the look of someone who had been beaten by life. This is her story:

I am from a village a long way from here in West Bengal. My family is very, very poor. There were four children in our family. My father is dead and my mother could not feed me and my brothers and sister. We did not have a proper house and we were always hungry. Everyone in our village looked down on us because we are poor and from a low caste.

When I was thirteen some youths from our village took me into a field away from the village and they raped me. There were five of them and they were from high-caste families. I was crying and I went back to the village but the youths said I went with them willingly. The village *panchayat* [council] said that I had a bad character and was not respectable and that I shouldn't tell lies about the youths. They told my mother that I had to leave the village because I was a bad influence. But no one wanted to marry me and my mother could not afford a dowry so she brought me here. There was nowhere else I could go. Sometimes I can send my mother a little money and this makes her happy. It helps to buy food for my brothers and sister. I can't go back to my village because they think that I'm bad and they know what work I do. This place is my home because I have nowhere else to go to. I'll go on working here for as long as the clients want me.

In Nepal increasing poverty is pushing women from a wide range of castes, including high-caste women, into selling sex.[32] But the majority of prostitutes are from the politically marginalised hill tribes, and almost all of the girls trafficked to fill north Indian brothels are from Tamang, Lama, Magar and Gurung ethnic minorities.[33] Their other distinguishing characteristic is that half of these girls come from families that are considered poorer than other families in their own communities.[34] As most Nepali households are grindingly poor, this is poor indeed.

Nepal's beauty hides desperate poverty. Tourists trek along scenic Himalayan trails taking photographs of charming villages, engaging children and breathtaking mountains. It is easy to see lots of smiles but so much harder to see the poverty that leaves 50% of children with stunting as a result of malnutrition.[35] According to the World Bank around 40% of people live in absolute poverty. In other words, their income will not provide them with enough food to meet minimum calorie requirements. Development has left many Nepalis far behind. A glance at national per capita income suggests that the average Nepali is better off now than thirty years ago. Many of the poor would dispute this, and anecdotal evidence indicates that the poor are getting poorer. Certainly the gulf between the 'haves' and the 'have nots' is increasing year by year. Girls from communities like these staff large numbers of India's brothels and the sex industry has grown fat upon the sale of their flesh.

The disadvantaged north and north-east of Thailand are traditional recruiting grounds for the sex industry. These areas of Thailand are poor compared with the more prosperous central and southern regions. They are areas in which the traditional rural economy has been weakened by decades of maldevelopment. As in most Asian countries a chasm has opened up between the urban areas, which have grown richer, and the rural areas, which have stagnated or, in some cases, declined. The sex industry has been a principal beneficiary of this division. In Thailand, the rural sector has been badly neglected. Just like in Nepal, scenic villages and traditional houses are charming to look at but they are horrible to live in. Pretty girls working in the fields look quaint and colourful on postcards, but a day's backbreaking labour in the sun is barely sufficient to provide them with basic subsistence. Around thirty years ago the introduction of a cash economy into the country's rice belt led to a breakdown in Thai farming. It made scratching a living from the earth in the poorer parts of the country even harder. Young people from the countryside have been leaving for the cities ever since. Some have gone to work in factories and in the service sector. Many of the girls are sent to provide sexual services to both Thai and foreign men. And the provision of these services, like the services provided by girls from Nepal, helps to prop up otherwise economically unsustainable family farms.

For two or three decades, large numbers of girls from north and north-eastern Thailand have been leaving home to work in the sex industry. Girls and their families understand the mechanics of the industry and most know how to manage their careers. So much so that brothel keepers began to think that ethnic Thai women were a little too assertive to be good for business. Their answer was to look for a new source of recruits, and they found a ready supply in the hill tribes of northern Thailand. These are groups that the development process has barely touched. They are people who are on the fringes of Thai society – ethnically, culturally, politically and economically. Many of these peoples do not even live within the territorial limits of a single state but customarily move backwards and forwards through the jungles that span the Thai–Burmese border. Their cultures are being undermined by the dominant culture of the Thai state and their cultural and economic integrity is increasingly fragile. The sex industry targeted girls from these communities because they were vulnerable individuals in the midst of a vulnerable people. Until recently girls from hill tribes did not even attend school. They lived in families that were wracked by poverty and in which there was a high rate of underemployment and drug addiction.

The exploitation of tribal girls was so blatant, and so abhorrent, that both Thai government agencies and non-governmental organisations stepped in to try and stem the flow of girls to the brothels. They established programmes to identify and help the most vulnerable girls by giving them protection, education and some vocational training. Campaigns were also started in the communities to raise awareness of the dangers posed to young girls who left their tribes. This had the positive effect of at least moderating the exodus to Thailand's brothels. But there is one thing about the sex industry that is very, very clear: it is always one or even two steps ahead of those seeking to control it. A new set of recruits had been found in women from Burma and to a lesser extent from southern China and Cambodia. They were cheap and plentiful and, in the case of the Burmese, they also appeared to be willing. Consequently the number of sex workers in the Thai industry who originate from the north of the country has been decreasing in line with a corresponding increase in the number of girls from other countries. Five to ten years ago around half of the women working in the brothels of Chiang Mai in northern Thailand were from Burma. Now 100% of brothel-based prostitutes are Burmese.[36] These women, especially from the

'Yai Thai' community, are in demand for their white skin and their delicate features. All of these girls are illiterate.

Yunnan is a peripheral and mountainous region of China. Its people have a low standard of living by Chinese standards, and educational levels and general statistics on human development lag far behind the rest of the country. What makes Yunnan a recruiting ground for the sex industry is its proximity to Thailand with its ever-expanding demand for fresh young bodies. Since the 1990s thousands of young women from tribal communities in the Yunnan–Burmese border area have been trafficked to Thailand.[37] According to official figures, which may well be an underestimation, around 2,500 women were trafficked out of Yunnan in 1995 alone.[38] Their main destinations were the Chinese marriage market and the brothels of Thailand.

Burma's bitter history of civil war and political repression by an authoritarian military government has left hundreds of thousands of people displaced from their homes and millions living in fear and appalling poverty. It is a dream for agents of the sex industry. There are thousands of young women without a home or a livelihood who are desperate to escape the depredations of the Burmese army. They have an unenviable choice. As one Burmese prostitute working in Thailand stated, 'Why should we stay in Burma to be raped by soldiers? If we come to Thailand we get raped as well, but here we get paid for sex – at least most of the time.' The refugee camps along the Thai–Burmese border are major recruiting grounds for prostitutes,[39] and the estimated two million people who have migrated from Burma into the surrounding countries since the early 1980s have formed an army of cheap male migrant labourers and the prostitutes who service them.[40]

The attractions of working in Thailand are obvious for young Burmese women. When you first cross the border from Thailand into Burma there is little difference in the infrastructure of buildings and roads. But there is a palpable sense of desperation. Ten miles into Burmese territory, however, and the poverty is shocking and inescapable. From the Burmese mountains overlooking the border with northern Thailand, you can see neatly cultivated fields, modern towns and roads that lead south. To the poor, and those who have lost faith in their country's future, it must seem like the Promised Land. For some women it will be just such a Promised Land and for many others it will be a hell.

It is a similar story for the dispossessed everywhere. They have little to fight with and few people to fight for them. The networks that supply the sex industry hover around these people. They hover, for instance, around the one hundred thousand people of Nepali ethnic origin who were expelled from Bhutan in the early 1990s in one of the world's lesser known chapters of ethnic cleansing. Today these people languish in refugee camps in the east of Nepal. These people do not have permanent homes and they do not have a nationality. They are of little interest to anyone. Except, of course, the agents of the sex industry.

Ethnic minorities and tribal peoples form an excellent recruitment pool for the sex industry because women's status in many of these communities is not quite as circumscribed as in the dominant national cultures. Women have greater economic power, more social standing and there are looser restrictions on sexual morality. Among the Tamangs of Nepal, for instance, there is no taboo on premarital sex. And in many of the poor farming communities of northern Thailand, the country's obsession with chastity and virginity does not have the same kind of resonance as it does among the middle and upper classes. This does not imply, however, that prostitution of girls from these communities is accepted as a customary norm. Ironically, the higher status of women in these societies and their greater freedom of movement rebounds to their cost because it means that the sex industry and its clients can manipulate this freedom and profit from it as a result of the communities' relative poverty. It is yet another example of the global truth that mainstream cultures twist and exploit minority cultures to their own advantage.

Poor urban slums are increasingly profitable recruiting grounds for the sex industry. Even so, most brothel-based prostitutes and streetwalkers have arrived in the city from the villages. There are many ways in which girls migrate to the cities and there are many means of trafficking. The 1980s and 1990s have seen a feminisation of migration throughout the world. In Asia this is a reflection of greater opportunities for women and well as their greater poverty. Crucially, in a social context in which women are viewed as either the possessions of men or as some collection of body parts for the use of the many, this feminisation of migration has left millions of women at risk of sexual abuse and general economic exploitation. The girls trafficked for prostitution are only the most exploited of many exploited women.

Girls and women in prostitution frequently relate similar stories about the background to their work. They say that their families sent them or at least gave them permission to leave home. Families waved them off happy in the knowledge that their girl was going to the big city to get a job in a factory or as a domestic servant. Many families are not dissembling. They really think that their child will have a better life away from the poverty of the village. But it is hard to believe that all are so ignorant of the fate that will befall their daughters. In northern and north-eastern Thailand, in parts of Nepal, Indonesia, China, Burma and India, families know that their daughters will become sex workers. Perhaps they do not understand the full implications of what this job will involve. Some families honestly believe that it is 'easy money' and they have a false idea of the conditions their daughters will endure. However, they do know that she will not simply be a waitress, or a dancer, or a maid in a rich person's house. The trafficking of girls is on too large a scale for it to be ignored and unnoticed. In some cases families pretend not to know in order to spare themselves the shame of sending a girl into prostitution. But be sure that for many – perhaps the majority – it is unspoken knowledge. Gossip travels fast even in the remotest villages of the Nepali Himalayas, and few will be totally unaware of what happens to girls who go to Mumbai.

The market for sex has made daughters a valuable commodity in some poor communities. A Thai official in a non-governmental organisation (NGO) explained, 'What it comes down to is that Thai country women are just another kind of crop.'[41] In northern Thailand a family with several daughters is considered lucky, and a community leader in Rim Mon in Chiang Mai province complains that 'some parents remain idle, just waiting for money from their daughters'.[42] Just as in Nepal and in India's prostitute castes, the birth of a daughter here is no longer a cause for lament. Sex work has given them a market value.[43]

Sending girls into prostitution, usually when they are between thirteen and nineteen, is not considered to be shameful in provinces of northern Thailand like Chiang Mai and Chiang Rai.[44] The whole community accepts sex work – and this includes officials and religious organisations because, ultimately, they all benefit financially from the trade. Evidence from Thailand, Nepal and Indonesia, among other places, suggests that a change in attitudes towards prostitution occurs after the women from a poor community have been involved in the business for a number of years. First there is the demonstration effect: girls return to poor villages with some money. Providing the money is substantial enough – and in a poor community it need only be a modest sum – the girl's shame is ignored because she has been successful and her money eventually buys her acceptance.

A crucial turning point comes when the daughters of former prostitutes are sent to the city for sex work. It takes a generation – perhaps two – and then prostitution becomes a profession and a standard career 'choice' for girls from poor communities who almost invariably have limited education and minimal skills. This process has only occurred in pockets throughout Asia but the phenomenon is spreading and a greater and greater number of girls are being reared for prostitution.

Amongst the Tamangs of Nepal the trading of girls is an open secret.[45] There are virtually no girls between the ages of thirteen and twenty in villages like Ichowk in Sindhupalchowk.[46] Similarly in northern Thailand and parts of the northern Philippines there are communities in which every family has a prostituted daughter. Initially girls were sold into the sex industry because families had few alternatives. They were desperately poor and the selling of a child made the difference between the rest of the family going hungry and providing them with just enough to eat. These girls were sacrificed so that others could survive. In some parts of Asia this is still the case but in those areas where prostitution is a career option for thirteen- and fourteen-year-old girls there is a complicating factor. Poor and marginal communities are besieged with the values, images and the materialism of affluent society and these disadvantaged groups have, inevitably, also desired the same symbols of status. One way they can afford at least some of the coveted commodities of a modern lifestyle is by trading a daughter into sexual slavery.

In Thailand this has become a sophisticated system of exchange. A customary practice known as *tok khiew* (which means 'green harvest') has been adapted to the needs of the sex trade. In the original version farmers pledged their unharvested rice crop in return for a loan. This system now also applies to girls. Agents place a kind of deposit on girls of twelve and thirteen, and sometimes even younger if they are exceptionally pretty and show promise of maturing into attractive teenagers. In return for this deposit the girl is pledged to the sex industry.

A study was undertaken in 1990 with the aim of establishing the reasons why some Thai families encouraged their girls to become prostitutes. It came up with some depressing conclusions. It found that 60% of families sending daughters to the brothels were not forced to do so because of acute poverty. Instead they were motivated by the desire to own consumer goods like televisions and videos.[47] There is competition among families to acquire household items. In some ways this consumerism complements traditional values which place a strong emphasis on external appearance.[48] All the young ethnic Thai girls who 'Go South' are not dragged screaming to the brothels. Only rarely are they held in captivity. Most would not claim to be forced or coerced, but their options are so narrow, and they are so young, that their compliance amounts to coercion.

Parents are not solely to blame. The perpetrators of the prostitution of young girls in places like Thailand are not just individuals but are entire social, political and economic systems. There is skewed economic development that leaves whole communities without access to the fruits of modern society while at the same time tempting them with its products. There is a social and sexual system that reduces women's utility to sex. There is a socialisation process which conditions women to accept that they must help their families by any means possible. There are men who demand the right to buy relationships of power with women and there is an industry ready to organise and profit from this demand. Parents and communities are only small-time traders in a much larger pattern of commerce created by vast social, sexual, economic and political forces.

I met a gorgeously beautiful woman in a Pattaya nightclub, where she danced in a tiny bikini and sold sex to foreigners. Once we had established that I did not want to buy sex from her she told me about her career and how well she had done for herself and her family.

I am from northern Thailand. From a little village. We were not rich but not poor. My mother was a sex worker in Bangkok during the time of the Americans [the Vietnam War]. I have two sisters and one brother. When I was at school I thought about getting a job in an office because I was quite good at my studies but when I was fourteen I started this work. My family said I could earn more money this way. I went to Bangkok and I worked in a massage parlour for a while but the work wasn't good: the clients were not nice and the pay wasn't enough. I worked there for three years until I paid off my debt. Because the customers like me, and I give good service, I got a better job in a bar and I entertained a lot of foreigners. One time I went to Japan for a few months and I earned a lot of money. This is good work for me because I can send money to my family. My brother has a motorbike and perhaps one day we can buy a car. My family has already made another room in the house with the money I sent them. They are very happy and proud that I am more successful than other girls in my village.

As you walk through the villages of Sindhupalchowk and Nuwakot in Nepal it is possible to pick out the families of girls working in Indian brothels. They have the houses with tin roofs and men lolling outside in the shade listening to radios and playing cards. This relative affluence and leisure is bought with the bodies of their sisters and daughters. In the lanes of Kamatipura red light area in Mumbai, I met a Nepali prostitute who looked around twenty-three but who said she was thirty-five. She was confident and heavily made-up. This is what she said:

I am from Sindhupalchowk in Nepal. My sister is also in the profession here. There are a lot of us from the same place. I came here about ten years ago with a *gharwali* [brothel manager] from my village.

It was clear from this young woman's comments that she was not physically coerced into prostitution and that she had started her career as a prostitute when she was a child.

The mixture of poverty, successful prostitutes and consumer

culture has dramatically altered societal values about prostitution in selected areas of Asia. But for most people, in most communities, it remains an unacceptable trade. This, however, cannot stop the desperately poor from trying to sell their children and often succeeding in the task. Poor families in Cambodia are aware that they can demand, and receive, a high price for their daughter's virginity and daughters know that this is a way they can help their families. In the Mekong Delta there are well-documented cases in which parents directly or indirectly are involved in selling children – some as young as twelve – into prostitution.[49] It is still possible, though more unusual, to find similar cases in Indonesia.[50] In the very poorest communities families are not even anxious to secure a payment for their girls. In Bangladesh, girls are taken from their families by agents who promise them jobs. Some of these parents and guardians are too poor to be choosy and cautious about what kind of work their daughters will do. As far as many are concerned they are happy to have girls taken away because it relieves them of another mouth to feed and another dowry to collect.[51]

Many trafficked girls and those who are directly coerced into prostitution in Asia share a similar set of characteristics. First they have low educational levels. In South-East Asia a report by the International Labour Organisation found that sex workers were less educated than the average woman.[52] In India, where most women are illiterate, brothel-based prostitutes and streetwalkers almost invariably have little or no schooling.[53] In Sonagachi, which is the biggest brothel in Calcutta, only 15% of the women are literate.[54] This pattern is repeated over and over again throughout South Asia.

Sompop Jantraka runs the Daughters' Education Programme in areas along the Thai–Burmese border and works with girls who are victims of trafficking for prostitution. His organisation tries to curtail the trade in girls by identifying those who are most likely to be trafficked. The girls are provided with a basic education and a training that might provide them with an alternative form of employment. Those who are in imminent danger are given a safe environment in which to stay. The programme identifies a number of common risk factors leading to trafficking and prostitution, especially among the tribal communities. A girl is more likely to be recruited into prostitution if she has a sister or relative who is already in the industry. She is especially vulnerable if alcoholism, drug addiction, divorce or the death of a parent shakes the structure of the family. The point at which these factors come into play is when the girl finishes compulsory education at the age of twelve or thirteen. Freed from school, girls from northern Thailand then 'Go South'.

Problems within the family, and not simply poverty, are the most important factors pushing girls into prostitution. This is borne out, time after time, by the experiences of women who were forced into prostitution by economic necessity and by girls who were trafficked and sold into prostitution. In Calcutta, for example, trafficked girls are often between twelve and fifteen years old. Trafficked Bengali Hindu girls are commonly from families in which a parent has died and the remaining parent has remarried. At this point the girl becomes subject to abuse from her stepparent within the reconstituted family. Among Bengali Muslims the situation is slightly different. Bengali Muslim men .commonly have many wives and many children whom they cannot support. Because children usually remain with their fathers after a divorce, new wives discriminate against the children of earlier wives. Girls report that they ran away from home because they could not tolerate the hunger and the beatings.[55] From there it is only a small step to being absorbed within trafficking networks and sold to a brothel. A study undertaken of prostitutes in Mumbai in 1962 discovered that the death of a girl's guardians and ill treatment by relations was the single most important factor pushing females into prostitution.[56] Almost forty years later the situation is remarkably similar. In interviews with girls rescued in a 1996 raid on Mumbai brothels it was found that over half of the girls had grown up in families in which one or both parents had died. Their home life was also marked by a collapse of family conventions. Some families, for instance, lacked the capacity, or willingness, to arrange a marriage for their girls.[57]

The experience of a woman who was trafficked into the Tanbazar brothel when she was twelve, and who now works on the streets of Dhaka, is a common one throughout South Asia.

My mother died when I was little and my father remarried.
My stepmother was cruel to me and my brother, but my
brother was lucky and my maternal aunt said she would look
after him. I had to stay with my stepmother and do all the
chores and look after my little half-brothers. She would beat
me for no reason and would not give me food so I was always
very hungry. One day I couldn't stand it any more so I ran
away from the house. I walked and walked because I had
nowhere to go. I met a woman on the road and she said she
could find me a job in the city. She seemed nice and kind and
not like my stepmother so I went with her and she sold me to
a brothel.

Marriages fail and parents fail and, inevitably, it is girls and women who carry the heaviest burden as a result. Sixty per cent of girls from northern Thailand enter prostitution in order to support their parents. A majority of Thai sex workers from the north-east do so after the failure of a marriage and the subsequent need to support their children.[58]

It is the same story wherever you go. Cambodia has been tortured by years of war and genocide. Basic familial relationships were irredeemably traumatised during the Pol Pot regime, when children informed upon their parents and parents upon their children. The fundamental building blocks of Cambodian society were torn apart as families unravelled. They have not yet recovered. This legacy makes the sale of children, and the buying of people, that much easier.

Troubled families are the breeding grounds for sex workers. And troubled families in poor, marginal and crisis-ridden communities generate the most reliable supply of cheap girls. Civil wars and natural calamities produce bumper harvests for the sex industry. Famine-struck North Korea cannot feed its people. It cannot feed the girls who flee across the Chinese border in search of food and who are met by sex industry entrepreneurs who take them to brothels in Chinese cities.[59] When Mount Pinatubo in the Philippines erupted and displaced thousands of people from their homes, it was the experienced agents of the sex industry who were some of the first to offer their sympathy and their own variety of support in the centres sheltering the victims. Like all successful business people they had their eye on a bargain.

Let us make no mistake, prostitution is not just about poverty. It is a business founded upon all sorts of inequalities. It is a business that is constructed out of the distorted relations of power between men and women, between the poor and the rich and between the minorities and mainstream of a society. The sex industry makes money because it buys cheap raw materials and packages them well. It turns vulnerability into a commodity and that commodity into a profit.

Chapter Three

THE AGENTS

Trafficking and the buying and selling of females for prostitution is an expanding trade run by a loose but gigantic web of people. Some of these are experienced professionals in the sex industry and some are small-time merchants making one-off deals with the bodies of children and young women.

The level of exploitation a woman will encounter in the sex industry is largely determined by the way she is inducted into the trade. Trafficking of girls and their forced entry into prostitution is a common method of recruiting new products into the lower echelons of the Asian sex market. However, it is not the only way that children and women are coerced into prostitution. In less-developed parts of the region urban slums are breeding grounds for girls who become absorbed within the sex industry. Hundreds of thousands of children living in miserable poverty on the streets of Asia's cities provide another vast reservoir of cheap bodies. Selling sex is the only way some of these children can survive.

Trafficking occurs because there is a large demand for cheap, purchased sex. In some Asian countries, like Pakistan and India, this demand is heightened because of the restrictions placed upon women and their limited interaction with men. In other countries, such as Japan, there is a shortfall in the number of local women willing to work for low wages in the sex industry. Most are safely ensconced in respectable marriages or they have alternative occupations. Importing women from other countries therefore makes up the shortfall. The advantage with this import strategy is that the imported women are significantly cheaper than the home-grown variety.

Contrary to popular myth, large numbers of girls are not abducted, drugged and then forced into prostitution. Agents do not need to go to such lengths. There is a ready supply of candidates for the brothels without engaging in risky abductions. Kidnapping does take place in some parts of China but this appears to be confined to the abduction of girls for marriage rather than prostitution. In these instances the young woman's body is purchased for the benefit of one man and not for the pleasure of many.

Trafficked women almost always end up in the very worst kind of brothel or club, servicing a large number of clients for very little money. Some receive no payment at all. The structure of the industry and the way in which women are duped, forced or enticed into it varies throughout the region depending on how highly developed the business has become. It makes sense to divide Asia into two main markets in order to understand how the sex trade networks operate. The first is the South Asian market, with India as its hub. The second is the South-East and East Asian market, with Thailand as its hub. These two giant networks are at differing levels of development, which are conditioned by the regions' general level of economic development and the cultural and social context. In South-East Asia the sex trade has assumed the proportions of a fully fledged industry and in parts of the region it is approaching the status of a 'normal' industry. South Asia's trade is less sophisticated, and there is greater cultural resistance to the concept of sex for sale but, even here, we can see that the industry is following a course towards normalisation that has been set by its South-East and East Asian counterpart.

First, let us look at the way that South Asian girls leave their homes and their path to the brothels. There is no consensus on the number of women involved in the sex industry in South Asia. All figures are estimates, and unreliable ones at that. Undoubtedly, however, the trade involves the entry of many thousands of new women each year. The majority of these are not in fact women but girls. Many of them will have barely entered their teens. Girls are taken from Nepal to India and from Bangladesh to India. The National Commission for Women in Delhi estimates that at least half of the girls and women in West Bengal brothels are from Bangladesh.[1] Women like these have been trafficked *internationally* and their plight has attracted some attention and media interest. However, *internal* trafficking of women is far more extensive and its victims experience very similar forms of exploitation. In Pakistan, for instance, internal trafficking of girls for prostitution is far more common than the trafficking of Bangladeshi, Indian and Afghani women. Indian brothels contain a large number of Nepali women but the vast majority of those held in systems of sexual slavery in India are Indian women. There are no major trafficking channels leading into Bangladesh and Nepal. The overwhelming number of sex workers there are local women as there is absolutely no one else desperate enough to compete for the dubious fruits of the sex trade in these poverty-wracked countries.

There is rarely anything approaching a well-defined sex trade organisation in the villages and towns in which the women grow up. Girls are usually first pulled into the sex industry's web by someone they know. The typical procurer is an older woman – a friend or maybe a relative – who has secured the trust of the girl and her family. Sometimes these women may run a small business that recruits girls now and again. Some may only ever recruit one young girl and send her on her way to a life in the brothels. This is how a fourteen-year-old prostituted girl explained how she had arrived in a Calcutta brothel from her impoverished village in Murshidabad, West Bengal:

> There was a woman in my village who was about ten years older than me. She had left the village a few years before and one day she came back and brought her husband with her. She had nice clothes and said she and her husband had good jobs in Calcutta and a beautiful house and jewellery and good clothes. She said to me, 'Come to Calcutta and I can get you a good job and you can help your family.' At first my mother said no but eventually she agreed because there was nothing else I could do and we did not have enough food after my father died.

From the rest of this girl's conversation it transpired that the woman who enticed her to Calcutta was a prostitute herself and that the husband was not a real husband but a *babu* (a regular client). This couple sold the girl's virginity to one of the woman's favoured clients, and afterwards traded her to a large brothel in Calcutta's Bowbazar red light area.

Most recruiters are not practising sex workers but many may be former sex workers who know the business and how to initiate new recruits into the trade. The women who manage significant parts of the Nepali sex trade are the best example of how this type of recruitment operates. Large numbers of Nepali girls from Himalayan hill tribes can be found in brothels throughout India's cities. The youngest ones are held in captivity and cannot be seen, but the older ones can be distinguished by their high cheekbones and Mongolian eyes. They work in all-Nepali brothels, which often look more prosperous than their Indian equivalent. The fact that there are so many

of these Nepali girls owes something to customer demand for submissive girls with fair skin and oriental features, but perhaps even
more to the efficient recruitment and transportation machinery
maintained by Nepali brothel owners and their *gharwalis* (brothel
managers). Girls have been trafficked from pockets of the Himalayas
for decades. The girls who first went to India are now elderly
women. A few became successful and now manage or own their
own brothels. These women send older prostitutes back to hill villages to recruit new staff for their establishment and it is rare for
them to return without a batch of fresh girls and young women.

Recruiters like these are professionals. But there is another
numerically more important group involved in the sale of children
and women in South Asia: ordinary people. They may be family
members: uncles, aunts, cousins, husbands, in-laws and even parents. They are neighbours and friends. Crucially they are the very
people their victims trust most. A study of sex workers in India
during the 1980s discovered that 33% had been pushed into prostitution by close friends and family.[2]

This was how a twenty-year-old woman from Karnataka
described her journey several years previously into prostitution in
Mumbai:

> One day I had finished working in the fields when my
> mother's friend suggested that we go for a bus ride and to see
> the city. I wanted to go because I had never been to the city
> and I was very excited. On the bus we had a good time eating
> snacks and talking. When we got to the city we went to visit
> my 'auntie's' friend. At first it was nice. We had tea but then
> my mother's friend disappeared and she didn't come back.
> She had sold me to a brothel.

By far the most common means of trafficking young women into
the sex industry throughout South Asia is to promise them a job.

Some know what sort of work they will do but I believe that the majority probably do not. The prospective job on offer may be as a domestic worker. In Nepal girls are frequently enticed with a job in the carpet factories of the Kathmandu Valley. In Bangladesh rural girls are lured with the offer of employment in a garment factory. A few of these jobs may actually exist – but for lots of girls they do not last for very long. The jobs are a kind of staging post on the way to the brothel. Once the girl is away from home and outside the protection of her family and community she is increasingly vulnerable, and it is only a short step from there into the world of the sex trade.

A recent survey by UNICEF of Nepali prostitutes working in India reveals that around 86% of them did not know that they were destined for the sex market when they left home.[3] Of those that were duped into prostitution 82% had been promised jobs.[4] And echoing the study undertaken in the 1980s, a large proportion of girls reported that they were trafficked by a close female friend or a person they considered to be well known to them.[5]

Very few prostitutes in South Asia make a conscious and positive choice to become a sex worker. Lalitha Nayak who manages the national anti-trafficking programme of the Joint Women's Programme in Delhi maintains that almost all girls in prostitution in India are either tricked, physically forced or pushed into the profession through dire poverty. Prithi Patak who, for the past ten years, has run an NGO aiding child prostitutes in the notorious Kamatipura red light district of Mumbai shares her opinion. 'Ninety-five per cent of girls here in Kamatipura were forced into prostitution,' she insists. 'They did not choose this occupation. The remaining 5% who did come here of their own accord did so by making a negative choice. They simply had no other alternatives.'

Virtually all of the prostituted women and girls I spoke to in Bangladesh had left their homes because they had been promised a job in the city. All left home willingly. Some wanted to escape beatings, some wanted to earn enough money to end constant hunger, and some left because they were told to go. Others went in the great hope that they would be able to help their struggling families and to better their own lives. Yet again, all left with someone they knew and trusted.

The poorest Bangladeshi families do not have to have the loss of a daughter assuaged by payment or what, in other countries, is euphemistically described as an 'advance' on her earnings. Those burdened by poverty and a surplus of daughters are glad to see them depart for the city where they will be able to feed themselves and may even send a little money home.

Marriage, rather than employment, is sometimes another avenue towards prostitution for unfortunate Bangladeshi girls. Professor Ishrat Shamim of the Centre for Women and Children's Studies in Dhaka relates this story and she believes that it is typical of the way in which marriage is used as a lever to bring girls into the sex trade: Rupchand was a poor rickshaw puller who had three daughters. He and his family were approached by an Indian woman who visited their house and who suggested that she should arrange a marriage between Fatema, Rupchand's fourteen-year-old daughter, and a man she knew in India who was looking for a bride. Rupchand accepted the offer on the grounds that it was 'the chance of a lifetime' for his daughter. Fatema left for India and nothing was heard of her again. Some years later the Indian woman returned to the area. By this time Rupchand had died and his widow had become suspicious about her daughter's disappearance. The Indian woman promised that Fatema was doing well but the girl's mother was not convinced. She believed that her daughter had been trafficked but she felt that it would be pointless to report it to the police, as her family was too poor and too powerless to matter.

In Pakistan new entrants to the sex industry are commonly recruited through the institution of marriage. Superficially, Pakistan is extremely conservative about sex. Apart from a few isolated and dying red light areas in Karachi and Lahore there is nothing to compare with the large brothels of India and Bangladesh. Pakistan has an extensive and growing trade in high- and middle-class prostitution that takes place in well-hidden brothels in the suburbs, but down at the lower end of the market, where the vast majority of sex workers operate, prostitution is very much a 'family' affair. This is the way the system operates: when a Pakistani woman marries she becomes the property of her husband. The extent and implications of this 'ownership' vary according to region, ethnicity and socio-economic class. Many wives are completely at the mercy of their husbands and this is particularly true of women from those areas in which a man will pay brideprice for his wife. What the businessmen of the sex trade do is to marry a woman and then pimp her out. What is more, they can legitimately have up to four of these wives. When the wife/prostitute becomes a little too old to attract customers she can be retained to do domestic chores or, just as likely, she can be divorced and a new wife can be recruited.

In Heera Mandi, the ancient red light district of Lahore, I interviewed a woman who had been a prostitute for many years and who had been owned and controlled by a series of men. As she aged she was rejected by her 'husbands' and was then picked up by another 'husband' who put her to work at a lower level on the prostitution hierarchy. She is now in her mid-fifties and is wracked by tuberculosis. She dresses in a tattered *shalwar-kameez* and lives in a tiny hovel of a room without water or electricity. In the darkness, and with a strategically placed candle, she tries to encourage clients to pay a pathetic handful of rupees for her services. Yet even now her new 'husband' continues to takes his cut.

A small but significant proportion of sex workers are girls who have eloped with boyfriends only to find that their new address is a brothel rather than a cosy marital home. Unmarried mothers and the victims of rape form another small but significant category. They are significant because apart from being the victims of awful personal tragedies their fate reveals some unhappy truths about South Asian societies. One of the most important of these is that many of the victims of trafficking are totally trusting. They trust the men who promise to marry them but who ultimately lead them to destruction. One of the roots of this trust and naivety is the manner in which girls are socialised to respect and to accord men a value that far exceeds the value they place upon themselves. So when a man flatters and pays attention to a young girl – especially if she is from an underprivileged community – she feels proud to be the recipient of this honour. In this context she can easily be duped.[6]

A common story repeated throughout South Asia is that of the failed romance as a prelude to prostitution. This is the story of a sixteen-year-old Limbu girl from far eastern Nepal. Unlike many of the other trafficked girls she has a moderate level of education and is not from a very poor family.

My job was to buy the vegetables for our family and I would go to the *bajar* [market] every day. One day there were some new men there drinking tea. They were army men [Nepalis working in the Indian Army]. One was very handsome and he started to talk to me. I ran away because I didn't know what to say. The next day he was there by himself and he told me that he was waiting for me. I thought he was wonderful because he was so handsome and he spoke so sweetly to me. He said that he loved me and that he wanted to marry me. I saw him every day at the *bajar* and I really loved him. Then after about one week he said that he was leaving because he had to do army work in Kashmir. He asked me to leave with him because there was no time to prepare a big wedding and he said not to tell my parents. He promised that we would be married in Kashmir. I was so stupid because I believed him. I packed a little bag and ran away with him. But he didn't take me to Kashmir. He took me to Mumbai. I didn't know that it

wasn't Kashmir. He said he loved me but all he wanted to do
was to make me a prostitute.

Strategies that use love and friendship as a means to procure and
traffic girls are far more common than the use of outright force. The
female migrant workers who arrive from their villages to work in the
carpet mills of the Kathmandu Valley or in Bangladeshi garment
factories are often little more than disoriented children. They work
in cramped unpleasant conditions for wages that hardly cover the
cost of board and lodgings. Frequently older male workers and the
management of the factories sexually exploit them. It is not surprising that they are homesick, however poor their homes and
families might have been. And then, as if by a miracle, they find a
special friend: someone who offers them affection and psychological support. This person also offers a solution to their financial
needs by suggesting that there is a better way to earn money. All the
girl has to do is go with them to another factory in a different town
or perhaps just across the border. At this stage, however, the girls do
not know that the factory does not produce carpets or garments but
that it packages girls for prostitution.

Procurers gather girls and young women from their villages. They
are the first link in the chain that takes the recruits to the brothels.
At the village level most recruitment does not take place as part of
some larger plan directed from the red light areas of the major cities.
It is a far more informal process. The sex industry does not have to
involve itself directly in recruitment of girls from their homes. There
are plenty of people already living within the community who are
prepared to do this. What is more, local people make better
recruiters. They have direct and personal knowledge of an area.
They know exactly which families to target. They know who is poor,
which family has too many daughters, which family has suffered
the death of a parent or a marital breakdown, which family is expe-
riencing the serious illness of a breadwinner, which family has an

alcoholic father, and which family cannot cope. In other words which families cannot, or will not, protect their daughters.

The most successful recruiters operate at times of hardship. In Bangladesh, for instance, they are most active between June and August when food is scarce. The pattern is common throughout South Asia. In Nepal the recruiters who offer jobs to girls, and who give their families an 'advance' on their earnings, do briskest business in the summer before the main harvests are brought in and when a household's food deficit is felt most keenly. Some recruiters do not even offer payment – but only the prospect of finding work for the daughter of a poor family. Others pay according to the age of the girl, her beauty and whether she is a virgin. An impoverished family will receive a reduced payment because the recruiters know that they are desperate. A family in Nepal may therefore receive anything from a few hundred to a few thousand rupees for their daughter. It is a pittance but, in the midst of acute poverty, even a pittance can be precious.

Small-time procurers may take a girl from the village to the city, and they may even sell her directly to a brothel, but they will rarely take her across national borders. This task is left to more organised groups of traffickers, and the further a girl moves from her home the more likely she is to become drawn into the network of professional traders. The role of these traders is a complicated one: recruiters and traffickers are vilified – but not universally so. Although the girls they recruit may be viciously exploited, some people within rural communities hold the agents in high regard. In India the image of the recruiter is generally poor but, in Bangladesh and Pakistan, the recruiters are sometimes seen as employment agents and facilitators offering the chance of a better life to the people who pass through their hands. Perhaps this view should be underlined to reluctant prostitutes.

In the parts of Bangladesh and Nepal that are not prostitute-breeding grounds, girls are recruited from their homes by a procurer. This procurer will then hand them over to an agent who takes them on the next leg of their journey. Typically they travel by bus and on foot. Sometimes they are transported in small groups and sometimes singly in order to avoid suspicion.

Border crossings are potentially the most dangerous part of the trafficking process, but generally South Asia's international borders are not rigorously policed and many border patrols find it hard to distinguish trafficked girls from the general population. Some that do distinguish the traffickers are paid to look the other way either in cash or in kind. Girls trafficked out of Bangladesh, for example, report being forced to provide sexual services to border patrols in order to avoid arrest.

The illegal migrants smuggled across the Indo–Bangladeshi border are known as *dhurs*. They include girls and women who are trafficked for prostitution and also other forms of exploitative labour. Another group of migrants is made up of poor men and older women who seek work in India and who cannot afford a passport to leave the country legally. A veritable industry has been made of this border crossing with local entrepreneurs acting as owners and managers of the transit points, or *ghats*. The border is not officially open but it is easy to cross with the help of the *ghat* men in places like Satkhira, Jessore, Meherpur and Chapai Nawabganj. In some places the migrants and the trafficked women simply walk though fields; in other places they wade through rivers.

The Benapole transit point on the Indo–Bangladeshi border reveals that illegal crossings are commonplace. It also illustrates how the traffic in migrants is well organised. The border area is dotted with houses which resemble small huts. During daylight these houses appear uninhabited but at night they are the scenes of feverish activity. A lot of food is prepared for a seemingly large number of guests. These guests are the *dhurs* and among them will be girls travelling to the Indian sex industry. A few may even go further afield to Pakistan. They wait in the houses until the *ghat* men take them across the border. For this service the *dhurs* pay a fee of 500 taka (£7), which is about half the average monthly wage of a female worker in a garment factory. This sum will form part of the debt the trafficked girls must repay by selling sex.

Trafficking of girls from Nepal is illegal, but crossing the border between India and Nepal is easy because the border is officially open and Indians and Nepalis can cross without passports. Halting trafficking along this five-hundred-mile open border poses considerable practical difficulties. Most trafficking, however, is conducted across the fifteen major border points between the two countries. In theory the border police monitor those who pass through the checkpoints very closely. But, in practice, this is not what happens. For example, Kakavitta is a border town in the far east of Nepal. It is a gateway through which many hundreds, and perhaps many thousands, of Nepali girls have left for India. The young and enthusiastic police officer in charge of the checkpoint is making a concerted effort to stem the flow of girls to India and traffickers have been arrested in the process of transporting girls south. But, unfortunately, traffickers do not necessarily have to face the rigours of the border checkpoint. What they do is to skirt the town, cross through the tea gardens and scramble down a path to the banks of the wide Mechi River that divides the two countries. Then they can either cross over the bridge or, during the dry season, they can wade across the river. The ease of crossing into India at Kakavitta is replicated all along the Indo–Nepal border and the majority of the Nepali girls I spoke to who had been prostituted in India seemed puzzled by my questions surrounding the difficulties of crossing the border. Many stated that they had been drilled to respond to the questions of the border police by claiming that they were the trafficker's cousin, or sister-in-law, and that they were on their way to visit family members living in India.

The agents who accompany girls to the cities are smart. They know how to avoid the authorities and the organisations combating trafficking. They do not take the girls along the most direct and obvious routes. In some places they take a detour and stop for a few days or weeks to avoid the suspicion that they are ferrying girls to market. Whenever agents believe that their movements have become exposed they switch to another route. This was the way one Bangladeshi woman described her ordeal:

> After we had been married for a few days my husband said
> that we had to go to India to look for work. We left our home
> in Dhaka and crossed the border. After that we travelled by
> bus to many different towns and villages. My husband knew
> lots of people in these places and we stayed in small hotels.
> My husband let his friends use me and they gave him money.
> At first I refused but then he would beat me. He was pleased
> with me when I earned money for him. After a few weeks we
> came to Calcutta and he sold me to a brothel. The work here
> is not much different than when I was married.

A whole series of agents may be involved in the trafficking process and they pass the girl from one to another. At each leg of her journey, her price increases because each of the traffickers wishes to make a profit from her. By the time she reaches the brothel her 'value' can be as much as a hundred times what her family received for her.

A high proportion of the traffickers – as opposed to the procurers – are full-time professionals. They are often the sons of sex workers. Some of the less professional traffickers force the girls to have sex with them on the journey, but most do not. Far from being a mark of respect for the girls, this restraint is necessary in order to preserve the men's own reputations. Their credibility within the sex trade would be severely dented if they were found trying to pass off used goods as high-cost virgins.

Girls have mixed recollections of their journeys to the brothels and this is especially the case if they were trafficked over long distances. Some said they were excited about going to the city, some were bemused at the new world they were seeing and others were frightened. Ironically, many claimed that they relied upon the person who was trafficking them. The trafficker helped them to cope in an alien environment: he or she gave them food, managed the transport arrangements, found somewhere for them to sleep and spoke the sometimes unfamiliar language. Many girls said that they could not have run away even if they had been given the opportunity, because they did not know where they were, who to speak to, and sometimes in what language to communicate.

Not all girls who are forced into brothel-based prostitution are brought by agents from the villages. Some arrive under their own steam. They are classic rural–urban migrants seeking work in the cities and they find themselves sucked into the sex trade because they are young and naive and vulnerable. A visit to the bus and rail stations of large South Asian cities is convincing evidence of the rich pickings awaiting canny agents. In Howrah train station and Esplanade bus terminal in Calcutta, tired and uncertain teenage girls arrive from their villages. Sometimes they come alone, sometimes with a friend. Waiting for them are pleasant, middle-aged women of respectable appearance who say that they know where the new arrivals can find jobs. To the girls it seems like an answer to their prayers and a path towards a new life. An eighteen-year-old girl described how she was approached in Howrah station.

I came from my village and travelled first by bus and then by train. My friend came with me. When we got to the end of our journey we weren't sure what to do. The station was so big. My friend said we could go and stay with her uncle who lived in Calcutta and that he would help us to find jobs, but we didn't know how to get there. Then a woman started to talk to us. She was very friendly and nice. She looked like a good woman because she wore nice clothes and jewellery and she wore *sindoor* in her hair [the sign of a married woman]. She promised us that she knew where we could get very good jobs and earn lots of money working in rich people's houses. The jobs were in Mumbai but she told us that she would pay for our train fares. So we went with her but when we got to Mumbai there were no jobs in rich people's houses. She sold me to one brothel and my friend to another brothel. That was about four years ago. A customer helped me run away from the brothel but my friend is still there. I want to help her to escape too but I don't know where she is.

Trafficked girls are frequently taken first to transit centres. These function rather like large clearing houses. From there agents will distribute them to the most appropriate market. Calcutta, Agra and Benares, among others, serve as significant transit centres in India. Karachi and Lahore are the Pakistani equivalent.

It is commonly assumed that girls and women who have been trafficked from other countries are inevitably destined for large brothels in major urban centres. This is incorrect. Many are, but an even higher proportion never make it that far. All Indian towns have brothels, and sex is a cheap and easily available commodity along Indian highways. Virtually every *dhaba* (a small restaurant or transport cafe) runs a lucrative sideline offering girls to truck drivers and men who are passing through. The most attractive trafficked girls do get taken to the big centres like Calcutta and Mumbai but those with lesser physical charms are sold off to these *dhaba*-affiliated brothels and to the red light areas of smaller towns. Everyone knows of the thousands of Nepali girls residing in the brothels of Mumbai, Calcutta and Delhi but very little is known about the thousands who work on the highways leading south from Nepal or those in the brothels of dozens of north Indian towns.

It makes sense for traffickers to diversify and not to depend solely on a few markets for young prostitutes in the big cities. There is increasing awareness of trafficking in these cities. In the well-known red light areas there are NGOs working on trafficking issues and child prostitution. These organisations are small in number and size but they can be an irritation for the sex industry. Even sections of the police seem more alert to the issues. This combination can create problems for traffickers, and many agents are now sending their goods to non-traditional red light areas. In sleepy towns and backwater brothels along the highways there is zero police interference. There are virtually no NGOs operating here. Even within cities the NGOs congregate in a handful of areas. Meanwhile the structure of prostitution is changing around them. To give an example, in Mumbai almost all NGOs working on prostitution issues are concentrated in Kamatipura. A survey of sex work in the city, however, has shown a proliferation of red light areas away from the customary centres so that there are now around thirty-three sites of brothel-based commercial sexual activity in the city.[7] There is a greater and greater demand for prostitution in a greater variety of locations throughout South Asia. The traffickers have simply responded to this demand by diversifying and targeting a wider market.

Agents arriving in towns and cities with a batch of new recruits may have an agreement to supply them to a particular brothel. Some agents may be affiliated with a single brothel. Others will have to negotiate a deal. They will take the girls to their contacts within the red light areas and see who is ready to buy. The merchandise is inspected and a price agreed. A teenager in a Bangladeshi brothel related her own experience.

The agent took me to the brothel. It was a very big building with two or three girls in each room. I was put in one of these rooms and then some people came to look at me and to ask questions about me. A woman pinched me and said I was

thin. Then they went out of the room. I heard the agent arguing with them outside the door and then he took me away to
another brothel. He was very angry and he kept twisting my
arm and slapping me and telling me that I had to smile at the
people. At the next brothel he was happy because he sold me
to a woman who had other girls working for her.

Brides are bought in large parts of South Asia. In parts of Pakistan
it is cheaper to buy a woman outright rather than to go through the
ritual of purchasing her through brideprice. Bangladeshi women
are sold as brides to the Indian Punjab. Some of these purchased
brides are happy with the transaction and lead more prosperous
lives in their new families than they could ever have expected if they
had remained at home. Many, however, do not. They are condemned to a terrible life of sexual and domestic exploitation in an
unfamiliar and hostile place. These women are undocumented and
unrecognised sex slaves. Hina Jilani, a lawyer and human rights
activist based in Lahore, believes that many of the Bangladeshi
women who were trafficked to Pakistan in the 1980s and early 1990s,
and who were forced into prostitution, are now living in horrifying
conditions of servitude in rural Pakistan. Many thousands of
women were allegedly transported across the subcontinent but have
now apparently 'disappeared'. After working for a spell as prostitutes these women are now too old to be lucrative sex workers for
their pimps. One theory suggests that they have been sold off as
wives/slaves to rural Pakistani men. There can be few more terrifying fates.

Clandestine auctions are held in Pakistan's North-West Frontier
Province. Women and girls form the merchandise and they are sold
to the highest bidder. Ostensibly they are sold for marriage, and the
auction process is explained as a simplified and quicker version of
the traditional payment of brideprice. It is also cheaper. An argument used to rationalise the process is that hardworking men cannot

afford to spend large amounts of time searching for a bride and negotiating the financial deal. An auction speeds up this process. It also has a singular advantage: the auctioned girls are highly vulnerable. No one is going to follow a purchased girl's fate. These girls can be bought for any purpose. And, in practice, they are.[8]

The sex industry does not place just one product on the market. Even within the brothel sector the product is not uniform. There are vast variations in the type of women or girls available: prices vary according to age, beauty, ethnicity, whether she is a virgin, whether she has had children, and what services she can perform. Women who enter prostitution in their twenties will fetch very little because they have limited working life left. A girl of about nine or younger will also be cheap because she will have to be supported for a year or two before she can start earning substantial sums on a regular basis. The price a brothel pays to an agent for an individual girl will depend upon these factors. It will also fluctuate according to the basic laws of supply and demand. Prices drop when there is a glut of girls on the market. Typically this happens when some crisis in the rural areas propels more young women to the cities. Similarly, they also decrease when seasonal food shortages in the countryside mean that procurement rates rise. Prices also vary according to the nature of demand. In Mumbai and Delhi, for instance, prices are higher than in less prosperous Calcutta. Consequently South Asian brothels do not pay a uniform price for their girls. In Calcutta girls can be sold for anything from a few hundred rupees to around 10,000 rupees (£7–£140). This is the way the dealers arrive at a price: the girl might be bought from her parents for somewhere between 200 and 2000 rupees (£3–£30). Then further 'value' is added. A procurer will charge between 1,000 and 2,000 rupees for their services. Perhaps a couple of hundred rupees will be paid out as bribes to police and border security forces. The trafficker will then add his or her own fee of 1,000 to 3,000 rupees. When this is totalled it becomes the cost of the girl. A similar accounting procedure is followed in Mumbai but here the total cost of a girl maybe as high as 30,000 rupees (£420). There are reports of Nepali girls fetching as much as 50,000 rupees (£700) but Prerana, the leading NGO in Kamatipura, has never come across payments exceeding 25,000 rupees (£550). This is the cost of purchasing a sex slave in India today. This slave then has to repay her cost by servicing any man who is willing to pay for her.

The South Asian patterns of recruitment, trafficking, sale and exploitation are repeated, with some variations, in South-East and East Asia. There are enormous differences between rich and poor nations in these regions. At one end of the spectrum is Japan; at the other end is Burma. In less-developed South-East Asia the sex trade bears comparison to that of South Asia in terms of the physical conditions under which the women are forced to live and work. But in the economically developed parts of these regions the sex industry has a different gloss. The business has been cleaned up. There is less squalor, more acceptance of the industry as a legitimate economic sector and a greater emphasis upon sex work as a career option for women. The principles of the trade, however, are identical. Relatively affluent men use their economic power to buy the bodies of poorer women and children. Women are brought from disadvantaged areas and less-affluent countries to more prosperous ones. The whole of this trade is underpinned by the principle that sex and women are commodities to be purchased.

Some women choose to become sex workers in South-East Asia, just as a few do in South Asia. In fact, a far higher proportion of women in South-East and East Asia have made a conscious, positive decision to make money from selling sex. Others, perhaps the majority, are forced by economic circumstances to join the trade. Others are groomed for prostitution from childhood and others are physically coerced. There is no lack of career opportunities in the sex trade. The sex business in South-East and East Asia is a highly developed industry and its reach and level of sophistication is awesome.

The industry finds its cheapest recruits in the poorest countries of the region. Impoverished countries like Burma and Vietnam are at the bottom of the regional economic hierarchy. They are sending countries and they export their women. Girls from northern Vietnam are sent as brides to China, and southern Vietnamese girls are channelled into prostitution in Cambodia. Between 1991 and 1994 the Vietnamese Ministry of Labour, Invalids and Social Affairs estimated that around five thousand Vietnamese women had been trafficked to China to become wives of men they had never met. Rich countries, at the apex of which is Japan, are receiving countries. In the middle is Thailand, which acts as a hub for the vast South-East Asian market.

Thailand has a well-deserved reputation as the world's brothel. It has an enormous domestic market in which the majority of Thai men are enthusiastic consumers. It also caters to a staggering number of sex tourists who fly in from all corners of the rich world to buy sex with young Thai women and sometimes children. Such is the demand for cheap young flesh in Thailand that women are sucked into the trade from all over the Mekong Basin. They come principally from Burma, Cambodia and also from southern China to join the thousands of Thai girls providing sex services to Thai and foreign men. The flow of girls and women throughout the Mekong region has accelerated in the past decade. The sex industry has thrived as borders between the countries have been opened and political relations have improved. Trafficking is, quite simply, easier now than it was a decade ago. Infrastructure and transportation services are better and commerce has expanded. Unfortunately this commerce includes a flourishing trade in people.

Thailand also functions as a transit country. Chinese girls, for instance, are transported through Thailand on their way to prostitution and marriage deals in Malaysia, Singapore, Taiwan and even further afield. Thailand is also a sending country. It exports its young women all over the world and especially to Japan. A few years ago a large proportion of exported Thai girls went to the Middle East but the structure of demand has changed with the expansion of South-East and East Asian economies. As the Asian tiger economies surged ahead in the 1980s and 1990s so did demand for commercial sex. Men in high-growth Asian economies decided to enjoy their increased affluence by spending it on the purchase of women. The economic miracle may have faltered during the crisis of the late 1990s but the demand for brothel-based prostitution has been only slightly dented. It seems that if Asian men are going to economise, it is rarely upon sexual services.

Japan is the region's most important receiving country. Its giant economy supports a lucrative domestic sex industry that has altered substantially in form, if not in substance, during the past fifteen years. Until the late 1980s tourism for the purpose of 'sex shopping' was a staple in the Japanese man's sexual diet. This activity was supported by the entire male-dominated culture. Companies treated their employees to annual sex tours to Korea, Thailand or the Philippines. This special kind of bonus included flights and accommodation together with the sexual services of local prostitutes. Tours like these were not run by shady organisations and indulged in only by a few dubious firms and their unsavoury employees. It was open, big business, involving prestigious companies and a sizeable proportion of the largely male workforce. Unsurprisingly Japanese and Korean feminists took great exception to this practice and they campaigned vociferously for it to be halted. Company executives returning from sex safaris were harangued at Japanese airports and there was denunciation of the tours in the media.

The response was entirely predictable: the tours adopted a lower profile and their presentation was altered. Men stopped travelling en masse. Now they go in small groups of perhaps four or five friends. And they purchase package tours that include a choice of girl along with other holiday options such as air-conditioning and minibars in their hotel rooms. Alternatively they make even more informal arrangements and just buy sex on demand. There was also another response to the curtailing of company-sponsored sex rewards. Instead of Japanese men travelling to buy sex in other countries, the sex industry decided instead to bring the women to Japan. So in the late 1980s thousands of Thai and Filipina women began to be imported. The mechanics of this import strategy were not too difficult for the industry to organise because the women came from countries where the Japanese were already famed as sex tourists and where the sex industry had established efficient networks of procuring, trafficking and marketing. In the case of the Philippines, the recruitment of women to work in Japanese brothels and clubs was facilitated by a labour export strategy conducted by the Philippines government as a path to development. For large numbers of Filipina women, however, this path led directly to sexual slavery.

Recruitment practices are largely open in those parts of South-East Asia where sex has been commercially marketed on a large scale for over thirty years. This applies particularly to northern Thailand. Here trafficking is not really the best description to apply to the recruitment and transportation of girls for prostitution. Rural–urban migration aided by a network of employment agents is a far better description of the trade. Coercion is rarely employed and girls are not deceived. Yet the absence of force does not make the sale of sex suddenly ethically legitimate – and this applies whether the goods on offer are children or women. It might make short-term economic sense for families and for individual women to sell sex. However, it is a travesty from the standpoint of human dignity and especially for the integrity of all women who must be allowed the freedom to aspire to be something more than a vagina with a price tag.

Thai recruitment patterns have changed in the last ten years. A

decade or more ago girls migrated to the cities to look for work.
They were then drawn into the sex industry when their employment
prospects appeared gloomy or when they realised that they could
earn substantially more by selling their bodies than by sewing garments in a sweatshop. Today this two-step pattern has been replaced
by a one-step pattern. Girls are delivered to the brothels directly
from their homes. The agents who organise the deliveries from
northern Thailand are significantly more organised than in South
Asia but there is rarely a single chain of procurers, agents and
brothel owners. Instead there appear to be many groups of agents
and sub-agents who are in close communication with each other
and with the brothels and clubs that will buy their merchandise. In
the north-east of the country, recruitment is less systematic, probably as a result of a greater resistance to the concept of commercial
sex.[9] Here daughters may work in the sex trade but many do not
want their families to know.

Northern Thai families are given an 'advance' on their daughter's
earnings. It is not a sale – or so the argument goes. In practice, however, it amounts to the same thing and we should not be fooled by
word games. Many new recruits to the industry are bonded labourers and the girls have to repay the 'advance' from their earnings.
They earn money by having their sexuality sold under conditions
that leave them little room for saying 'no'.

Sompop Jantraka, who runs the Daughters' Education
Programme in Thailand, describes the web of interests that lock
girls into prostitution as the 'blood-sucker cycle'. It is a perfectly
worked description. He has a deep knowledge of the mechanics of
the trade in the region and explains how large sections of the community are overtly or covertly involved in the sex business. Agents
work openly in the villages and compete with one another over the
deals that they can offer. Parents looking for the best deal for their
girls manipulate this and in some cases may sell their children to two
separate agents, spend the money and then leave it to the agents to

fight over the resultant contractual mess. In parts of Thailand, as well as in other countries like Vietnam, the family's attention is not focused on safeguarding their daughter from prostitution. On the contrary, the critical issue is the kind of brothel she will work in. The measure of concern is the reputation of the brothel and the reliability of the agent who takes her there. Canny fathers take their girls directly to the brothels. This way they can cut out the middle man and make a higher profit. And then there are the mothers, themselves former sex workers, who deliver their own daughters directly to the sex industry. Such stories are a sad and disturbing reflection on a society that offers girls such limited options. They also illustrate the ugliness of a vicious circle in which families perpetrate upon their children exactly the same set of pressures and abuses that they themselves were exposed to as children.

Girls are recruited in their early and mid-teens and they are collected from their villages in the back of vans and pick-up trucks. Jantraka is able to monitor the surges in demand for girls when brothels in the cities place 'rush orders'. On such occasions girls leave in batches. Deposits are also placed upon especially pretty ones while deals are negotiated with those affluent clients who express interest in deflowering virgins. For some families who have qualms about sending a daughter into prostitution there is now an increasingly favoured and more socially acceptable alternative. Teenage girls conclude serial marriages with elderly men. It is not uncommon for a sixteen-year-old girl to be the bride of a sixty-year-old man. The marriage rarely lasts long and the price for this short period of conjugal bliss comes at an unbeatable 500 baht (£8.30).

A recent study of the handling of trafficked children in the Mekong Basin found that agents used a variety of techniques to market their goods.[10] Some delivered to order, others contacted employers to offer children for sale, and others touted the children from place to place in a van. Those left at the end of the day, and whom no one wanted to buy at the recommended retail price, would have their cost slashed in order to secure a sale. Others took their children directly to employment agencies where the children would wait until selected by an employer.

Not all Thai women who work in prostitution were groomed for the trade. Not all families of sex workers sent their girls off to earn money on their backs. Some really did choose to become prostitutes. And some, on the other hand, had absolutely no idea at all that they would be required to sell sex in the city or abroad. Those girls who have no choice in the matter of their new occupation are recruited by the same kind of duplicitous means seen in South Asia. Agents hang around bus and train stations awaiting the arrival of country girls seeking fame and fortune – or more often those who are simply looking for a basic job to pay for food and lodgings. In areas where prostitution is not accepted, recruiters weave the same kind of stories and tell the same kind of lies as they do to poor Nepali, Indian and Bangladeshi girls: they offer them the prospect of a job and a way to help their families. This is a typical story of a girl from a Thai village who was trafficked to Japan and reduced to a sex slave. Her story appeared in a pamphlet warning other girls of the fate that might be in store for them.

> '[The agent] told us his own daughter also went to Japan and sent him 10,000 baht each month . . . He showed us her photos and her letter which said she was fine and not to worry. He tried to convince us that the young girls should go to Japan because it took a long time here to get rich. So we should go and find a husband and send some money for our parents to build a new house . . . All my life it was a dream of mine to work and send large sums of money to my parents. I thought it was a good chance for me as I was not educated and this way I could help them to have comfortable lives.'[11]

Beauty contests are a favoured and often-practised method of trawling for pretty girls. The lucky winner will receive a cash prize, a sash, her picture in the press and ticket to the world of prostitution. Some forward-thinking agents use other clever tactics to improve their market share. They take pictures of the raw materials and send the photos for approval to the brothels. Girls are also advertised on the internet to attract potential clients, particularly sex tourists. Thailand is leading the way in making commercial sex a mainstream, professionalised and technologically sophisticated industry that befits the twenty-first century.

The trafficking of girls in South-East Asia is relatively easy. This is especially true of migration into Thailand from Burma. There are three major entry points: in the north of Thailand at the Tachilek–Mae Sai and Myawadi–Mae Sot crossings, and in the south between Kawthaung and Ranong. In the north the migrants are mainly members of minority groups and tribes such as the Akha, Lahu, the Tai Yai and women from the Shan State. In the south they are mostly Indian-Burmese women and those from southern Burmese states. Many work in and around Ranong but others are sent to fill the brothels on the Thai–Malaysian border. A proportion of the Burmese women are brought openly across the border in pick-up trucks. In these instances an arrangement is made between the agent and the local border police. If the agents wish to avoid involving officials in their business they can easily take girls across the border by using jungle trails. A similar process is found on Thailand's border with Cambodia. Girls are trafficked into Thailand using the transit points at Poipet and the island of Koh Kong, which faces the town of Kompong Som. In addition to these supposedly controlled crossing points there are other smaller transit points that are rarely monitored. The Mekong Basin that incorporates Cambodia, Laos, Vietnam, parts of China and Burma, and which has Thailand as its economic axis, is a vast area dissected by rivers and jungles. Girls can be successfully trafficked within this region along tiny trails, in boats and in buses and in the back of trucks. Thailand is a magnet for peoples from the poorer countries around it and its borders are porous. Thailand is easy to enter. So is its sex industry.

Almost all the girls and women working in the very cheapest Thai brothels come from Burma. They are at the ultra-economy end of the market. Thai girls tend to dominate in the better-paid call girl and bar girl sector. Some of the Burmese girls know that they will be prostitutes when they leave their homes but very few will have any idea of the appalling conditions that they will have to endure. Many are deceived about the nature and conditions of their work.[12] Some girls are even brought by desperately poor parents to brothels in the border towns.[13] Extensive networks of agents bring women across the Thai–Burmese border. Like the agents operating in northern Thailand, these people are not always exactly 'traffickers'. The majority transport 'willing' women, and the women even pay them for their services. They are called 'carrymen' and can charge as much as 3,000–5,000 baht (£50–£83) for taking girls into Thailand. The Burmese prostitutes I spoke with in northern Thailand described the traffickers as 'facilitators' who helped them to cross the border.

Traffickers are people who are native to the area. They are often of mixed Thai and Burmese origin and they belong to communities that straddle the modern-day territorial boundaries of the state. Very often they are women. They know the geography, the culture and the language because they have grown from it. They know the area so well that it makes them good agents. Trafficking and the illegal crossing of the border are easy for them because they are things they have always done. Many of these agents are involved in other illegal activities. They are involved in drug and gem smuggling and they use the same trails and contacts to smuggle their human merchandise. Unsubstantiated (but highly likely) reports suggest that the people who run these networks are closely associated with Burma's military regime.

A similar pattern is found in Yunnan in southern China, where girls are increasingly 'trafficked' willingly because of their desperate need to escape poverty at home.[14] Here too the agents are native to the region and have an intimate local knowledge. This makes them highly effective traffickers along what is one of the region's least understood trafficking routes.

The picture in Cambodia is less complicated, in part because the trade is largely domestic and not so well developed. The Cambodian sex industry is truly horrible. In Thailand greater affluence gives high-class sections of the industry a veneer of sanitised order and pleasantness that is wholly lacking in the Cambodian case. Few of the Cambodian girls I interviewed had any idea that they would become prostitutes. The vast majority detested what they were forced to do. The vast majority were also barely more than children when they began sex work.

Around 50% of the young women who were sold to brothels in Cambodia were sold by someone they knew.[15] In November 1997 the police raided brothels in Phnom Penh and rescued 439 women and children. Half of these were sent to the Cambodian Women's Crisis Centre, where interviews revealed that 86% had been tricked or sold into prostitution.[16] There is a tendency for rescued women to insist that they were forced into prostitution. This saves them from at least some of the shame associated with being a prostitute because they can claim that they had no choice in the matter. But even if we allow for a degree of inflation in this figure it does suggest that a substantial proportion of women have been sold and forced into the Cambodian sex industry. This is corroborated by the experiences of girls and young women in prostitution. A fifteen-year-old girl explained how she was fooled into leaving her home.

I lived with my mother in a little village in Kampong Chhnang. Our father had left us and we found it hard to manage. My mother sold porridge on a stall in the road but we never had enough food to eat and we were all hungry. There was a woman who sometimes came to our village. She was rich with jewels and beautiful clothes and she said she could find good jobs in the city for some of us girls. I wanted to go with her so when she came back I went for an interview with some others. There were two men with her and they asked us lots of questions. I was really happy because they chose me and two others to get jobs. We left the next day in a taxi and we went to Phnom Penh. We thought we were going to work in a shop but instead they sold all of us to different brothels.

There is disagreement over the nature of the sex industry in Cambodia. Some observers think that it is tightly organised, especially in provincial capitals. Others believe that it is informal and loosely structured and that there are few tightly meshed sex trade organisations working in the rural areas. This second view is probably correct: there seem to be lots of small independent operators working alone or in very small groups. The sex industry simply does not need to get itself well organised to be successful in Cambodia. There are thousands of poor and vulnerable girls who are easy prey. It does not need an army functioning with military precision and efficiency to recruit them. Even those Cambodian women and girls trafficked across the Thai border do not appear to be transported by a highly organised operation.[17]

Prostitution and trafficking in the Philippines follow many of the patterns common in mainland South-East Asia. An increasingly large proportion of women and girls who are forced into the sex industry come from the shanty towns of the big cities, but the rural areas remain the principal recruiting grounds for trafficked girls. A brothel manager, known as a *mama-san*, explained her experience of the trafficking process in this manner:

Sometimes the traffickers are employed by a single brothel and they go to the villages to recruit girls for their own business. But most of the traffickers are independents. They get about 500 pesos (£7.40) for each girl they can sell. What they do is to recruit them in batches, transport them in groups and then sell them to clubs, bars and *casas* [closed brothels].

Agents tour the rural areas. There are some parts of the Philippines where sex work is accepted and here there is no need to concoct stories about fictitious jobs. But, as elsewhere in Asia, large numbers of girls are lured by the promise of respectable jobs. In the Philippines they are usually offered something better than domestic work: perhaps a job as a waitress or a singer in a club in the city.

A proportion of the girls is trafficked abroad – particularly to Japan where there are thought to be many thousands of Filipina women working in the sex entertainment sector. Some of the girls are already working as prostitutes before they leave for Japan and so know of the nature of their employment. But, as a rule, traffickers prefer to recruit and traffic women who do not have long prior experience of the sex industry: hardened and knowledgeable girls who know the ropes are far more hassle and difficult to manipulate.

According to Amparita St Maria, Director of the Ateneo Human Rights Centre in Manila and the leader of a team that has researched the trafficking of Filipina women to Japan, many of the girls who go to Japan know that they are courting danger of some kind. They convince themselves that nothing bad will happen to them. She believes that perhaps half of all the girls who are recruited to go to Japan have no conception of what they will end up doing. What is more, even after they have been trafficked most of the girls remain disoriented and unaware of the structure of the organisations that took them to Japan and then profited from them once they were there.

I visited a small town about two hours' drive from Manila where

I met a group of young women who had been trafficked to Nigeria to work in a club for Asian businessmen. The town was poor and the women were anxious to earn a better living and to pull themselves and their families out of poverty. So when an older woman from the town offered them the chance to work in Nigeria in a restaurant owned by her German husband they were keen to go. One of the women explained her view of the opportunity.

> My father didn't like the idea but I told him that it would be OK as eight other girls from the village were also going to go and that we would all be safe if we were together. I had heard that it was dangerous for girls to go abroad but I thought it couldn't happen to me – especially as I wasn't going alone. I had worked as a seamstress for a couple of years, and no matter how hard I worked my life never got any better. So I decided to go because it seemed like the best dream in the world.

The opportunity turned out to be a nightmare rather than a dream. There was no restaurant. Instead there was a club in which the women were forced to sell sex. They were originally offered $350 per month, plus tips, for waitressing. In reality they were delivered to a businessman who told the women that their Filipino employment agent and trafficker had sold them for $21,000 each. They then had to repay this cost by entertaining clients. For the first four months they received no money for providing this service and thereafter were given $25 a month.

South-East and East Asia's sex industries are even more highly differentiated than their South Asian counterpart. Prices for commercial sex vary wildly from the peaks amongst elite Japanese call girls to the rock bottom prices of Burmese prostitutes along the Thai–Burmese border. Consequently there is a lot of movement of trafficked girls to ensure that they are placed in the right market and at the right price. For instance, Chinese girls are trafficked south from Yunnan, through northern Burma, into Thailand and then south to the provinces frequented by Chinese tourists. Many are moved on to Malaysia and Singapore. There is a sound economic logic to this. Chinese men will pay handsomely for sex with Chinese girls. They will pay even better rates for white-skinned Chinese beauties and a fortune for virgins in their early and mid-teens. Agents are well aware of this and will therefore grade their girls according to these criteria and send them to an appropriate market. Grade 'A' Chinese virgins may fetch between 50,000 and 100,000 baht (£830–£1,660) if they are traded in Malaysia to service men from the Chinese community. By contrast, it would not be economically feasible to transport a dark-skinned Cambodian girl that far. She can make a greater profit for her pimps and owners in Thailand's budget brothels.

Trafficking of women into Japan is a more difficult activity. The rewards, however, make it enticing for traffickers and the sex industry. It is difficult to estimate what proportion of women go to Japan with the intention of selling sex. A significant percentage think they will be waitresses or singers rather than sex workers. One Columbian woman believed rather bizarrely that she was travelling to Japan to be a fishmonger.[18]

It is certain that some of the women who are taken to work in Japan know what they are going to do and, if they know the ropes and have some good luck, they make what they believe to be a good living from selling sex. But lots of others are not so fortunate. Even though some women realise that they will be prostitutes many find, once they are in Japan, that they have to work under terribly exploitative conditions akin to sexual slavery. Women such as these often receive scant sympathy on the grounds that they are not 'innocent' and that they deserve abuse and exploitation because they are prostitutes. According to this viewpoint a prostitute is not worthy of possessing basic human rights. Other girls and women have no inkling when they leave their homes of the fate that will befall them. But whether the women chose to sell sex or not is immaterial. When women find themselves in conditions of extreme exploitation their human rights are infringed. No one asks to become a sex slave. And no one deserves to be one either.

Because Japan is a collection of islands, the only ways to enter the country are by boat or by air, and potential entry points are limited and closely monitored. Prostituted women have therefore usually entered on legitimate visas – either as tourists or entertainers. These allow them to stay for three months, and they can be extended to a maximum of six months. A few of the women vanish when their visas expire and will stay on illegally. Others return home. Another group enter the country on expensive, false passports that have been produced by the criminal underworld's lucrative forgery department. This is especially true in the case of Thai women and is one of the main reasons why they incur such high debts.

A large proportion of the Thai and Filipina women who are trafficked to Japan realise that they have been sold only after they arrive in the country. The usual scenario is that they fly in to Narita airport with a minder and are taken to one of the big hotels surrounding the airport. They then witness a transaction in which they themselves are the merchandise. They find that they have been sold to a 'snack' – a euphemism for a brothel or a bar in which sex is as easily available as the drinks. Even those women who agree to go to Japan to provide sexual services are frequently deceived because many are not told of the extortionate fees charged by agents until after they reach their destination. By then it is too late for them to change their minds.

For some women, the risk that they take in going to work in Japan is offset by the potential financial rewards that await them. I spoke to a Romanian woman who had been trafficked to Tokyo. Her story reflects the gamble that women take in deciding to travel to Japan.

This is my third time in Japan. The first two times were good and I was not forced to do work I didn't like. Everything was well managed and the organisation I worked for sorted out my travel arrangements. I came back to Japan because the work is well paid. But this time it was different and the girls were forced to sell sex.

Rutsuko Shoji of the HELP Asian Women's shelter in Tokyo repeated a story told to her by a Thai woman who had been offered an office job in Japan. This woman accepted the job because, although it was similar to the one she did in Bangkok, the salary in Japan was considerably higher. In order to take up the appointment she paid an agent 400,000 yen (£2,350) to arrange her transport, and a Japanese man then accompanied her to Tokyo. Once past immigration the woman was taken directly to a large hotel where another Japanese man and a Taiwanese *mama-san* cornered her in a room. The trio forced her to count out four million yen (£23,500) and to give it to the man who had brought her to Japan. This was the price the *mama-san* had agreed to pay for her. The shocked woman, who had paid her own trafficker, was then forced by the Yakuza (the Japanese mafia) to repay the four million yen by selling sex in one of their brothels.

This Thai woman was rather expensive. Typical prices for new recruits vary from 1.5 million yen to four million yen (£8,800–£23,500). The total varies according to the likely earning potential of the woman and the cost of transporting her to Japan. A small number of Colombian women work in Japan and they tend to be among the most expensive because of the high cost of their airfares. In middle-income Thailand the prices of girls vary according to the usual criteria of race, beauty, youth and virginity. But in the budget brothel sector a Burmese girl can fetch anything from 10,000 to 30,000 baht (£170–£500). An ethnic Thai girl can be expected to realise far more. In impoverished Cambodia prices are even lower and brothel owners usually negotiate a sum of between $150 and $500 and occasionally more if the girl is deemed to have significant sex work potential.

Although the environment in which these girls will work ranges from the luxury of clubs for Japanese executives to a Cambodian shed-like brothel sectioned into tiny cubicles by flimsy plywood, all these girls sell the same product. And all are bonded to stay in their new profession until they can repay the price of their purchase. Their first challenge, however, is to condition themselves to the only means by which they can earn their freedom. They must acclimatise themselves to selling their bodies to a stream of unknown men. They cannot resign because of poor working conditions and the unreasonable conduct of their employers and clients. Slaves do not have a choice.

Chapter Four

SEASONING

Few experiences in the world can be quite as bad as being a poor virgin girl in a cheap Asian brothel. It is the stuff of nightmares. Every day thousands of girls and women are initiated into prostitution through acute physical and psychological violence. And every day men are willing to pay to enjoy the violence of this initiation. What do these appalling facts tell us about the real substance of Asia's dual sexual codes?

Experience is considered to be an advantage in most occupations. Paradoxically, the value of the average sex worker in Asia is greater the less she has plied her trade and the more ignorant she is of sex. This does not find a clear parallel in the Western sex trade. In general, female sex workers in the West have to be young and sexually attractive but they also have to have a good idea about techniques and what the customers enjoy. In Asia many sex consumers find the prospect of a knowledgeable and sexually experienced woman highly intimidating. They do not wish to buy a woman's sexual experience as most of their Western counterparts do. They would far rather buy sex with a girl they can control and dominate. A virgin is best of all. She is largely clueless, almost always frightened and she is also likely to be supplied with an Aids-free guarantee. Such thrilling sexual privileges come at a price . . . and it is an expensive one.

A high degree of coercion is needed in order to supply the large numbers of girls and women required by mass-market prostitution. This is especially true in societies such as those in South Asia that have very rigid rules of sexual conduct for women. It is not a form of work that women would flock to if they had many alternatives. A thorough process of re-education is necessary in order to turn the average woman into a 'willing' prostitute. It is called 'seasoning'. It is rather like preparing a piece of meat for the dinner table – or in this case the clients. At the end of the process the reluctant prostitute will accept sex work as her profession. In many places she will have absolutely no alternative.

Seasoning is achieved in different ways according to the sex establishment, the way the girl arrived there and her own personal character traits. Almost all seasoning, however, involves some form of coercion. Sometimes the girls are physically forced to sell sex and are tortured in order to make them compliant. They are raped repeatedly by numerous men until their will to resist is broken. In highly traditional societies the rape of a woman can lead to a destruction of self-esteem. Women may therefore accept prostitution as their way of life because they cannot escape from the psychological prison created by their experience of rape and its associated shame.

Other women are forced to sell sex because of the economic pressure created by debt. Once they have been sold to a brothel, the brothel owner will demand that the girl repays this outlay by servicing customers. She thereby becomes enmeshed in a highly exploitative system of debt bondage that, in its worst forms, is indistinguishable from slavery.

The initial exposure to prostitution and the seasoning process takes place in a variety of locations. Sometimes it is in traditional red light areas but, increasingly, young girls are initiated into the sex business in other more low-profile venues, perhaps in safe houses or hotel rooms.

The physical environment in which the girls and women first find themselves varies according to the country. Victims of trafficking for prostitution are usually recruited for the brothel sector. That is to say, they will be used in one of the poorest parts of the sex industry and they will cater to those sex consumers who have the least spending power. Understandably, the poorer the country, the poorer the environment in which prostitutes live. For example, it is tough to live in Bangladesh under the best of conditions. It is difficult to be a poor Bangladeshi and it is even more difficult to live the life of a poor Bangladeshi woman. Imagine what it must therefore be like to be a poor Bangladeshi prostitute. The physical conditions under which these women work are the worst I have ever seen. Quite simply, they defy imagination. Brothels are overcrowded and unsanitary. Street prostitution takes place in the gutter and the women do not even have a place to bathe and clean themselves. Although the squalid surroundings of brothel prostitution in developing Asian countries are atrocious they are comparable with the living conditions of many other poor people, and for some young prostitutes they may even be an improvement on what they had known before. In the midst of so much general poverty the environment in which brothel prostitutes live is unremarkable. What is remarkable, however, is that so many men should visit these miserable places to buy sex and should then heap scorn upon the women who pleasure them there.

India has a large brothel sector. There are red light areas in virtually all towns and cities. Brothels crowd around bus terminals and railway stations. Behind teashops and *dhabas* (highway restaurants) are little rooms where a handful of women will be available for purchase. Boys may also be offered in the same *dhabas*. The brothel quarters in the big cities are well established and some have been in existence for centuries.

Mumbai (Bombay) is the commercial heart of India and the centre of its exuberant film industry. It is therefore entirely logical that it is also the capital of its sex industry. Kamatipura and the area around Falkland Road are the most closely watched, researched and written about red light areas of the city. The streets of Kamatipura are lined with brothels. Most of these are small. There is an open-fronted room looking out onto the street and this is lined with small benches. Perhaps six to ten girls sit or stand around in this entrance waiting for customers. Behind the reception room are tiny cubicles that are usually constructed of wood. Most of these are around a metre wide and two metres long. There is just enough space for some unimaginative sex on a thin, bare mattress. A light bulb hangs from the ceiling and, in some more prosperous establishments, there might be the luxury of a fan. The sex workers have usually made an effort to make the surroundings more inviting. Pictures of plump Indian film stars are pinned to the wooden partitions and there may be a bunch of plastic flowers and some little ornaments next to the mattress. For modesty's sake the cubicles have a door or a curtain but sound travels fast and easily in these places and the practice of sex is a loud one, especially when there is a surge in demand and a number of customers are buying simultaneously. Other brothels are a notch more sophisticated. They are also more of a prison for their inmates. There are some brothels that do not have an entrance room but only a gate with a guard and a bell. Girls in these brothels do not come out. And they do not sit on benches waiting for the customers. It is for the customers to come to them. In total, two thousand women work in the brothels of Kamatipura.[1]

Falkland Road, and its surrounding warren of lanes, lies close to Kamatipura. The two red light areas form one large, almost continuous commercial sex market. In the brothel hierarchy, however,

Falkland Road and its environs occupy an even lower rung than Kamatipura. Here the women may not necessarily have the benefit of a cubicle in which to service the clients. A shabby curtain divides the beds and some rooms resemble a closely packed dormitory. Desperate women and girls stand on the streets shouting out to passing men to whom they will sell budget-price oral and anal sex. Some will offer services for as little as 5 rupees (7p). It is rare to find lower prices or a sadder product.

In the interior lanes off Falkland Road, and in the more inaccessible brothels, there are special rooms reserved for newly procured women. Children are kept in attics. It is very hard to prove this because the business is so highly secretive. The best sources of information on this subject are the sex workers themselves. I have heard reports of child prostitution from completely independent informants. Some of these reports were from the children involved and at other times adult women, some of them practising sex workers, would express their anguish at the lives that these prostituted children lead. A Nepali prostitute who had worked in Mumbai for several years told me this:

Most of the time you never see the very young girls – the children. They are kept separate from the rest. For a long time I never saw any really young ones but then I began to see them sometimes at night. I could hear them. They were allowed to go and play on the roof [a kind of roof terrace]. I could hear their voices and they were just little girls. Whenever we asked about them we were told that there was no one there and that we had made a mistake ... Then another time there was a girl with us who was young – about eleven. She was always kept inside and if the *gharwali* thought there was going to be a raid she was squeezed into a little hole under the floor. She was told that she would be killed if she made a noise.

Girls and young women are often kept in 'closed' brothels in Kamatipura and Falkland Road. This is particularly true when they are very young, when they have been trafficked and when they are physically coerced into prostitution. Nepali girls form a significant proportion of this category. The brothels in which they are kept are frequently of a superior standard: they have running water, maybe air conditioning and, most importantly, a reliable supply of fresh teenagers. The inmates of this type of brothel are commonly described as the 'caged prostitutes' of Mumbai. They do not literally live in cages but the analogy is apt. There is a narrow and dark staircase leading up from the street, there is a guard at the door and there are iron grilles at the window. Occasionally you can see the girls peeping out between the bars. That is as near as they will get to the outside world until their process of seasoning is completed. It is a process that, for many girls, will take years.

Brothels in big Indian cities are little more than variations on the same unpleasant theme. Conditions are marginally better in Calcutta although the money a sex worker can earn here is generally less then her counterpart in Mumbai. Sonagachi is the largest brothel area in Calcutta. Sex workers in Sonagachi are divided into three classes. 'A' class is the highest and 'C' class is the lowest. The 'A' class girls are young and pretty and have rooms with decent furniture and sometimes even adequate sanitation. Girls, however, do not stay in the 'A' class for long as there is always competition from new and younger girls coming on to the market. When this happens the established girls are downgraded to 'B' class and then to 'C'. Women in the lower classes usually share a small room measuring six feet by ten feet. Two or three women will share this space with a far greater number of rats. It is both their home and their workplace. Their beds can be separated by little curtains and, when this is not possible, the women and their clients take it in turns to use the rooms. As the sex for cash transaction is often a very hasty function, they do not have to wait very long.

Sonagachi is a maze of alleys and lanes flanked by two- and three-storey buildings. Dark passages with uneven floors and more uneven steps lead into lots of tiny rooms. Each decrepit building is constructed around a dark, dank courtyard in which there is a central tap or water pump that all the inhabitants use for washing. There is usually one toilet for around twenty women, and they cook their food in their own rooms. Just as in the other red light areas of the city, women stand in lines in the streets and passageways in bright saris and Western dresses, their faces heavily made up even in the early morning. They call to clients, encouraging them to go inside. Pimps lounge around watching and looking for customers. They explain that upstairs, in one of the back rooms, is a very young girl who can be had for a knock-down price. Some people will tell you that the horrors of child prostitution are a thing of the past in Sonagachi. This is wishful thinking. Listen to the words of one of these children:

> I was sold to the brothel when I was twelve and I started
> work right away. There were other young girls like me but the
> *malkin* [brothel manager] used to hide us. She made us say
> that we were eighteen. There were some that were a lot
> younger than me. They were like small children but they were
> kept separately and we only saw them sometimes.

Delhi presents a slightly different picture but it illustrates the direction in which the sex market is moving in South Asian cities. GB Road is the traditional red light area and its three- and four-storey buildings contain around four thousand girls in eighty-five brothels.[2] Typically each brothel is reached from the road by a narrow, badly lit and dangerous staircase. Upstairs there is a room about twenty-five metres square and this has a sleeping platform above it. There is a toilet and a kitchen and, around the outside of the main room, there are six to eight tiny, and usually windowless, rooms that are just big enough to take a small bed. Around twenty-five to thirty-five girls and young women are crammed into this space, which functions as a living area and also a viewing arena for the customers. Girls sit on the floor while clients come in to look them over and to make their selection. It put me in mind of dealers coming to select and buy some colourful animals in a cattle market. The women and the clients then disappear for a few minutes into one of the small rooms. For this service the customer pays about 70 rupees (£1).

New recruits to Delhi's sex industry are not often seasoned in GB Road. Trafficked girls may end up there but they are increasingly broken in elsewhere, in places that are safer and where there is less likely to be interference from NGOs or the police. This is consistent with a new trend in the industry. Prostitution is becoming more diversified and sophisticated and it is expanding out from its customary locations. In many ways this makes it more difficult to assess. It also makes the perpetration of abuse considerably easier because fewer people are on hand to witness it and the victims are almost totally isolated. No one is even aware of their existence. Commercial sex, even at the lower end of the market, is no longer confined to traditional red light areas but is moving out and dispersing throughout the cities. It is found in 'respectable' areas. Brothels no longer necessarily look like traditional brothels. But for the sex slaves that fill them, the experience of being seasoned must be much the same whether the establishment is in GB Road or in some more salubrious middle-class suburb. This diversification of prostitution, even within the lowest tier of the industry, is repeated all over Asia.

A good example of the growing complexity within the industry can be seen in Cambodia. Many Cambodian brothels are little more than hastily constructed shacks. They have the same utilitarian design. There is a large room in which the waiting girls can be observed and then selected. And behind this are a number of cubicles. Often these cubicles are the girls' home as well as their workplace. Some areas of Phnom Penh are well known for providing fresh new girls – or whatever else should take the consumer's fancy. Svay Pak, just outside the city, is unbeatable for Vietnamese teenagers – a fact attested to by the cars streaming out of the city. On my visits to Svay Pak it was noticeable how many groups of Chinese and Japanese men arrived in expensive cars and minibuses because there was frequently a problem with parking. The Seventh of January Market in the centre of Phnom Penh specialises in Khmer virgins. Toul Kork, a muddy, potholed track bordered by dozens of small shed-like brothels, offers just about anything. Guards and pimps monitor the girls and there is little opportunity for escape.

The Cambodian sex industry has perfected a lucrative means of initiating its young recruits without having the painful process undertaken within the brothel itself. The youngest girls – those under thirteen – plus older virgins who possess considerable sexual charms, are kept in separate locations. These act as a form of holding pen. The brothel management then negotiates deals with clients and will deliver the girls to them for defloration. Typically a businessman will purchase not just a girl's virginity but also her services for a few days and perhaps a week. During this time he has frequent sex with her secure in the knowledge that she is not infected with HIV or other sexually transmitted diseases. A senior employee in one of the biggest luxury hotels in Phnom Penh said it was common for businessmen, and particularly ethnic Chinese businessmen, to purchase a girl and have her brought to the hotel. She remains in his room, often under guard, until the week is up. Most of these girls are village girls between twelve and fifteen years of age and their customers are usually wealthy middle-aged men. The hotel staff know of these arrangements because they are obliged to clean the rooms and to take food to the girls. This is not a one-off occurrence: it is absolutely typical of Cambodia today. It is also a phenomenon observable throughout the rest of the region. The girls these men enjoy are destined for the mass market. They are not elite prostitutes but, for a while, they are of interest to the more discerning consumer. While they remain virgins they are of value and their sale can command a high price. Once they have been initiated into the pleasures of sex their value plummets. A virgin in Cambodia costs approximately $500. Sex with a girl in her first two months of prostitution may cost around $10. After that she will command a price equivalent to that of a bottle of beer. Wealthy and respectable men would not dream of visiting the kind of low-class brothel these girls will eventually work in. They would consider it beneath their dignity. However, it is quite within their dignity to purchase her virginity and enjoy the triumph of its possession in a well-appointed room in a luxury hotel.

It is useful to describe the sex trade in Mae Sai in northern Thailand in order to amplify this point. Mae Sai is a charmless frontier town on the border between Thailand and Burma. The only reason people could possibly have for going there is to shop in the markets on either side of the border, which sell cheap merchandise and rather crude handicrafts. The other kind of shopping is sex shopping and the goods are Burmese virgins. The town is an important entry point into Thailand for Burmese girls and women fleeing from poverty and a vicious military regime. Some of these women are illegal migrants, some are refugees and some are the victims of trafficking. No one is quite sure where the boundaries between these categories are to be drawn and, very often, women fall into more than one category. Some, confusingly, fall into all. Lots of these young women end up in the sex trade. Even those who intended to sell their bodies, however, rarely realised the dreadful conditions under which they would have to work.

Mae Sai is a breaking-in station. Some girls go directly to brothels further south but many spend around six months in the town before being moved to sex establishments in Chiang Mai or

Bangkok and Phuket. There are no sex workers older than twenty-two in Mae Sai because there is absolutely no demand for them.[3] Mae Sai is a magnet for men wanting to buy virgins, and at the time of writing a girl could be purchased for around 25,000–30,000 baht (£420–£500).

Commercial sex does not happen in the brothels or bars. Instead it happens in hotels. The town has six main hotels and guesthouses and the more organised of these have separate floors. Some are for the tourists seeking nice views and a bit of local culture and the other floors are for Thai men and those tourists seeking a bit of bought sex with girls from the local brothels. Who buys Burmese virgins? The question elicited laughs from women involved in the management of Mae Sai's sex trade. 'Everyone,' one of them said. 'Thai men . . . And of course foreigners including Westerners. But especially Japanese. Japanese are number one.'

Closed brothels exist all over Asia. There is not one Asian country that does not have a substantial brothel sector and many establishments within this sector will be 'closed'. That is, they are open for customers but closed should the inmates wish to escape. Thailand's brothel sector is dominated by Burmese women and those from Thai hill tribes. These women are the main victims of sexual slavery in Thailand. Ethnic Thai women work in the better class clubs and bars – although this does not necessarily mean that they escape from physical abuse and exploitation. Brothels vary in size from those employing a handful of girls to those employing a hundred or more. Although the physical environment in which the girls find themselves is often a lot better than that of South Asian sex workers the methods of control and the economic and sexual exploitation are remarkably similar. Just as in South Asian brothels there is a 'room for opening virgins'. The new recruits sit on a bench in a back room. Their health is guaranteed and their price is very high.

Casas are the closed brothels of the Philippines. They differ from the 'a-go-go' bars and karaoke clubs in that they cater specifically to local men. Foreigners can be admitted only if they are introduced by a regular local client. Japan's closed brothels are slightly different but they too are closed to foreigners. Japanese brothels like to pretend to be something better: a club for successful executives, for example, or a karaoke bar or a cabaret. Something to make the client think – momentarily – that he is heir to those powerful men of the past who were graced by the company of *geishas*. Yet, rather than a highly trained *geisha*, the modern-day *samurai* is much more likely to be paying for an intimidated Thai or Filipina woman who was duped into the job.

Women who are trafficked to Japan and those who are held in sexual slavery are not concentrated in the main red light areas. Kabukicho, Tokyo's principal and very loud commercial sex market, is reported to house a few sex slaves but most are scattered liberally throughout the Japanese islands in what are known as 'snacks'. There are 'snacks' everywhere: in small towns and especially around *onsen* (hot spring resorts). Some of these are small, and offer the services of only six or seven girls but some can provide as many as fifty. The physical surroundings in these establishments are totally unlike those in South Asia: the Japanese are fastidious people and it would not be good for business to offer sex for sale in a hovel. However, if we strip away the veneer provided by greater affluence, the processes of seasoning and control, and the manipulation of the debt bondage system are remarkably similar whether we are in India, Cambodia or Japan.

Bemusement, disbelief and shock are the initial emotions that the new recruits experience when they enter the world of the sex trade. They are almost always totally disoriented. While they are in this vulnerable state the seasoning begins. The following story is that of a twenty-year-old Cambodian woman who left her village in search of work and found herself rapidly absorbed within the sex industry. It is the kind of story I have heard repeated on countless occasions all over Asia. She was born near Battambang and her father was a refuse collector who died when she was thirteen. She had nine siblings and her mother sold vegetables. Even though they worked hard the family did not have enough money, so when she was fifteen she and her sister decided to leave home and look for work in the town. They arrived late in the evening and had nowhere to stay. Then a friendly man and a woman approached them and said that they could help. They offered the girls some food and said that they could stay overnight in their home.

> When we were in the house the woman put me in one room and my sister in another. Then later the man came to my room and raped me. His friend raped my sister. The next day they took us in a car to Poipet (on the Thai–Cambodian border). They sold us both to a brothel for 100,000 baht (£1,600).[4] I was locked in a room for three or four days and then I was put into another room with some other girls. A Thai man came and looked at us and he chose me. He took me in a car to Thailand and paid some money to the police to let me in.
>
> We went to a hotel but I don't know the place because I was so scared and the man said that if I tried to run away the police would catch me and put me in prison because I didn't have a passport and papers. The man raped me many times and every day for four days lots of his friends did too. Maybe five or six different ones. Some of them were policemen.

Although the minor details in this type of story vary, the structure is almost identical and the outcome is always the same. This was how a sex worker described her initiation into prostitution when she was fifteen years old.

> When I got to Calcutta my friend took me to her house.

I thought it was very strange because my friend didn't wear her clothes and spent all her time in a blouse and petticoat. I asked her about this and she said, 'Why should I wear a sari when I am at home? Here I can relax and wear what I want.'

She started cooking some food but then a man arrived and asked if she had any time for him. She said yes and told me to finish the meal. Then she took this man into another room and shut the door. I didn't know what they were doing and when they came out I said, 'Who was that man, what were you doing and where has your husband gone?' She laughed and said, 'There are no husbands around here. That other man was not my husband he was my *babu* [regular client].' Then another man came and started talking to my friend. And my friend said to me, 'Go into that room with this man and stay with him for a while and do what he wants. He says you are pretty and he wants to marry you. Afterwards he will give you some money.'

She pushed me into the room with the man and locked the door so I couldn't get out. The man started to touch me and he said he wanted to marry me but he said, 'First I have to get to know what you are like.' Then he raped me in that room.

When he was finished he gave me fifty rupees and left and then another man came. I was very upset and crying but my friend said, 'Go with this other man.' I said, 'But that man wants to marry me and he will be angry if another man touches me.' My friend just laughed again. I said I would not do it and I said I wanted to go home but my friend said, 'This is a good job. See how much jewellery I have. If you go with him think how much money you will make and you can have nice things like me.' I didn't want to do it but they pushed me into the room again and the other man raped me.

Then another man came to the house and I refused to entertain him. My friend said that if I did not do it she would tell my family that I was a prostitute and that our family would be shamed in the village. I could not bring shame on my family so then I began to take clients and I did not refuse any longer.

Threats to inform a girl's family of her involvement in prostitution are one way to tie her into the trade – and this applies even to those girls who were forced into prostitution. Girls who joined the trade when their families accepted an 'advance' on their earnings are taught to fear retribution against their families if they should decide that the work is not something they actually wish to perform. This can range from the threat that a girl's family must repay the advance to threats that relatives will be targeted for physical punishment.

Brothel owners and managers use varying levels of brutality to season new girls. Arati has yet to reach adulthood. She was sold into prostitution in Mumbai when she was nine years old. She is now living with the first stages of full-blown Aids in a safe house after being rescued from a closed brothel. This is how she described her experience:

The *malkin* [brothel manager] was from Nepal and she was very cruel. She liked to torture me. I was put in a little dark room with a chain around my ankle. I could only go out of the room to go to the toilet. Then one of the guards would undo my chain and take me and watch me. The other time my chain was undone was when the customers came to my room. My first customer was a very old man. He beat me very hard and then he had sex with me. Some of the customers were not cruel but others liked to hit me. The *malkin* hit me many times so that I would be good with the clients.

Arati remained chained in her room for five years. She was never fully seasoned and she will never live to be an adult. Her story is one of the worst I encountered but it is by no means unique. It is a horrifying personal tragedy and, if it was an isolated horror story, we could explain it as the terrible product of a few sick minds. Shockingly, there are repetitions of Arati's experience and countless echoes of her terror all over Asia. We cannot dismiss these girls' ordeals as awful but unrepresentative cases that distract us from analysis of the broader patterns and themes in sex work. It is unforgivable to concentrate on the economics of prostitution as if the people at the sharp end of this trade are a nuisance and a distraction from the big picture. They are the big picture. Sexual slavery is not really something that is best analysed simply in terms of statistics. Human misery is not a substance easily measured by plotting numbers on a graph. When the stories of girls and young women like Arati are analysed together they amount to a damning indictment of prostitution and the principles that sustain it.

The following story is that of a young woman initiated into prostitution by a combination of acute poverty and physical force. It is a common story and comes from Dhaka in Bangladesh.

I worked at the factory for about three months and I earned about 500 taka a month [£6]. I shared a room with another girl but then she said she did not want to share with me any more because I did not have enough money. So then I had nowhere to live. I was feeling very bad and was walking in the street when a woman started to talk to me. She said that she would look after me and find me a good job so I went with her. She took me to a room and gave me some food and then two fat veiled women came in and the woman told me to go with them because she said that they would show me the city. It was dark and they put me in a scooter. We went to a very busy place and it was very gloomy. There were many girls there wearing strange clothes and they wore makeup. When we walked down the alley one of the women pulled off my

orna shawl and said, 'You don't need to wear it in this place.'
They took me into a big building and talked with another
woman about me. I was very frightened. They gave me a
tablet and asked if I felt dizzy. I didn't but then they left me to
sleep for the night.

In the morning lots of other girls came to talk to me. They
told me that I would be all right if I did what I was told and
that I would get used to it. I didn't know what they meant.
They said it wasn't so bad in this place and that you got good
food and clothes to wear.

That night the woman who was in charge locked me in a
small room and after a while a man came in and tried to rape
me. I fought with him and he was very angry and said, 'I have
paid for you, so do as I want.' The madam was so angry that
she beat me all over my arms with a stick so that they were
bruised and swollen. Some of the clients were good. When
they saw that I did not want to have sex with them they
would not say anything to madam. But most were bad. They
complained to madam that I did not give good service and so
madam would start to beat me again. She shouted, 'How long
will it take you to accept this?' After five days of beating I
accepted it.

Even in benighted Bangladesh the sex sector is undergoing a
metamorphosis. Girls are sold into prostitution – but not necessarily to a traditional brothel. Instead they are initiated into 'hotel
prostitution'. This is something of a misnomer and it gives a misleading impression of the scene in Bangladesh. It should read
'grubby little lodge' or 'large unsanitary hostel' prostitution. The
structures of the trade are exactly the same as in traditional brothel
prostitution but the business is movable and more discreet. Clients
are saved the embarrassment of visiting notorious areas. Instead the
girls are delivered to them. A similar phenomenon is found in

Pakistan where girls from brothels are delivered to hotels for the enjoyment of the guests. During one of my stays in a luxury hotel in Lahore a distraught thirteen-year-old girl was taken away from the hotel lobby. She was the daughter of a sex worker from the main red light area and the event was supposed to be her initiation into prostitution. Her clients were two wealthy local businessmen in their sixties and they were haggling over the price of the deal with the girl's own grandmother. Clearly this sobbing girl was not the kind of exciting sex partner the two men had in mind.

This type of sex work is an extension of the virgin purchase in Cambodia and Thailand. All countries in Asia have this system of hotel prostitution, but in some instances the girls have a measure of freedom in part because they cater to a higher class sector of the market. In impoverished Bangladesh this higher class sector is very small. Instead, this is one girl's experience of seasoning within the hotel prostitution scene. It comes from an eleven-year-old girl who was promised a job as a domestic servant but whose cleaning job never materialised.

> The husband of the lady who employed me said, 'You don't have to do jobs in the house. I have a much better job for you.' The next day he took me to an agent and sold me. This agent took me to a hotel where there were some other girls. Most of them were older than me but there was one that was just the same as me. I was taken to a room in the hotel and a young man came in. He was about twenty or twenty-one. This man made me have sex with him. Every day after that I was taken to hotel rooms and men would visit me in the room. All the time I was guarded. There were guards who watched us eat and took us to hotel rooms. We were never alone.

In societies in which prostitution is becoming an open business, the more sophisticated players in the sex market do not need to use physical force to tie young women into prostitution. Market forces achieve this and the owners of the sex establishments can relax and keep their hands clean. In Thailand, for instance, many bar and club owners do not want to sell the sexual services of girls who have been coerced into prostitution. Instead they recruit girls who are gradually absorbed into the industry as a result of peer pressure and, crucially, because they have acquired some unexpectedly high debts to pay off.[5] Remarkably, these debts have to be paid to the bar or club owner. Initially therefore they may work in a fringe trade – as a waitress for instance – but within a short time they too become sex workers.

One of the Filipina women who was trafficked to work in a brothel in Nigeria catering to the Asian community explained how she and her friends were coerced into selling sex.

> We were sent into a big compound surrounded by high
> fences and it was very heavily guarded. There were three
> houses in the compound and all were filled with other
> Filipinas who looked at us. We were told that we had to work
> in a club so that we could pay back our airfare and the money
> that the club owner had paid for us. We had to entertain the
> clients because how else could we pay back the debt?

This strategy of burdening a girl with a massive amount of debt is commonplace. The girl is then given only one realistic way of clearing the debt: she has to sell her body. A Romanian woman trafficked to work in a Japanese sex club described the methods that the club owners used to encourage her into prostitution.

> For the first few months we weren't given any wages for being
> dancers. They said we had to pay back the expenses for our
> training and airfare. We just had a tiny amount of money –

not even enough to buy food, and I was always hungry. If we
wanted some more money we had to go with clients and then
we could get some tips. We couldn't leave because we had a
legal contract to stay at the club, and besides we had no
money to pay for the airfare home.

Debt bondage is the name given to this system. It is a widespread
practice throughout the global sex industry and is common in Asia.
At its best it can be seen as a way a girl can secure an advance upon
her earnings. At worst it is akin to sexual slavery because the brothel
and club owners manipulate the debt. The debt is not fixed and it
expands at the whim of the brothel owner or manager. In essence
debt bondage is used to force women to become prostitutes and to
make them accept customers and comply with sexual acts that they
would otherwise refuse.

Some of the worst examples of debt bondage are found in South
Asia. In Calcutta a system known as *chukri* operates among new
entrants to the profession. A brothel owner buys a girl from an
agent. The girl then comes under the complete control of this owner.
The owner pays for all of the girl's requirements – her food and
clothes and general living expenses. These costs are added to the
girl's debt together with various other unspecified sums that are at
the discretion of the owner. The new prostitute must then repay
this nebulous debt by servicing customers. The trouble is that she
will rarely know how much she owes, how much will be deducted
per client and how much will be added for her expenses and the
'gifts' which the brothel owner will give her. It is not uncommon, for
example, for a girl to be given some cheap jewellery that she will
then have to pay for with the sale of her body. The *chukri* system is
sexual slavery.

Very similar arrangements are found throughout the subcontinent. In Mumbai's Kamatipura a girl will receive half of the fee the
customer pays for sexual services. Out of this she must pay for her

សេចក្ដីណែ NOTE

១ -សំបុត្រគ្មានលក់មិនអាចយកប្រាក់មកវិញបាន
   -Ticket sold is not refundable

   -សូមរក្សាសំបុត្រសម្រាប់ត្រួតពិនិត្យ ។
   -Please keep ticket for inspection.

៣ -អ្នកដំណើរត្រូវឡើងឡាន ១៥ នាទីមុនពេលចេញដំណើរ ក្រុមហ៊ុន
   ឥតទទួលខុសត្រូវចំពោះ ។
   -Passenger must be on board 15 min before departure. Our
   company is not responsible for late passengers and has to
   leave on time.

៤ -សូមពិនិត្យកន្លែង, ម៉ោង, ថ្ងៃ, ខែ, ឆ្នាំ, និងតម្លៃឡានមុនពេលចេញ
   ដំណើរ ។
   -Please check destination, time, date of departure, and fare
   before leaving

៥ -កុមារមានអាយុ លើ ៨ ឆ្នាំ ១.៣ ម៉ែត្រត្រូវទិញសំបុត្រ ។
   -Children are over 8 years old or 1,3m all must buy one ticket.

៦ -ក្រុមហ៊ុនឥតទទួលខុសត្រូវចំពោះការបាត់បង់សំបុត្រឡេ
   -Our company will not be responsible for any loss of ticket

៧ -ក្រុមហ៊ុនឥតទទួលខុសត្រូវចំពោះការបាត់បង់ឥវ៉ាន់របស់អ្នកដំណើរឡេ
   -Our company will not be responsible for any loss of luggage

៨ -សំបុត្រនេះសំរាប់ប្រើតែម្នាក់បុគ្គល។
   -This ticket is valid for one person only.

៩ -សូមទាក់ទងមកលេខទូរស័ព្ទ (855-23) 210 359/ 210 859
                              (855-12) 631 545

168

ក្រុមហ៊ុន ផលិតក្រុងសូរិយា ដឹកជញ្ជូនអ្នកដំណើរ
PHNOM PENH SORYA TRANSPORT Co., Ltd

No.SRY **N: 138151**

គោលដៅ៖
Destination:

ថ្ងៃចេញដំណើរ Departure Date	ពេលវេលាចេញដំណើរ Departure Time	លេខកៅអី Seat No

ថ្លៃ
Fare _____

ថ្ងៃចេញសំបុត្រ
Issued Date _____

ចេញសំបុត្រ
Issued by _____

CUSTOMER COPY

living expenses including rent, electricity and food, and she must also pay off her debt. For some girls this will take many years. In Bangladesh it is not unusual for the debt to be settled only after four or five years. During this time the young prostitute works as a kind of apprentice under the control of the brothel manager. She is not free to leave and she must service all clients that are given to her.

The basic structures of the debt bondage system are identical in South-East Asia. The costs for trafficked girls, for instance, usually have to be repaid with 100% interest.[6] A Burmese girl who is trafficked across the Thai–Burmese border may cost the brothel owner around 10,000 baht, but the girl herself will have to repay the brothel owner 20,000 baht. She will have to repay this sum by selling sex. Half of the customer's fee will be given to the girl and from this she is expected to pay off her debt.

Perhaps the most perplexing aspect of the debt bondage system is the way that it is accepted as inevitable by those girls who have experienced it at its most vicious and exploitative. In the initial phases of my research I found it almost incomprehensible that a young woman should believe that a third party had the right to sell her. I expected them to be outraged or at least angry at the fact that they had been sold. Very few, however, questioned either their sale or the debt bondage system. When they did express an opinion it was to state their obligation to clear the debt. A Bangladeshi sex worker in Calcutta, for instance, thought that it was unjust that a neighbour had sold her into prostitution when she was a child, but she did not question the need to repay her debt to the brothel owner. 'I hated the work,' she explained, 'but I had to repay the money.' I have heard similar views from Cambodian sex workers who felt bitter that friends and relatives had sold them to brothels but who, at the same time, never, ever questioned the fundamental assumption that they could be bought and sold. After a while it made sense to me: these girls do not question the principle of their sale because they accept what they are. They are a commodity to be traded. They are not angry at being dispossessed of their rights because they never had believed in those rights in the first place.

The second – and most profound – shock I had during the field-work for this book was the ages of the girls involved in the sex trade. In recent years the Western media has placed a spotlight upon pae-dophilia. In the West it is an acknowledged problem and the perpetrators of this evil are known to travel to Asia, as well as to other less-developed parts of the world, to liberally indulge them-selves in a vice that demands far greater discretion while they are at home. From coverage in the Asian press you would suppose that paedophilia was a perversion confined to the West and perpetrated upon Asian children only by Western tourists and expatriates. I want to be the last person to defend these pathetic and deeply sad men, but the Asian media should be more honest. Paedophilia among Asian men exists on a large scale, but the problem of men's sexual attraction to children is simply not acknowledged. In some coun-tries this is because sexual relations between men and children are institutionalised.

To give an example: there might be public distaste in Bangladesh when twelve-year-old girls are prostituted. But this is because pros-titution is stigmatised and not because twelve-year-olds are having sex with adult men. Why should there be outrage? In Bangladesh ten-year-old girls become wives in consummated marriages. Fifteen per cent are married at twelve or younger and 57% are married by the age of fourteen.[7] In South Asia girls are sold into prostitution when they are children and they are married when they are children. What is the difference?

To be fair, we have to make the distinction between preferential sex abusers and situational sex abusers. Preferential paedophiles are those people who seek sex primarily with prepubescent children. Situational paedophiles are those people who have sex with children but who do not necessarily seek children out as victims. I believe that most of the customers of Asian child prostitutes fall into the second category. They have sex with children because they are available and, once the girls' virginity has been sold, they are also cheap. When men do wish to have sex with a girl they tend to desire those who are pubescent as opposed to those who are prepubescent.

In Bangladesh, like in other developing countries, there is no recognised intermediate stage between childhood and adulthood. Instead there is a sudden transition, which takes place at either puberty or marriage – whichever is the sooner. Similar patterns apply in the rest of South Asia. The age profile of sex workers within the region illustrates the early age of initiation into prostitution. A study of two hundred child prostitutes in Rajasthan by the Indian National Commission for Women found that 64% of these girls had entered prostitution before they were fourteen.[8] The overwhelming number of prostitutes entered the profession as children and most at around the age of puberty.[9] In 1999 Bangladesh's Department of Social Services undertook a survey of over one thousand women in the Tanbazar and Nimtoli brothels. Four hundred and fifty of these inmates were in fact children. Similarly, in a survey of street prostitution in Dhaka, involving over 180 women, almost 30% were found to be under sixteen. A counterpoint to this is that there is a dramatic decline in the number of prostitutes who are in their mid-twenties. There are virtually none above the age of thirty.[10] This is not because the women have found a happier and more socially acceptable occupation; there is simply no one prepared to buy them.

This point is worth repeating and illustrating. Reports suggest that over a quarter of the prostitutes in Phnom Penh are under seventeen.[11] This may even be an underestimate because many child prostitutes are not visible and therefore not calculable. In Malaysia virgin girls who have not yet reached puberty carry a premium.[12] In Nepal 48% of sex workers enter the profession between the ages of ten and fifteen.[13] Twenty percent of those who are trafficked to India are thought to be below fifteen,[14] and in Indonesia a quarter of all brothel-based prostitutes begin work when they are under seventeen.[15] The girls who are found in *casas*, the closed brothels of the Philippines, are also very, very young. Seventy percent are believed to be under twenty, with the majority being in the twelve to eighteen age group. A *mama-san* with extensive experience of various sectors of the sex industry in the Philippines, and who had managed a *casa* for several years, explained that the girls in the brothels were from very poor families. This is how she described the demand for them:

> Things are the worst for girls in the *casas*. They have lots of clients, especially on Friday and Saturday nights when they have ten to twelve men. It's especially bad for the new girls because all the regulars want to try her out. Twelve to fifteen is considered the best age. They are called 'cherry girls' but only the richest customers can afford to buy her 'cherry'.

In the past few years there has been a crackdown on child prostitution in Thailand. This initiative does seem to have had some impact – but not necessarily in the way intended. Child prostitution has been moved out of many brothels and is now made available in more discreet locations. I have therefore heard complaints from Thai sex workers that there are fewer customers visiting the brothels because the clients are going elsewhere in search of younger girls. This belief is corroborated by a survey by the International Labour Organisation, which noted claims by brothel owners that the ban on hiring women under eighteen was bad for business as most customers wanted to buy sex with younger prostitutes.[16]

It is often suggested that the emphasis upon very young prostitutes is a product of fears about Aids. According to this argument clients are demanding sex with younger prostitutes in the belief that these girls will have had less exposure to the virus and so will be less likely to be infected. This is certainly true in South East Asia where the average age of girls on entrance to prostitution has been declining. In South Asia, however, there has always been a premium placed on very young girls. Traditional religious prostitution such as the *devadasi* system demanded induction into the trade by puberty at the latest. Today's emphasis upon teenage girls therefore has a long pedigree and the contemporary worries about disease are a convenient additional justification for men's desire to have sex with girls who are children.

A major selling point for virgin girls is that they are not infected with HIV and other sexually transmitted diseases. The health-conscious consumers of virgin prostitutes therefore pay a premium not only to deflower the girls but also to enjoy them without nagging doubts about unpleasant diseases. Condoms are therefore disposed with. But of course this safety assurance applies only to the clients. The girls, on the other hand, are highly vulnerable to infection because they are having unprotected sex on a critical occasion with a man who is likely to have had multiple sexual partners.

Fresh young girls who find themselves in a cheap brothel will not stay fresh for very long. This is because there is greater demand for the services of younger and newer girls. A study of sex work in Calcutta found that prostitutes usually serviced between two and ten clients per day, with the average number being three.[17] However, there was a very wide variation, with some unfortunate Nepali girls servicing as many as ten to fifteen clients.[18] Invariably the younger girls have the most customers. It is a similar scene everywhere. In Cambodia brothel owners force teenage prostitutes to take anything between seven and fifteen clients a day. This is far more than the numbers serviced by adult sex workers. I met one girl who had been blessed with features considered to be highly attractive in Cambodia: she was pretty, plump and fair-skinned. During her captivity in a Phnom Penh brothel these desirable qualities also blessed her with twenty customers a day and HIV.

Seasoning can take anything from a few weeks to a few years. Some entrants to prostitution do not need to be seasoned because they have chosen to sell their bodies. But for many others there is a period of adaptation. This also applies to girls who knew that they would sell sex but did not know of the conditions under which they would have to do the selling. They must all adapt to captivity and to the psychological and physical toll that prostitution will take upon them. Their will to resist has to be broken.

For the youngest girls, the physical scars of a brutal initiation into prostitution can never be healed. They suffer irreparable internal injuries. Efforts are made by brothel owners to prepare younger girls for prostitution. In Calcutta, for example, dried and tightly packed pith, which expands when water is applied to it, is used to widen the vaginas of young girls who are to sell sex to adult men. But even this is not sufficient to stop serious damage. The staff at Sanlaap, an NGO working with child prostitutes in the city, has evidence not only of maiming and grievous injuries to young girls but also of their deaths.

Psychological conditioning is every bit as brutal as the physical coercion of girls and women into the trade. Its long-term effects are often just as serious. A principal tactic in the brothel owner's battle to turn reluctant prostitutes into willing sex workers is to strip them of their previous identities. They are often given new names and they are denied contact with their homes and families. Until they are seasoned their whole world will be centred in the brothel. This has the effect of isolating the girl and making her feel vulnerable while simultaneously divorcing her from the patterns of thinking and feeling that make her hostile to the idea of sex work. She is provided with a new pattern of behaviour. Women who refuse to adopt these new patterns are beaten, tortured and sometimes killed. How often such killings take place is unknown because the women who are the victims are invisible once they have disappeared into the opaque world of the sex trade. Virtually every sex worker will tell you that she knows a woman or girl who refused to comply with her brothel owner's expectations and was killed as a result. Whispers about killings and a regular dose of beatings by pimps are marvellous incentives to keep prostitutes working. Most new recruits, however, do not have to endure months of sadistic torture. Burdened with debt and threatened with violence, they adapt to their new situation. They have to if they wish to survive.

Escape is impossible for the victims of sexual slavery. Brothel owners have paid for the new recruits and they are unlikely to let their investment simply walk away. The girls will only be free once their purchase price has been recouped and a substantial profit has been made. Until then they are watched and guarded. This involves far more than simply placing a tough guy on the door. A red light area is home to a large network of criminal gangs and people who are affiliated with the trade. So if a girl manages to escape from her brothel she will rarely get very far. She will be picked up by some of the local youths who patrol the streets and who can be found loitering at every street corner. Nervous girls and disoriented young women are very easy to spot as they try to make a hurried or confused getaway.

One of the great advantages of using trafficked girls is that they rarely know where to escape to. This is especially true for those who have been trafficked over substantial distances and particularly across international borders. They may not know the language and they may not know the city they are in. The HELP Asian Women's Shelter in Tokyo gives assistance to women in prostitution and receives telephone calls from trafficked Thai women pleading for help. Some of these women are so isolated that they do not know where they are. They have been brought to Japan and sold to a 'snack' in some Japanese town. They do not speak the language and cannot read any signs. They do not even know which part of Japan they are in. They have seen the telephone number of the shelter in a Thai newspaper and have run away from the snack to make a call from a public telephone box. Even those women who know where they are and how to get back to their own countries are stopped from doing so by a basic law of economics: they cannot afford the airfare home.

Nepali women who have been trafficked to brothels in Indian cities report that they did not know how to get home. Many are unfamiliar with urban life and are confused by the environment outside the brothels. Inside the brothel are many horrors but, for some, this may be preferable to taking their chances in the unfamiliar and hostile world outside its doors.

Brothel owners frighten trafficked women by telling them that they will be identified as sex workers and picked up and then sold to another even worse brothel if they try to escape. Alternatively they are told that the police will arrest them for being illegal immigrants. This is a real threat for many women trafficked to countries such as Thailand and Japan and they have good reason to be fearful.

The seasoning process is completed once the woman accepts that she has absolutely no alternative but to be a sex worker. At this point some will seem genuinely to embrace their profession. This is because they are survivors. They have been forced to become prostitutes and, as they have no other options, they make the very best of the situation. This process can be seen at its most poignant in South Asia. In most parts of the subcontinent there is no way back to 'respectable' society for a woman who has sold sex. How she entered the profession is seen as totally immaterial. She is marked out for social death. However, once they have been seasoned and have come to accept that they are locked into the trade, women can be very philosophical about their lives and their work. The attitude expressed by this successful prostitute in Calcutta is typical:

> I did not want to do this work. I was sold to a brothel and then I could not go back to my village and live like an ordinary woman. I could not have a husband and a family. But if I can't return to society then I can support my family. My life

is ruined but at least I can help my mother and my brothers
and sisters. I am good at my job and I have a lot of regular
clients who are generous to me. With the money I earn I have
paid for my sister to be married. I gave her a dowry and my
brother is going to school.

Women can be conditioned to accept even the most dehumanising prostitution as their occupation if they are pushed by poverty
and by debt and if they are coerced by violence and by threats. They
will survive and accept sexual exploitation and brutality. And most
will do so with dignity and, eventually, with a perceptive humour.
But in many parts of Asia they become, in the process, irredeemably
stigmatised. They are a group of social outcastes fashioned from
poor and vulnerable women. The societies that create them condemn their very existence. The men who enjoy them will be exactly
the same men who, once back in their roles as model family men
and good citizens, will recoil with distaste from such moral degradation. No wonder Asia's prostitutes have to be seasoned so well.

Chapter Five

THE CUSTOMERS

Some magical things happen in the sex industry. One of the most remarkable tricks is just how often the customers vanish from both analysis and censure. It is almost as if they were not really that important. Only a few of the many reports written on the trafficking of women and prostitution pay any attention to who is buying sex as opposed to who is selling it. From most of the available research on the subject you might begin to believe that the sex trade involves only poor women and an array of criminal elements. Yet it is obvious that prostitution would not exist without demand from the customers. Commercial sex is an industry and, like any other successful industry, there has to be a sufficiently large number of people who are willing to become consumers. In Asia, the sex trade may have encountered a few problems of distribution and merchandising, and the law is sometimes an irritation, but the industry cannot complain about insufficient customer demand. On the contrary, more men than ever are buying sex.

To understand prostitution, sexual slavery and the trafficking of women and girls we need to shift and widen the parameters of the debate. Some frequently sidelined questions need to be dusted off and answered. Who, for instance, are the customers? And who buys the girls and women who are locked into sexual slavery? We know a great deal about the girls who become sex workers but next to nothing about the men who buy them. We should ask what these consumers think about prostitution. And why they have to buy sex.

Questions like this remain unaddressed for the simple reason that it is incredibly difficult even to begin answering them. There is an astonishing lack of information on the consumers of commercial sex. What information there is on prostitution is focused upon trafficking and child prostitution. With a handful of notable exceptions, the published books on prostitution in Asia are abysmal.[1] Many are exposés, principally of the call girl and bar girl sectors, and aim to titillate. Or they amount to sex guides for visiting foreigners. From these books it would seem that all prostitutes in Asia are having riotous fun and earning a steady income to boot. Sex slaves do not figure prominently in these accounts. And the customers, of course, are fundamentally decent men looking for a bit of harmless adventure.

There is a profound reluctance in the region to research and discuss matters relating to sex. It creates acute embarrassment. Prostitution, I was told by people in countries as far apart as Pakistan and Japan, is not a subject worthy of study – especially for a respectable woman like myself. Presumably being in the mere vicinity of prostitutes, or even talking about them, was enough to brand a visiting academic with the stigmatised brush of whoredom. Debates on prostitution in most Asian societies are usually muted. When the subject is considered worthy of discussion the discourse centres upon prostitution as a symbol of an individual sex worker's moral degradation or, in more progressive circles, prostitution is interpreted as a development issue. According to this perspective, prostitution is intimately related to poverty. Of course it is: poverty creates a steady and reliable source of prostitutes. But poverty is just one factor in a much more complicated story. Sex work is just as much about the way sexuality is constructed, commodified and sold.

There are lots of explanations for why men buy sex. Sociobiology provides us with some interesting although contentious arguments about human sexuality. The crux of the argument is that sexual behaviour is designed to maximise an individual's ability to pass their genes on to subsequent generations. For men this means mating with a large number of fertile women with a reliable gene supply: they have to appear to possess a minimal quota of intelligence, be reasonably physically attractive and capable of caring for offspring. For women these biological imperatives mean mating with a man who will provide protection and an environment in which she and her offspring can flourish. There is a solid and convincing foundation to this logic, but it is not faultless. It does not make genetic sense, for instance, for a man to spread his genes too widely. He cannot help in providing protection and material support for the hundreds or even thousands of children he is capable of fathering. Likewise, for women, the socially and economically powerful men who can provide the best environment for rearing children may not necessarily be the ones with the most enticing gene bank. Even for women, who are supposedly monogamously inclined, it might make genetic sense to sleep around.

The transition from primitive communities to settled agriculture, the development of patriarchy and the emergence of private property created a problem. If property was to be passed from one generation of men to the next, men had to be sure that the inheritors carried their own genes. Women's sexuality therefore became more tightly controlled. Yet if men were still to continue with their genetically programmed and fairly indiscriminate mating patterns certain provisions had to be made. The results were prostitution, polygamy and concubinage.

Both prostitution and traditional marriage can be interpreted as a continuation of a primitive form of human transaction whereby women exchanged sex for food and protection. These sociobiological and functionalist explanations for prostitution are convincing but they need to be more nuanced. The foundations and parameters of sexuality are set by biology. The cultural construction of sexuality works within these guidelines, although culture also causes the parameters set by biology to be modified and reinterpreted. Basically, there are consistent patterns and types of behaviour which boil down to exactly the same thing: all over the world men seek to dominate. They seek to dominate women and other men. It is a biologically driven need and its goal is to enhance reproductive success. This need makes power, domination and sex inextricably linked. What happens in cheap Asian brothels is just one of the most unpleasant manifestations of a universal theme. Man is an animal. The girls in closed brothels are treated like breeding mares because their vulnerability allows men the licence and opportunity to behave like animals. And these girls are vulnerable because intensely male-dominated Asian societies have created cultures that keep many young women powerless. Biological pressures and male-dominated cultures are, unfortunately, a largely inevitable and very bad mix – especially if you are a poor, vulnerable girl approaching puberty.

Prostitution flourishes in societies that are sexually open and it also flourishes in societies that publicly espouse strict sexual and moral codes. We can draw two interrelated conclusions from the Asian prostitution scene. First, the sex sector thrives in places where women's sexuality is under tight control. And, second, the greater a society's rhetorical commitment to conservative sexual mores the greater is its degree of hypocrisy. There is a neat symmetry: the more repressive the sexual morality and the more rigid the social conventions, the greater is the tendency to buy sex. This is entirely understandable. As men cannot openly enjoy a biologically driven need they will do so in secret and will pay for this pleasure because it is not one available for free.

I spent several weeks researching prostitution in Pakistan but found it very difficult to make significant progress. It is hard investigating prostitution in a country in which sex for sale is not supposed to exist. The Pakistani government has only recently acknowledged that such vices do, perhaps, occur. Previously it was considered unthinkable that sex could be bought and sold in an Islamic state. Unsurprisingly, however, prostitution is as extensive in Pakistan as anywhere else. In fact the practice of commercial sex may be even higher in Pakistan than in most other Asian nations. What is more troubling is that terrible abuses within the industry are all the more common because the trade is so highly secretive.

Sex workers are essential to the functioning of Asian societies. If men want to control women within their own families and yet still have sex with multiple partners there has to be a pool of prostitutes. In terms of numbers this pool is really quite small but it services lots of men. In most respects men benefit from this system because it is one they have made to suit their needs. But, in other ways, it lets down some individual men. They cannot, for instance, have legitimate sexual relations before they marry. Plenty of them nevertheless decide to have illegitimate ones both before and during marriage. Among the Indian prostitute users that I interviewed were a small number of unmarried educated young men who bemoaned their inability to have sexual relations with women before they married. This, they explained, was why they bought sex. It would be much better, they maintained, if they were free to form casual relationships with women from their own social circles, but, alas, the young women in question were sadly and frustratingly unavailable. I thought this sounded like a seed of progress and an indication of changing attitudes, but their reaction to my next question threw the thesis into doubt. They were outraged at my suggestion that they should marry a woman who was not a virgin. Impossible, they insisted. When I asked why, I was met with some evasive replies along the lines of 'How could I trust her?' and 'She wouldn't be respectable'. One young man said that his wife had to have no prior experience of sex, otherwise, 'She might have enjoyed sex with another man more than she enjoyed sex with me.' It appears as if the sexual double standard has a lot of life left in it in India. So, therefore, does prostitution.

Most customers have no qualms about buying sex as long as their activity can be hidden. The unofficial codes of Asian societies sanction the buying of sex providing that this activity does not disturb the surface appearance of the respectable social order. It is not so much the act that is bad. What is bad is getting caught.

It is assumed by a majority of people in many Asian societies that men have enormous sexual appetites that can be satisfied only by frequent intercourse – preferably with a large number of women. A very senior Bangladeshi police officer, who was genuinely concerned about the problems associated with prostitution, explained earnestly to me that the whole business of sex and the commercial sex sector was complicated by the weather. Apparently, Bangladesh's high temperatures stimulate men's passions and contribute to the demand for sex workers.

In Cambodia male sexual desire is considered insatiable. One woman simply cannot satisfy the average man. A Cambodian proverb, 'Ten rivers are not enough for one ocean', expresses this very aptly. Men believe that they are entitled to have sex and they believe that they have a right to buy it. That is not all: they believe they have a right to cheap sex. Their beliefs are then validated because there are lots of poor women ready to sell cheap sex to them. Assumptions about the boundless limits of male sexuality feed into an argument that has common currency throughout the world. Prostitutes are needed as a kind of safety valve, allowing men burdened by awesome libidos to have a sexual outlet. If this outlet did not exist then 'innocent' women would inevitably be raped.

Prostitution in this context changes from a social vice into a worthy social service. Rather than being exploiters of poor women, the customers are, in fact, socially responsible citizens seeking to curb their own potentially destructive sexual behaviour.

It is risky to suggest how many men buy sex in Asia because there is a woeful absence of firm statistics. Figures are impossible to derive because the sex trade is hidden and often illegal, the acts are done in private and few clients are willing to identify themselves. Very few studies on prostitute use have been attempted and these are usually micro studies and are open to question. Thailand is perhaps the best analysed country. In 1990 a study by the US Agency for International Development concluded that 75% of Thai men had purchased sex and that 48% of men had had their first sexual intercourse with a prostitute. These figures have not been seriously challenged and they are corroborated by other small studies. For example a survey in the Klong Toey slum in Bangkok found that 82% of men and 66% of women thought that it was normal for men to visit sex workers.[2] Similar statistics can be found in studies undertaken in neighbouring Cambodia where a survey discovered that 60–70% of men were thought to visit prostitutes.[3] Thai male sexual culture actively promotes male promiscuity and the purchase of sex. Such values are rapidly being exported to neighbouring countries of the Mekong Basin.[4] Comparatively rich and culturally dominant Thailand acts as a magnet for the poor and also as a promoter and distributor of an unhappy sexual code.

My own guesses on prostitute usage in Asia are highly impressionistic and are based upon interviews with people who have extensive knowledge of the sex industry within their own countries. They include humanitarian agencies, non-governmental organisations, human rights groups, government officials, journalists and health care professionals working in the field of reproductive health and the control of HIV and sexually transmitted diseases. On the basis of their information I believe that the proportion of men who buy sex is very high but that it also varies between Asian countries. Towards the high end of the scale are societies like Japan, Thailand, the Philippines, Cambodia and Pakistan. And towards the lower end are countries like India, Bangladesh and Indonesia. Informants in Japan and Pakistan were extremely insistent that the scale of commercial sex was enormous in their own societies. Comments that the purchase of sex was 'universal' among men, or that it involved 'all men' at some point in their lives, were repeated by informants who worked in different fields and who arrived at this verdict completely independently of each other. Although it is extremely unlikely that such sweeping generalisations are true, these opinions suggests that the scale of the commercial sex sector within Asian countries is extremely large. In most Asian countries, most men will pay for sex at least once in their lives. Many, moreover, are habitual buyers.

The perceived rate of prostitute use in Asian societies bears similarity to that of men in Western societies during an era which was far more sexually repressive than today and when women's sexuality was tightly controlled. Social reformer Robert Dale Owen estimated that half of the adult male population of New York City in the 1830s visited prostitutes on a regular basis.[5] In 1948 Alfred Kinsey's report on sexual behaviour suggested that 69% of the adult male population had purchased sex on at least one occasion.[6] A number of small-scale studies on contemporary prostitute usage suggest that a smaller percentage of men are now buying sex in Western societies. Estimates understandably vary. One report in the US in 1993 suggested that around 20% of men buy sex.[7] In 1997 a study by Middlesex University claimed that 80,000 men purchase the services of prostitutes in London every week.[8] This would indicate that around 10% of London's male population are prostitute users. These statistics are open to question but they do prove that although prostitution exists everywhere, it is also less common in more sexually relaxed societies where there are greater opportunities to enjoy sex outside marriage.

Who are the men who buy women enmeshed in systems of sexual slavery? There is not a stereotypical Asian sex consumer, just as there is not a stereotypical Asian prostitute. Some clients would be appalled if they thought they were buying women who had been forced into the profession but I fear that, for all too many customers, this kind of consideration is totally immaterial. All classes, religions, ages and ethnic groups are represented among sex workers' clients. Wealthier men frequent clubs and purchase high-class call girls while the cheaper brothel sector tends to be patronised by the less affluent. There are, however, no fixed boundaries. A *casa* owner in the Philippines revealed that some of her clients were wealthy men:

My best regular client is the mayor. He likes to visit the *casa* every fortnight or so. He often telephones to see when I have new virgins in because they are his favourite.

A cross-section of males visit closed brothels. This is how a sex worker in Dhaka described the clients she had entertained during her period of debt bondage:

My clients were all ages. Some were boys and some were old men. A few were rich and some were college students. Well-off university students would come in a group to the brothel for the whole night. They would sit and talk and joke together and have sex with the girls.

The age of some of the customers is corroborated by other sources. An HIV/STD intervention programme, known as the Shakti Project and targeted at sex workers and their clients in Bangladesh, found that a minority of customers were schoolboys of twelve to thirteen years of age. A young Burmese woman who worked in a Thai brothel made similar observations about her own customers.

I had all sorts of clients including boys who were still at school. A few were only about thirteen. There were old men and middle-aged ones. Some had white hair and looked like a grandfather.

It has been estimated that between 60,000 and 80,000 men buy sex each day in Calcutta.[9] This is astonishing when we remember that in 1993 – and in the midst of the global Aids epidemic – the Indian Minister of Health said that the country would be saved from the scourge of Aids by strong family values.[10] Either the assessment of prostitute use in Calcutta was uncharacteristically sloppy or the Minister of Health needed a more professional briefing. If we look at HIV infection rates in terms of the percentage of the adult population who are infected, India is not suffering the misery of many sub-Saharan African countries. Even so, the disease is beginning to spread very rapidly in India and four million people are now thought to be infected.[11]

Heterosexual commercial sex plays a significant part in the spread of HIV in the country, and prostitute users are taking the disease both to the women they buy and to the women they marry. A recent survey of four hundred women who were treated for sexually transmitted diseases in Pune found that 93% were married and 91% had never had sex with anyone other than their husband. Almost 14% of these women, however, were HIV positive.[12] In 1997 4.3% of women attending antenatal clinics in Mumbai were also found to be HIV positive.[13] We can infer many things from this but the most persuasive point is that a sizeable number of Indian men must have a seriously muddled impression about the requirements of family values.

A large proportion of Calcutta's prostitute users will buy from the brothel sector. The Sonagachi red light area caters to middle- and low-income groups. In the superior brothels girls say their clients are businessmen and professional people: they are government officers, lawyers and doctors. In the cheaper brothels the clients are rickshaw pullers and petty traders. It is hard to categorise these men because they belong to many different professions and classes. The one thing they have in common is that they buy sex, and the women that they buy are both poor and from despised communities and castes.

Inexperienced sex workers appear to be very confused about why so many customers want to buy them. One terribly distressed Cambodian prostitute questioned me on this subject.

> Why did these old men want to have sex with a girl like me?
> They have wives. They have daughters like me at home. I
> don't know why they come here. They have nice houses and
> money. Why do they have to spend it on me?

An older, well-seasoned prostitute in Calcutta had a much clearer picture of her customers.

> Men come here because maybe their wife doesn't like sex or
> they don't like their wife. Or their wife is pregnant or she
> lives in the countryside. But I think for most it's just like a
> kind of hobby.

Male migrant workers are some of the best clients of brothel-based prostitutes. These men are often poorly paid and so when they buy sex they patronise the lower end of the market. Many of the women who service these migrants will be held in a form of slavery. There are large populations of male migrant workers throughout Asia. They work in badly paid jobs that the local people shun. They work in factories and on construction sites. Most are unaccompanied: they might be unmarried or they might have left their families back at home. In Calcutta, for example, the 1991 census revealed that there were 1,000 men for every 799 women. In other words there were lots of men in Calcutta who did not have partners.

Frequently, these men buy sex with women and girls who are from their own communities. In the last century Chinese migrants bought young Chinese prostitutes and today Burmese men working in Thailand buy Burmese girls. In Ranong there is a large population of Burmese men working in the fishing industry, and a large number of Burmese prostitutes have been imported to service them. These men buy women from their own societies for two main reasons: first the girls are likely to share the same language and they will be familiar with the men's customs. They will provide, in some measure, a little of the comfort of home. Secondly, like the male migrant workers themselves, the women's labour will also be cheap.

Many migrant males work under very poor conditions. They are exploited and far from their families and communities of their birth. In Cambodia the youths who ride motorbike 'taxis' are one of the main client groups of cheap local brothels. One youth, who was really little more than a boy, explained why he visited prostitutes with his friends.

Often we are lonely so we go to see the girls. Our families are not here and we don't have girlfriends. When we go to the brothel we can have some beers and have a good time and forget about our troubles.

The ritual of the brothel visit is vital to many of these men. An indication of this is provided by a glance at the economics of the transaction. In Thailand a young Burmese girl in a brothel will cost around 150–250 baht (£2.50–£3.50) for 'short time', that is one sex act. A Burmese migrant worker, however, might earn only 100–150 baht per day. He then budgets for his sex and will save up for a monthly visit to the brothel.

A lot of these workers are lonely boys and men. They might not realise that the women they buy have very little control over their lives. Many will not care, partly because they suffer from similar problems of disempowerment too and partly because purchasing sex grants them, for a moment, the unaccustomed thrill of power over another human being. We can understand why they might want to buy sex, and we can sympathise with their often miserable lives, but this does not absolve them from responsibility when they buy girls who are held in sexual slavery. Inside a brothel even these relatively powerless men can exercise control because they have the power to buy women.

Prostitution flourishes wherever there are imbalances between the sexes and a higher proportion of men than women. It is also common in those societies in which young men cannot afford to marry because of a lack of employment opportunities or the inflexible system of landholding and inheritance. A concentration of unattached males will commonly be complemented by a concentration of prostitutes. This is the case with male migrant workers and also with prostitution catering to military personnel. It was no coincidence that the Cambodian sex industry blossomed during 1991–93 when a 22,000-strong United Nations peace-keeping force was stationed in the country to oversee general elections. The number of women and girls in prostitution sky-rocketed in line with the demand from troops. A large proportion of the girls who serviced these soldiers had been sold into prostitution.

Marked imbalances in the sex ratio are looming in China. The combination of a traditional preference for sons and the One Child Policy is a particularly nasty one for female Chinese babies. Put simply, lots of daughters either do not make it into the world or have a brutally short stay. China is breeding an army of bachelors. There are simply not enough women to go around. If we looked at this in terms of supply and demand we might assume that a scarcity of women would increase their value. It has – but not in the most beneficial way for women. In some rural areas a shortage of women has led to the purchasing of wives, and in the cities it has contributed to the demand for prostitution. Today, women are more valued in China because they can fetch a higher price in the country's liberalising markets.

Buying sex may not be part of Asia's official social and moral codes, but it is intricately and firmly woven into the pattern of men's behaviour. Sex workers are important in framing the sexual lives and identity of large numbers of men all over the region. Prostitutes initiate many young men into their sexual lives. A visit to a brothel is a rite of passage for young men in countries like the Philippines and Thailand, and is confirmation of their arrival into adulthood. Close friends and even members of the family may arrange an excursion to the brothel. It is a celebration and a matter of importance from which the young man cannot escape if he wishes to establish his reputation as a real man. He must go through the ritual in order to save face. This sexual initiation sets the scene and the tone for the rest of his sexual life.

Wealth and social status are associated with sexual access to women. Sexual potency for many men is the most profound symbol and measure of their identity as males. This is not exclusive to Asia. The power and ability to have sex with attractive young women is a status symbol. It is a proof of masculinity and is one of the most important markers of a man's position within male hierarchies. It is also a marker that needs constant reaffirmation because hierarchies are never static. Men may be encouraged by biological imperatives to mate with as many women as possible, but to do this successfully they need to prove, establish and maintain a dominant position within their own peer group. Buying women achieves both of these aims simultaneously. In Cambodia, high-level business deals are sealed by having sex with virgins. It is considered auspicious; it is proof of considerable financial security and it is also enjoyable. Chinese businessmen measure their success by their company's balance sheets and also by their tally of deflowered virgins.

Buying sex projects an image of a potent, powerful man. Buying sex proves a man's dominance within the public world: it proves he has money and power (although it also reveals his own inner weaknesses and vulnerabilities). The very limited number of studies undertaken on men's attitudes to prostitution indicate that buying sex is seen as the inevitable result of male instincts. In the mid-1990s a survey by the Asia Japan Women's Resource Centre at Ryukyu University in Japan's Okinawa Prefecture found that a majority of male students had a positive view of prostitution. The findings of this study are entirely consistent with perceived rates of prostitute use by Japanese men.

A number of clients honestly believe that prostitutes enjoy their work. Perhaps a few do, and for some it is a nightmare. But, from what I can gather, most seasoned women just find it rather repetitious. Those clients who have been impressed by the responsiveness of their purchased sex partners are forgetting the economic foundations of the sex business. Simply: men who make return visits tend to be those whose egos have been massaged along with their penises. An inadequate man who is made to feel even more inadequate by a wooden prostitute will not pay tips and he will not become a regular client. For women in need of money it is very bad for business to remain unmoved by the man who pays the cash. Successful prostitutes learn techniques and modes of behaviour that make men feel masculine. And because the cultural construction of masculinity varies (within parameters set by the need to prove dominance) prostitutes adopt different behaviours when they service different nationalities.[14] The sex workers who survive and prosper in the long term are those who are the most highly accomplished actresses. Consequently, they are also the ones who are perpetually thrilled by their clients.

Many of these same clients also believe that they are doing the women a favour. Most of the girls and women in prostitution are poor and the clients believe that they are giving them the means to make a living. The customers are not exploiting prostitutes; in fact they are giving them a helping hand. Prostitution thereby becomes a kind of convenient welfare service. This belief is encouraged by the fact that so many sex workers in Asia are from poor and despised communities and the fact that girls and young women are trafficked from poor to richer countries. It must be heart-warming and immensely satisfying for those men who buy the daughters of impoverished families to know that they are doing their bit to redistribute wealth in an unjust world.

All kinds of men purchase intimacy. It makes little difference whether they are married or not. The married clients of Asian sex workers buy sex because they can get away with it. Even in those countries where the legal apparatus allows a woman to divorce her husband for adultery, the social implications of this decision are so disastrous that few women will contemplate it. A majority of women continue to derive their social status from men and a divorced woman is a very sad figure to be pitied or sometimes scorned. Wives may also be economically reliant upon their faithless husbands because society offers them few opportunities to be financially independent. Basically, there is not a lot a woman can do if her husband frequents brothels. For some women the fact that their husband visits prostitutes is the lesser of two evils. In Thailand, for instance, wives would prefer their men to purchase sex from prostitutes than for them to establish 'minor wives' or mistresses, as these would pose a greater financial and emotional threat to an established marriage. Setting up a second household is much more expensive than a twice-weekly trip to the local brothels.

Marriage and sex are compartmentalised aspects of life for many Asian men. Thai men, for example, may not consider that they are being unfaithful to their wives when they visit prostitutes. Japanese men will depart with friends on sex tours and will buy sex in a variety of establishments and yet they will not really think that this activity threatens their marriages. And they are quite right. In general, Japanese women turn a blind eye to their men's infidelity. In part this is because they have no other option. And partly it is because a large portion of Japanese women have chosen their husband not for love but because of criteria such as the man's earning power and his potential for career and social advancement. Japan's rigid social structure then keeps them locked into dysfunctional relationships. It may sound unsympathetic, but many women end up with exactly the kind of faithless husband they deserve.

Not all of the men who visit prostitutes are going simply for sex. A few go in search of comfort and love. Many experienced sex workers claim that their best and most regular customers are those men with unhappy but unbreakable marriages. They say that they visit to talk, to be cuddled and also to have sex. Some men want to buy romance as well as passion. How sad that the brothel is the only place they will find it. This is particularly true in South Asia where there are very strict rules about the interaction between men and women. India has a strangely ambivalent attitude towards the idea of romantic love: social conventions firmly prohibit it, while it is simultaneously portrayed as an incomparable experience in popular culture. Indian films heave with pretty girls and portly heroes in the throes of passionate, if cinematically chaste, romances. The plots are unlikely in the real world. For most women the yearning for romantic love will remain just that – a yearning. But for men there is the option of indulging in passion outside marriage: relationships with sex workers are one of the easiest ways of achieving this.[15]

Because women are largely divided into 'good' and 'bad', or, more pointedly, into the wife or whore category, there is confusion about women's sexuality in large parts of Asia. Good women are not supposed to like sex. If they do they are suspect: perhaps they are whores dressed up in respectable women's clothes. Cambodia provides a good example of the way this reasoning operates.[16] Here, wives are blamed for not having sufficient technical expertise to keep their husbands faithful. Presumably only a whore could possess the requisite sexual repertoire and enthusiasm. A wife, by definition, could not possibly have such skills because that would make her a stigmatised prostitute. Of around one hundred and fifty women who took part in focus group discussions during an in-depth survey, only one thought that a woman's sexual desires could be natural.[17] This incredibly restricting and deadening attitude is compounded by similar feats of self-serving male logic. The Cambodian idea of beauty is that of a young, fair-skinned and made-up girl. Yet a wife would be ridiculed as an immoral woman if she should ever dare to present herself in this manner.

A similar phenomenon is found in the Philippines, where the Catholic church has done a splendid job of turning sex into a mortal sin. Within this repressive context ignorance of sex is seen as a virtue. The purest are those who have the least experience of the sordid business. Even asking questions about sex can be interpreted as evidence of loose morals. The ideal wife is therefore a sexually illiterate virgin upon marriage and a devoted wife and mother thereafter. There is no space for anything else: the choice is to be either a good wife or an insatiable and irredeemable whore.

It is grossly unfair of men to complain about the sexual passivity of their wives and to posit this as an explanation for their own prostitute use when they also demand that these same wives adhere to a sexually repressive code. This is especially true in countries where marriages are arranged. It is inconceivable that a sexually inexperienced woman who is married to a man she barely knows will be a spontaneous and energetic sex partner. It is only a little less conceivable that a man will find long-lasting sexual sparkle with a partner his parents have chosen for him. To prove the point, ask experienced South Asian prostitutes about their regular clients. They will tell a familiar story of unhappy men in dead and unrevivable marriages. I am sure that the wives of these men would tell an even sadder tale.

Arranged marriages remain common in large parts of the region – particularly in South and East Asia. Even when this system of mate selection has become more relaxed single people typically have to choose from a very small pool of socially suitable potential partners. Although the Western variety of mate selection on the basis of romantic love has considerable drawbacks and makes its own sizeable contribution to the sum of human unhappiness, I believe the practice of arranged marriages and outlawed divorces is a greater source of misery. It has a public relations advantage however: it looks a lot neater and more civilised. Couples do not tear each other apart in horrible public displays: instead they do it within the intimate privacy of the family. Under the happy, harmonious togetherness of lots of families in countries as far apart as Japan and Pakistan – and especially in these two countries – there is a bitter but far quieter tune being played.

Men are the architects of this social and sexual system and women are its principal victims. Individual men suffer from the restrictions of the system but we can say, with complete certainty, that it is women who suffer the most. Both wives *and* prostitutes.

The 'dominant mother complex' is frequently used to explain problems and dysfunctionality in sexual relationships in South Asia and East Asia. According to this hypothesis, men are unable to have sexual relations with women they feel they cannot successfully dominate.[18] The socialisation process in many Asian societies is thought to lie at the root of this failure. One of the weakest bonds within the family is the relationship between a husband and wife. Men engage with the broader public world while women's lives are more restricted and confined largely to the domestic spheres of family, household and friends. While men may be free to indulge in fleeting extramarital activities women must abide by a double standard and remain faithful to their husbands. This results in a distortion of the most intimate of familial relationships. If a woman's emotional energies cannot be absorbed by her conjugal relationship then her greatest attachment is redirected to her sons. In traditional societies a son provides status – proof of her success as a woman – and he becomes the vehicle through which her own ambitions will be fulfilled. A tight bond therefore develops between sons and mothers. This bond is so tight that when the sons become men they cannot distance themselves from their mothers. They are fearful of women because they are reminded of the suffocating maternal embrace.

In India the dominant mother complex leads to anxiety over encountering female sexuality. There is a widespread and pronounced dislike of sexually mature women in many parts of India. Its counterpoint is men's special fascination for the very young and a sexual preference for immature girls. Adolescence is considered the ideal period of female sexuality.[19] The sexual demands of mature women are seen as threatening to men who have not yet acquired sexual and emotional maturity. Such men then avoid having sex with women who are in their own age groups. Behaviour like this creates a vicious circle: adult women who feel rejected by their husbands will then smother their sons. This, in turn, creates men who fear sexually mature women. This complex is common in middle-class Indian families and less so among the poor who do not have the financial resources to allow the luxury of such an exclusive mother–son bond to develop. However, when we consider the age profile of Indian sex workers and the high demand for purchased sex with teenagers the thesis has a convincing tone.

Very similar patterns of behaviour are common in Japan. A mother who pushes her son to achieve high levels of academic performance and who combines this pressure with a smothering love will produce a sexually and emotionally inadequate man who cannot relate to sexually mature women.[20] A significant proportion of Japanese marriages are sexually sterile after a few years.[21] This is because Japanese husbands are unable to perform sexually with their wives after a period of time, as their wives have substituted for their mothers.[22] In order for men to separate their sexual partners from their mothers they need to feel a sense of power and independence they did not feel when in their mother's presence. They need to feel dominant. In the initial years of a marriage a man might feel in control of his bride but very quickly the power dynamics of the relationship change. The wife gathers power as she establishes and extends her influence over the household. Within the home the husband is no longer master. And if he is no longer master he becomes, at least psychologically, his own wife's son.

Dysfunctional relationships that grow out of the dominant mother complex might appear to be the product of tyrannical, overbearing women. We should remember, however, that mothers behave in this ultimately damaging way because the parameters of their lives have been set by a patriarchal society. Women smother their sons and are often dictatorial within the confines of their own families because, for very many, this is the only space where all their hopes, ambitions and longings can be played out. If restrictions are placed upon their sexual and emotional lives and if they are confined by social convention to a world of domesticity, it is no wonder they channel their energies into sons. Sons provide emotional bonds and they provide physical intimacy. If they are successful they can fulfil their mothers' ambitions. They become the adoring lovers these women never had. Asian mothers are made to love their sons too much.

This discussion may seem a long way from prostitution and an even longer way from sexual slavery, but in fact one flows from the other. Japanese men buy sex for the same reason that most men throughout the world buy sex: they want to purchase dominance. As so many Japanese men can function sexually only when structures of dominance are in place it is unsurprising that prostitution is so common. In Japan, as in India, there is a pronounced desire for very young women. Mainstream Japanese men's magazines are filled with pictures and profiles of girls who either are, or who pretend to be, adolescents. Favourite outfits include school uniforms and sailor suits or tiny shorts and socks. These magazines are not catering to a specialist paedophile niche market. Teenage girls take the leading roles in Japanese men's fantasies, and Japan is the world's largest producer and exporter of child pornography.

Image clubs provide a revealing example of the way that Japanese men's sexuality is constructed. These clubs provide sexual services but they do so in a themed setting. A room is furnished to look like the inside of an underground train, or a doctor's surgery, or any number of other favourite sites for men's sexual fantasies. The customers and the sex workers then adopt roles reflecting the dominance/subservience motif. For example, train passenger and uniformed schoolgirl, headmaster and female pupil or important doctor and student nurse might be the roles and sexual harassment would be the plot.

An element of sadism runs as an unpleasant undercurrent through Japanese society. *Manga* are like giant comics principally produced for Japanese men and boys. Torture, mutilation and rape of young women and girls are a regular feature of the storylines.[23] This interest in violence and the high incidence of prostitute use appears strangely at odds with a society that is so ordered, and where crime rates – including statistics on rape and murder – are so low in comparison with Western societies. On my visits to Japan I never encountered any form of sexual harassment. The Japanese men I met were formal and unfailingly courteous and, despite warnings about gropers, I was never molested on the Tokyo metro (although that may have been because I was twenty years older than the average sexually desirable female). Unlike any other major city I have visited, a woman can travel alone around Tokyo late at night without feeling the imminent victim of some form of assault.

This is not the picture of Japan and Japanese men that is painted by sex workers, and particularly sex workers from other Asian countries. One of the most common explanations for the duality in Japanese behaviour is that the violence portrayed, for instance in *manga*, is a kind of safety valve. In a tightly structured, intensely competitive, conformist society people need some avenue for individual expression and the release of tension and anti-social behaviour. Violence, just like conformist behaviour, is rigorously structured and is channelled into distinct paths. The purchase of sex is one of these paths.

Many of the prostitutes who serviced Japanese men either in Japan or when the men visited the women's countries as sex tourists insisted that their clients did not know how to behave. These criticisms applied to educated and well-off men as well as to the less affluent. This was how an East European woman described the way that the Japanese clients treated the hostesses in the club where she worked:

> They are always so rude. They get drunk and talk about the girls and say horrible things but the girls can't understand because they don't speak Japanese. They talk about the size of their breasts and try to touch them.

I have heard similar descriptions time after time. Inadequately socialised men like these are unable to engage with women as equals and so are unlikely to find partners who genuinely enjoy their company. Instead the men can go to a hostess bar and pay women to pretend to like them. That way they can avoid the embarrassment of being rejected.[24] To Japanese men who are deprived of a sense of control over their own lives by an intensely hierarchical and rigid power structure, the purchase of women, and the exertion of dominance over them, also serves to endow these men with a measure of confidence in their social and sexual potency.

One of the most interesting things to emerge from discussions with women who are trafficked to Japan was the very demanding nature of the customers. This did not apply only to the sex acts the women were requested or forced to perform but also to the customers' selection criteria for girls. Very few Japanese men would buy the same prostitute twice. Regular clients would visit a club once or perhaps twice a week but they would want a new woman and, supposedly, a new experience each time. Consumer fads are big business in Japan and products with novelty value have a great attraction. The sex market is no exception to this. One wonders however, how new these sexual experiences are after a time and how many variations on a theme there can possibly be. Clubs are, nevertheless, under great pressure to find fresh recruits in order to stop customers taking their money elsewhere in the search for superior new sensations.

Racism complicates and deepens the domination theme in sex purchase by Japanese men. The Japanese consider themselves to be the 'whites' of Asia. And they are every bit as racist as old-time Western colonialists. Japanese customers treat prostitutes differently according to the colour of their skin. Japanese and Caucasian women are treated far better than dark-skinned Asian women. White women's experience of sex work in Japan tends not to be as negative as that of Thai and Filipina women. I assume that this is because the men do not feel in such complete control of these women that they can do anything to them and still get away with it. Japanese prostitutes dominate the higher class sectors of Japan's sex market while the lower end is staffed principally by Thais and Filipinas. Although all nationalities complain of poor treatment there is a close correlation between the scale of abuse and the depth of skin colour. Colombian women have suffered from some of the most degrading treatment and, in the months preceding the writing of this chapter, young Colombian women have been gang raped on stage. Thai and Filipina women report beatings and threats with knives and guns.

In general the behaviour of Japanese sex buyers deteriorates when they leave Japan. Perhaps it is the effect of being released from the tight restrictions of a conformist, group-centred society. Alternatively, perhaps it is the result of being surrounded by so many racially inferior people who can be bought. A prostitute in the Philippines expressed her fears about Japanese clients:

> The Japanese treat us really badly – and so do the Arabs. I am
> always a bit frightened to go with a Japanese customer
> because some of them are really crazy. They seem OK and
> then something happens and they go crazy. My friend was
> burned by cigarettes on her nipples by two Japanese men.
> They treat us like animals.

So many women mentioned similar worries about Japanese customers that it was rarely necessary to ask specific questions about Japanese clients. Throughout South-East Asia Japanese men emerge as the biggest international consumers of commercial sex and the men who are most frequently brutal in its enjoyment. They are major purchasers of virgins. When the Japanese buy sex it is likely to be a more discreet arrangement than that of Western sex tourists. You do not see many middle-aged Japanese men carousing in the streets with young prostitutes, although you will occasionally spot a decrepit Japanese pensioner-businessman being nursed by a beautiful young woman in an exclusive restaurant. Japanese men have girls brought to their hotel rooms or they go to karaoke bars and clubs. Many also go to brothels. Most of these clients do not care about the girls they buy. They do not care if they have been forced into the business. Why should they? They consider foreign sex workers to be unimportant, racially inferior beings who deserve to be dominated and used. On a number of occasions the prostitutes who service these men asked me why their Japanese clients treated them with such contempt. Did they think, the women asked with a mixture of despair and annoyance, that they were not really human?

My own guess is that these clients are very much aware of their sex partner's humanity but that they put it on a far more primitive level than that of their own humanity. The women are of sufficient value to be possessed but do not have sufficient power to pose any kind of threat to the inadequate men who buy them. Young women are exciting for the Japanese men who buy sex because they are also comforting. No illiterate sixteen-year-old Burmese prostitute who depends for her own and her family's livelihood on her client's money is going to make any complaints about his sexual performance. Neither is she going to make any emotional demands upon him. She is not like his mother.

In some respects this concentration upon Japanese men as the consummate purchasers of commercial sex is unfair. Japanese men figure so prominently among the clients of Asian sex workers because Japanese men have infinitely more spending power than men from most other Asian nations. Japanese men buy lots of sex because they can afford to. Other men might do exactly the same if they had a similar financial capability.

The explanations for men's promiscuity and prostitute use are not uniform throughout Asia. The dominant mother complex is a useful tool in helping to understand some of the themes in gender relations in Japan and India but it needs to be modified and reinterpreted elsewhere. In some societies it is not really very relevant. In the Muslim-dominated regions of South Asia – in Pakistan, Bangladesh and among the Muslim community of India – the dominant mother syndrome is crucially important, but there are also additional factors to be considered. One is the segregation of the sexes. Men and women do not know how to interact with one another in a relaxed manner. There are only two forms of legitimate male–female relations. Either the relationship is one between family members, or it is an entirely formal interaction that never strays beyond strict guidelines. Anything outside these two spheres is inevitably interpreted as an invitation to unrestrained lust.

Segregation exists amongst Hindu communities – and especially amongst higher castes that have more to lose by inappropriate sexual liaisons between their own women and members of lower castes. But, as a rule, segregation is primarily a feature of Muslim societies and the more conservative the society the stricter are its rules of segregation. Pakistan is the very best example. Here the products of segregation are obvious and severalfold: young men and women cannot have informal relationships. Women have to be hidden away to keep them quiescent and so that they cannot draw men into temptation, and a group of prostituted women has to be created, and simultaneously stigmatised, so that a man can have plenty of sex while appearing to be sexually abstinent or faithful to his wife (or wives). The Japanese may be the biggest spenders in the sex market but the Pakistanis are the biggest hypocrites.

A second consideration in Muslim societies is the abrupt social and psychological rupture that a boy experiences at around the age of five. At this point he is transferred from the cosy, protected and segregated world of his mother and the women of his family to join the equally segregated, but much more public and competitive world of men. This rupture thrusts male children into an arena in which they have to learn very quickly how to cope with and compete in very strict male hierarchies. One result of this traumatic transition is a precarious sense of male identity.[25] Rather than emerging naturally from the developing confidence of a maturing young man, this identity takes the form of macho behaviour, conformity to male patterns of behaviour, fear and hatred of women, intense competition with other men, and the cultivation of an image of invulnerability. For some men a fragile sense of masculinity may be bolstered by frequent visits to prostitutes. Prostitution is necessary to keep the sex segregation system working and, ironically, prostitutes are also needed to provide sexual and emotional therapy to those men who, at least superficially, benefit from these distorted forms of human relations.

Filipino society does not have a pronounced dominant mother complex but many men still buy sex. Here the culturally specific explanations for this global practice are found in a mix of Catholicism and *machismo*. The cult of the virgin, idealisation of female chastity and consequent rampant prostitution were all bequeathed as an inseparable package to the Philippines by Spanish colonialism. The same package was also delivered to Latin America. Clearly, Asian societies, cultures and religions do not have a monopoly on hypocritical sexual morality.

Filipina prostitutes and *mama-sans* with long experience of sex work are dismissive of men and the clients they serve. I talked at length with a group of women who catered both to foreigners and to Filipinos in and around Angeles. They saw men's desires and need to purchase women as fortuitous because it provided them with a living. Yet at the same time they thought the clients foolish and like children. There was great hilarity when I asked why the clients wanted to buy teenagers. This was the reply:

Because the men are pathetic. They want a girl who doesn't know anything. It makes them feel like big men. If they go with a grown-up woman she will tell him to do it like this . . . and like this . . . and not like that. But men are frightened by this and they think that they can't be as good as all the other men the woman has known. They want a girl to just lie there. They say they want girls because they like 'tight pussy' but we all know it's because they are scared.

Biological imperatives dictate that the most sexually desirable females will be young. But these imperatives do not also dictate a preference for children and adolescents. Most females are not fully capable of sustaining pregnancy and successfully delivering babies until they are around seventeen years old. Buying sex with an eighteen-year-old woman makes genetic, if not ethical, sense. Buying sex with a thirteen-year-old does not. Prostitution and the consumer demand for sex with very young women and girls are created by cultural adaptations of sexual instinct and the psycho-sexual problems that grow out of, and reinforce, distorted patterns of human relations.

A lot of ridiculous old myths are trotted out to explain men's purchase of sex with children. An absurd, and suitably favoured, one throughout Asia is that having sex with a virgin can cure a man of sexually transmitted diseases. Such are the miraculous powers of virgins that they can even cure a man of Aids.

Among Chinese men there is a belief that regular sex with very young women – especially virgins – will rejuvenate an ageing man. According to this ludicrous theory everything has either *yin* (hot) or *yang* (cold) properties. A man can slow down the ageing (*yin*) process by drawing upon a girl's virgin youth – or her *yang* qualities. This would explain why so many middle-aged and elderly ethnic Chinese sex tourists from Taiwan, Hong Kong, Singapore and Malaysia, and men in China itself, visit brothels to have sex with virgin girls. And, of course, the theory does have some validity – but only to the extent that it provides a sad and temporary psychological crutch. Buying sex with virgins presumably makes these men feel young because it gives them a buzz and a kick from their physical proximity to youth and their power to buy and control what they themselves have lost.

I am sceptical as to whether men really believe these myths. Instead the myths provide a convenient rationale for what might otherwise be interpreted as a weakness. Better for a man to say that he needs to deflower a virgin to rejuvenate an ageing body or to cure Aids than to say that only a teenager can provide enough stimulation to counteract creeping impotence. It is far more soothing for men's egos to repeat a traditional myth than to analyse why they need to buy these pathetic and singularly unimpressive forms of dominance.

The debate on the relative importance of biology and culture in the construction of sexuality is an interesting academic exercise. We can debate whether men are biologically programmed to want to buy sex and we can debate why, and in what ways, cultures encourage prostitution. These arguments can be used to explain why there is a market for commercial sex and why there are women in sexual slavery. However, they cannot be used to justify prostitution. We cannot shrug our shoulders and say that such evil happens because we live in a genetically determined world. Our responsibility is to focus upon the reality of the lives of those women and girls in prostitution and particularly upon those in the lower tiers of the industry. It will not be much comfort for a sex slave to be informed that her suffering is a product of men's natural instincts. I am sure she is aware of this already. Nor will it be of consolation to be told that her stigmatised status as a whore is culturally defined. Our responsibility instead is to change men's behaviour and the cultural frameworks that give it such destructive shape. We all have a very long way to go.

Chapter Six

THE MANAGEMENT

Prostitution is not a peripheral area of society. It is not simply a nasty, remote corner into which all the social, sexual and emotional detritus can be thrown and safely ignored. Prostitution is an essential part of the social fabric of most societies – and especially Asian societies. It is part of the weave and an organic part of social, economic, political and cultural patterns. Directly or indirectly, it affects everyone.

Anything this important has to be lucrative. An enormous industry thrives by providing girls, young women and sometimes boys for sexual recreation. Yet the procurers, the agents, the traffickers and the brothel managers are just the bit players in an epic drama written by men. The rest of the cast is harder to identify. The leading roles are taken by people who do not appear on stage and the organisers never even get a mention in the credits.

The Asian sex industry makes a lot of money for a lot of people. The biggest financial winners in this industry, as in any other, are the senior management and the major shareholders. The workers, as usual, get a very poor deal. As for the slaves, they do not get paid at all. Among the world's illegal and morally suspect businesses, the sex industry probably has one of the biggest financial turnovers. It is also a lot less risky than the other big time money-spinners like trafficking and dealing in arms and drugs. It is easier to traffic humans than it is to traffic drugs or guns and, although women's value steadily decreases with age and experience, they can, unlike drugs, be consumed by the punters time after time.

Several attempts have been made to gauge the economic size of parts of the sex industry in Asia. This kind of analysis is extremely difficult because the business is often hidden and illegal. Despite this qualification the figures suggested by the latest research indicate that the size of the commercial sex market in the region is vast. Yearly profits from the Japanese sex trade in the mid-1990s were thought to stand at around 4.2 trillion yen.[1] Indonesia's sex industry accounted for between 0.8% and 2.4% of Gross Domestic Product during a similar period. Pasuk Phongpaichit, a specialist on the economics of the Thai industry, estimates that profits from prostitution between 1993 and 1995 were around three times the size of profits from the drugs trade.[2] There is less information on the South Asian industry but what little there is gives us a glimpse of the economics involved. In impoverished Calcutta alone, the sex industry has been estimated to generate around 720 million rupees (£10 million) each year.[3] We can guarantee that the women who are held in sexual slavery see very little of this.

Statistics such as these on financial turnover include all branches of the sex industry: they include the high-class market, and the mass market, plus profits from the industry's advertising department, pornography. The contribution that is made by the practice of sexual slavery to these profits is unknown, but is likely to be a relatively small proportion of the total. However, the economic significance of sexual slavery lies in the fact that it is an important way of initiating women into the industry throughout the region.

Once they have been initiated and properly seasoned they are no longer defined as sex slaves. They become voluntary sex workers.

Organised criminal networks control large sections of Asia's sex industry. In general they do not manage the day-to-day running of the industry but provide it with protection and take a substantial cut of the profits. Brothels and clubs in towns and cities could not operate without the consent of organised crime. Big gangland bosses do not make decisions on recruiting girls from the countryside. Nor do they decide on the methods of trafficking and who should become a sex slave. All these stages in the chain of supply are accomplished either informally or, alternatively, by the small fry in the criminal network. The result, however, is that girls who are recruited by minor traffickers through informal means will ultimately find themselves in brothels that are owned by big-time mafia-like organisations, or whose owners themselves pay homage – and cash – to criminal networks.

Very little information is ever forthcoming from brothel managers and owners about the shadowy people and organisations associated with the sex trade. And it is not surprising. Those who speak out about the trade are the ones who invariably end up dead. It is significant and inevitable that less information on the sex trade is available in areas where there are very strong criminal networks and where these networks have strong political backing. Non-governmental organisations and human rights groups working on prostitution and trafficking are scarce in countries with weaker civil societies. It is no accident that these are also the countries with the most serious problems of organised crime, and of abuses in the sex industry too.

Pakistan has a thriving sex industry but, sadly, very few organisations working to combat it. Pakistan's authoritarian governments do not like NGOs who speak out about social issues because these are invariably political issues as well. Successive Pakistani governments have played the card of religious conservatism to mobilise support for their regimes and to deflect citizens' attention from their political and economic failings. A key aspect of this process, known as Islamisation, is that greater restrictions have been placed upon women in the belief that such restrictions are an essential part of Islam. Associated with this is a greater rhetorical commitment towards conservative sexual morality. In this kind of environment debates about prostitution, and NGO activity on the issue, are anything but welcome.

What is more, other problems of gender discrimination and the generally abysmal treatment of women in Pakistan seem to attract the attention and energies of progressive NGOs. Women in prostitution are part of a much bigger and very depressing picture. Pakistan boasts a couple of organisations working on HIV intervention programmes in Karachi, there are privately run shelters for distressed women, a few government-run homes, and a handful of good NGOs focusing on human rights and gender-related issues. There is, however, nothing even vaguely comparable to the organisations that deal directly with prostituted women in India. Some NGOs exist on paper and a few have received money from donor organisations, but even limited field research reveals that women in a red light area such as Heera Mandi have had zero contact with those people supposedly fighting for their rights and for their access to health care. Presumably the funds had run out before the plucky teams had made it to the brothels. The donors must console themselves with the knowledge that the money was spent on offices, brochures and four-wheel-drive vehicles. It is a similar story everywhere: plenty of people feed off the work of prostitutes. Sex work is an industry and, like all other major industries, it is not sealed off from the world around it.

In Thailand NGOs working on trafficking and prostitution are concentrated in Bangkok and in the north. This is not because their work is not needed in the south of the country. In fact, abuses within the industry may well be even more severe in southern Thailand. However, organised crime is also stronger in the south and so there is far less opportunity to develop the activities of organisations promoting human rights and sex workers' rights.

Awful abuses are perpetrated in Japan's enormous sex industry. Yet there are only a handful of small organisations working on sex-industry-related issues. Partly this is because highly conformist Japan does not have a long tradition of NGO activity and partly because the Yakuza tightly controls the industry and access to the women who work in it. The Taiwanese mafia and the Hong Kong triads also manage large sections of the sex industry in their own countries but perhaps not with quite the same degree of organisational sophistication and success as the Yakuza do in Japan.

Ruthlessness and brutality are the two best descriptions of the way that the Yakuza manages the Japanese sex trade. A Thai prostitute who worked in Japan explained the management style of the Yakuza members who 'protected' the club where she worked.

> The Yakuza are good if you obey all the rules. There are lots
> of rules and you have to learn them very quickly. If you are
> not good and you don't do what they say you get your throat
> cut and they don't give you a second chance. If you do exactly
> as they say and you earn a lot of money by going with clients
> and giving them what they want, they will treat you nicely.
> They are a lot better than Thai men.

A Thai woman who was trafficked to Japan related her experiences of the Yakuza in a book which was published by a women's rights organisation, and which tried to warn other young women about the dangers of going to Japan.

> Many times I had seen the Yakuza rush into the bar.
> Whenever they came in, we were all trembling with fear and
> wondered what was going to happen. They would throw the
> glasses away and kick chairs over. After they sat down, they

would use their toes to call any woman to sit with them [the use of the feet in this way in Japanese and Thai culture is extremely rude. You would not do it to a human being] ... Occasionally, there were some women who ran away so the boss or the man who had selected and bought these women would pay a gang of Yakuza to trace them and return them for punishment. They would lock the woman up in a small room in which she had to sleep with any customers they commanded. If she disobeyed, she would have only one choice – death.[4]

The vast majority of women who are trafficked to Japan will end up in a 'snack' that has Yakuza connections. This is because the Yakuza and the sex industry are inseparable. A study undertaken by the International Organisation for Migration, of one hundred Filipina women who were trafficked to Japan, found that forty-six of the women were aware of the involvement of the Yakuza in the process.[5] In all likelihood the real rate of Yakuza involvement is probably even higher.

Organised crime's connection with the international trafficking of women for prostitution is not surprising, and it is not new. In the nineteenth century, Chinese secret societies – the forerunners of today's Triads – were heavily involved in the trafficking of women. Today, in those more economically developed parts of Asia that have strict immigration policies, it is essential for the trafficking business to be well organised. This is especially true of trafficking to Japan.

Typically the process of recruitment is subcontracted out. Girls in Thailand will not be recruited directly by the Yakuza. Instead they find their way into the sex industry's web through existing Thai networks. They are then recruited for the Japanese sex industry by Yakuza-affiliated traffickers. Often these are Thai women who have close links to a Yakuza member. Perhaps they are the wife or mistress of a Yakuza boss whom they may have met when they themselves were working as prostitutes and entertainers in Japan. In general the Yakuza do not work with the Thai mafia. In part this is because the Japanese consider the Thais to be unreliable. In part it is because they would have to contend with inevitable squabbles over status and precedence in the criminal hierarchy, and partly it is because any loss of control over the business can lead to a dilution of profits.

Different branches of the Yakuza compete with one another as well as with different branches of their Taiwanese and Chinese competitors. Kabukicho, Tokyo's main red light area, is a scene of intense international competition between criminal gangs. The clubs that these organisations control, here and throughout Japan, are not micro-managed by Japanese men. This is left to *mama-sans* usually from Thailand and Taiwan. These are the people whom the trafficked women deal with on a daily basis. A gangland member or the owner – typically an important figure in the underworld – makes periodic visits to collect dues and to make sure the business is on a sound footing. This was how a Thai woman described the management structure:

Our big boss was an important man. I think he was Yakuza. But we didn't see him very often. He was quite young and he would come in expensive clothes and call in and talk to the people in the club. We were always nervous when he was in the club. He walked round and looked at us and the club. He talked to the *mama-san* and to the men who worked there for security. If the *mama-san* was angry with a girl she told the boss and then the girl was in big trouble. Most of the time he was really nice to us but if he was angry he used to kick us and say he would get some of the boys to kill us.

A number of women do not have bad memories of working in Japan but they were shocked by what the Yakuza did when they left the country. This Thai woman complained of being cheated:

I went to Japan to work in a club and was promised 230,000 yen [£1,350]. I went on a three-month tourist visa and worked as a hostess [i.e. prostitute]. The work was hard but was better than being in Thailand. Then when I had finished the three months I was taken to Narita [Tokyo's international airport] and the man from the Yakuza only gave me 60,000 yen [£350].

As the woman's ticket home was already booked, and as her visa had expired, she could not stay to argue her case.

Lots of women who are trafficked to Japan do have a legitimate visa. They arrive with a three-month entertainer's visa. These visas are supposed to be granted to artists with recognised talents and professional qualifications. In practice, if a girl is trafficked by a Yakuza-linked network, she can be given an entertainer's visa providing that she has enough talent to walk. The power of Yakuza money makes this possible as does alleged corruption within the Japanese immigration department. Others arrive on false passports. A roaring trade is done in Thailand and in Taiwan where specialist agencies produce counterfeit passports and visas. The price of this documentation is high and the cost will be added to the debt that the woman has to repay once she is in Japan. The biggest financial beneficiaries of this arrangement, of course, are the forgery departments of the criminal networks and the brothel owners who demand interest payments on the debt.

Some brothels are part of large networks. For example, in Japan girls are moved from one 'snack' to another in order to provide a steady stream of new bodies for the novelty-seeking clients. Several women reported being moved between a number of different towns in the space of a few months. Sometimes these were transfers and exchanges between brothels that were operated by a single owner or organisation. Sometimes it was as a result of direct selling and then re-selling of women between loosely affiliated snacks. A similar practice occurs in Thailand. Girls arriving from Burma, for example, spend around six months in the brothels of towns like Mae Sai. They are then moved south to work in brothels in Chiang Mai, Phuket or Bangkok or in a host of other towns that have sex establishments belonging to the same owner or network.

In less-developed Asia the control that crime syndicates have over the sex industry is not as extensive. Like much else in these countries, the sex industry runs along an ad hoc and often confused path. The reach of the sex industry is extensive but often much of the groundwork is done by the forces of poverty and not by the underlings of organised crime. The dons of the Indian criminal networks would not have to bother making provision for complicated trafficking arrangements. All this is handled at a very low level of management, in part because the legal complexities of trafficking women into Japan or Singapore do not have to be addressed in places like India. In India, however, the trafficking of Nepali girls from established prostitute-recruiting grounds is sometimes very well organised right from the girl's home to the brothel. Maiti Nepal, a Kathmandu-based NGO that works to prevent trafficking and to rescue girls from prostitution, has been able to identify networks of traffickers run by Mumbai brothel owners. Many of these owners. are Nepali women – some of them former sex workers themselves – who transport girls out of Nepal and then profit from their exploitation as sex slaves in Indian brothels. Anuradha Koirala, who runs Maiti Nepal, a shelter for prostitues returning from India, claims that the profits are sufficient for these brothel owners to own luxurious houses in Kathmandu, to drive air-conditioned cars and to send their children to expensive private schools.

If brothels are synonymous with organised crime, then organised crime cannot operate without the connivance of politicians. In large parts of Asia – as in the rest of the world – there is a symbiotic relationship between gangsters and politicians. In some places you might have good cause to think that they were the same people. To give just a couple of examples: the Japanese Yakuza is reported to have high-level support within the political system and most Pakistani politicians are believed to be corrupt.

The strength of the links between the sex industry, organised crime and the political world is based on the power of the purse. Political success is largely dependent upon finance. Asia is no exception to this. What is more, aspiring politicians, and even established ones, cannot go around upsetting important people. The people who manage and profit from the sex industry, and other forms of organised crime, are just such important people.

The pattern found in Dhaka, Bangladesh is replicated elsewhere, albeit with minor variations in line with cultural practice and levels of economic development. Organised crime has a foothold in all parts of the city and criminal gangs exert a significant degree of control over some neighbourhoods. Local leaders, businessmen and even religious figures may be in the pay of the network. Others may be intimidated into compliance and support. At election time this translates into backing for a particular political candidate with whom the leaders of these gangs know that they can come to some harmonious arrangement. In some instances this informal agreement is not necessary because the gangland leader may be the political candidate. In most cases, however, the meshing of the political and criminal worlds translates into votes for favoured candidates because gangland-leaders have large vote banks at their disposal. Duly elected politicians then have an obligation and a vested interest in allowing the activities of the underworld to carry on unhindered – except, of course, for the occasional crackdown to give the impression that they are active in the fight against crime.

Gangland bosses control the sex industry in Dhaka and in Bangladesh's other large brothel areas. These men have enormous power and leverage. In woefully poor Bangladesh they are rich. They control the sex industry not by running brothels but by owning the buildings in which they operate and by extracting a variety of charges from the women working there. The houses are rented out to tenants who then sublet the rooms to brothel managers who in turn recruit prostitutes. This practice of having the real owners of brothels hidden behind several curtains of tenants and sub-tenants is very common in South Asia. In cities like Mumbai, politicians and leading figures are rumoured to own buildings in red light areas. In a legal sense the owners do not operate brothels: they only own houses in which brothels are run. But this is a poor defence, especially when the owners wield so much power and know exactly what is occurring in their property.

The fate of the Kandupatti brothel in central Dhaka provides an interesting example of the way in which this power can be used. Kandupatti was a large brothel housing about five hundred women and girls and had been established by the British during the colonial period. It was overcrowded, unsanitary and typical of the worst type South Asia can offer. Girls shared tiny dingy rooms and most of the women who worked there had been physically coerced into the trade or forced into the business by acute poverty. Almost all had started work when they were children. Kandupatti, in other words, was like lots of Bangladeshi brothels.

It became different, however, when the women in Kandupatti began to challenge the power of the influential man who owned and controlled the area. Mumtaz Begum, a leader of the Kandupatti Council of Evicted Sex Workers, explains that this man extracted 'savings' from the women and portrayed himself as a kind charitable financial institution aiding the prostitutes. But when he became a successful politician and refused to hand back any of the women's savings, trouble began to brew. The result was that in May 1997, the brothel was suddenly closed down. A local citizens' movement was orchestrated to rid the neighbourhood of the undesirable women and religious sentiments were mobilised to turn the endeavour into a virtuous crusade. A community that had tolerated a large brothel in its midst for over a century shut it down within a day. The women did not even have time to collect their personal belongings. This was not because the community had suddenly become hostile to the concept of commercial sex; many of its men, after all, had been regular clients of the brothel and local traders profited from the women's money. Instead, the brothel was closed because the landlord had withdrawn his favour. He must have calculated that there were easier ways to generate a profit from the prime site land than renting it out to troublesome prostitutes who demanded the return of their money. The local opinion-formers and religious leaders then followed his lead. The effect of this clampdown on vice is that the dispossessed women of Kandupatti now live on the streets and they service men in the filth of the gutter and in the park. Is this supposed to have been a victory for virtue?[6]

Two years after the closure of Kandupatti, the Tanbazar and Nimtoli brothels near Narayanganj were also shut down with similar speed and lack of concern for the welfare of the inmates. These brothels contained an estimated three thousand women and, just as in the case of Kandupatti, their closure had far more to do with politics and the mechanics of the criminal underworld than worries over the conditions under which the women worked. Supporters of the Bangladesh Nationalist Party controlled the Tanbazar and Nimtoli brothels. The MP for the area, however, was Shamim Osman, a member of the ruling Awami League. Shutting down the brothels was seen as a legitimate way in which to weaken the political opposition within his constituency and to deprive it of the considerable financial resources generated by the sex industry.[7] Interestingly, MP Osman commented that 'prayers were offered at mosques in the town for the closure of the two brothels ... It was a long-felt demand of the people of the town.' Presumably not all the pious citizens were equally enthusiastic about the closure: three thousand prostitutes require more than a handful of clients.

In some countries the established leaders of society are big-time players in the sex industry. And this is not just as consumers but also as owners and managers. In places where the democratic process is weak, high-ranking military and government officials are involved in running the sex industry. In Cambodia, Burma and Pakistan, for instance, there is no real clear line of demarcation between the criminal underworld and the respectable world supposedly above it. They merge into one.

Local politicians frequently offer *de facto* support to traffickers and to key figures in the sex industry because they have no alternative. Prostitution is woven into the fabric of society. It is woven into economic patterns. It is therefore logical that it is woven into the political fabric too. It is a seamless web. Politicians, sex industry bosses and criminal networks are parts of a power structure that constantly reinforces itself. They do not care about women in prostitution because these women are considered unimportant and disposable – even though they are also profitable. In Nepal the member of parliament who represents a constituency with one of the worst reputations for trafficking girls to India has been in the business of politics for years. He is a powerful and influential man. It is thought that he could help to reign in trafficking within his constituency if he wished. He does not do so because this action would upset the balance of power within his carefully cultivated and managed constituency. His political opponents are not much better. They will not, for example, go on record as saying that families sell their daughters into prostitution. Political expediency requires them to be mindful of the public's sensitivities. Families are therefore described as being duped and girls are the unwitting victims of depraved Indians.

Not all politicians are corrupt and not all are willing to ignore the unhappy fate of the poorest and most vulnerable women they represent. But we can guarantee that many of those who preach conservative moral values, and who would be the first to condemn prostitution, will also be supported indirectly by criminality of some kind. And if they are supported by criminal networks they will also be supported indirectly by the sex industry. It is unjust to condemn all Asian politicians for being involved in systems of sexual slavery but far, far too many are complicit.

This charge can be laid at the feet of many people who benefit either directly or indirectly from the practice of forced prostitution. We can include in this a whole range of services that cater to sex workers as consumers and to the customers of sex workers during their visit to the brothel. We can also include the communities who benefit from the sale of women's bodies. When we look at the management of the sex industry we have to look a lot further than just the brothel hierarchy and the traffickers. Girls and women are exploited not just by clients, brothel owners and managers, they are exploited by an entire society and sometimes even by their own families.

Brothel managers in Calcutta claim that the mothers and brothers of girls from impoverished families in Murshidabad visit the brothels periodically to ask for money. Sometimes this will be part of the money that the girl has earned and sometimes it will be an 'advance' on her earnings and the sum will then be added to her debt. The male relatives of girls from Nepal's Nuwakot and Sindhupalchowk districts visit the brothels every few years to collect their young relatives' earnings. A similar phenomenon is seen in Thailand. It is very difficult for an outsider, living the comfortable life of a middle-class academic in a developed country, to criticise the decisions taken by families living in destitution. Ethically it is untenable. But equally, it is also difficult to draw a dividing line between those whose poverty can in some way excuse the otherwise morally inexcusable decision to send a child into prostitution and those who can afford not to. The measurement of poverty is flexible and open to many interpretations. I can say with confidence, however, that some families sell a child into prostitution not to avoid starvation but, instead, to buy consumer goods.

This question is very relevant in northern Thailand where whole communities are sustained by the prostitution of daughters. This is not part of the sub-culture of an underclass but is a major feature of normal society in many villages. It involves the police, the schools, the temples and the village leaders. It is part of the power structure. Only twenty kilometres from the Thai–Burmese border there is a village in which the daughter of the headman has joined her school friends as a prostitute in Bangkok. Sompop Jantraka of the Daughters' Education Programme estimates that in many of the villages of northern Thailand one third of families have daughters in prostitution. No one speaks out about this because everyone benefits: families can build nice houses and offset the losses from unsustainable farms, and priests do not condemn the money that sex workers give as donations to build temples and to do meritorious works. Just like anywhere else, the people with power in northern Thailand's villages are the people with money. Unfortunately, anyone with money here almost invariably has links to the sex industry because there is so little opportunity to earn money in any other sector. Finance from the sex trade creates, legitimises and reinforces a power structure that tells young women that prostitution is the only way to escape poverty.

An appalling perspective on the link between poverty and the legitimisation of prostitution among the desperate is illustrated by an interview that was given to Justice Kirby, the UN Human Rights Ambassador to Cambodia, in 1995. A brothel owner was reported as agreeing that the minimum age for girls entering prostitution should be eighteen. However, she claimed this principle was difficult for her and her peers to adhere to because it was very hard to refuse the pleading of impoverished parents who wanted their young daughters to start work in the brothel.[8]

In Bangladesh there are occasional reports of traffickers being beaten to death by members of local communities.[9] On the other hand, there are significantly more instances in which the local communities know of, and ignore, the activities of trafficking gangs. A research survey conducted by the Centre for Women and Children's Study based in Dhaka discovered a profound reluctance on the part of local people to divulge information on suspected traffickers.[10] This suggests that people were either ignorant of the process, intimidated into silence or were protecting those involved. I suspect that it was the last of these reasons: traffickers are shielded because it is a local business from which lots of people benefit. In the thick of poverty, high-minded ethical sentiments about trafficking and prostitution are a redundant luxury.

A whole host of trades and professions profit from prostitution. In South Asia women depend to a significant extent upon door-to-door vendors because they are either unable to leave the brothel or unable to leave the red light area. Vendors sell everything the women could want. They sell cosmetics, jewellery, clothes, trinkets and snacks. The cost of these items is frequently highly inflated because the salespeople have, quite literally, a captive market. When, as is often the case, the women do not have enough money to purchase the goods, the vendor will offer partial credit at high rates of interest. They are guaranteed repayment because the brothel owner or manager will settle the bill and add the sum to the debt that the girl owes to the brothel.

A Nepali woman who had worked in both Calcutta and Mumbai described the attraction of consumer goods and the high price she had to pay for them.

When I first came to the brothel I didn't have any nice clothes and jewellery. At home I never had shoes and I only had one sari. The brothel owner said that if I worked hard I could have lots of nice things. Some salesmen came to the brothel and they brought some pretty dresses – saris and Western dresses. I choose two. I don't know how much they cost but the brothel owner said I had to serve lots of clients to pay for them.

Dubious financial institutions and loan sharks offer loans to women in prostitution. The rates of interest are usually astronomic because the women are unable to approach reputable financial institutions like banks. Loans might be needed for a variety of reasons: to help with a family crisis, and especially to pay for medical treatment. The medical profession and the pharmaceutical industry reap regular profits from sex work. Lucrative private practices cater to communities of prostitutes. This includes fully qualified, bona fide doctors and, in less-developed parts of the region, a bizarre array of quacks and traditional healers. Abortions and the treatment of sexually transmitted diseases are the stock in trade of these practitioners although, in the poorer parts of Asia, most of the women also suffer from the many diseases associated with poverty, poor nutrition and an unhealthy environment.

In India, for example, sex workers spend a large proportion of their income on medication and doctors' fees. Abortions are performed in grim clinics and women will call upon the services of a known and trusted – but not necessarily qualified or competent – health care practitioner to deal with their frequent bouts of STDs. A number of doctors visit closed brothels to treat the inmates. Some children are injected with hormones to stimulate sexual development and hasten their full-scale entry into the trade. A number of reports, which are often repeated but which I have yet to substantiate, suggest that a small number of doctors perform reconstructive surgery on deflowered girls to recreate the illusion of virginity.

The Indian National Commission for Women estimates that the medical profession makes an annual sum of Rs 20 crores (£3 million) from women in the sex sector. The pharmaceutical industry makes another Rs 80 crores (£11.5 million).[11] In Japan abortionists carry out a vast and lucrative trade. A proportion of these terminations are performed on sex workers. The high cost of these terminations is added to the debt the women owe and will be obliged to pay back through the sale of sex. There are two ways of interpreting these facts: either the medics, pseudo-medics, pharmacists and pharmaceutical companies are providing a vital service and helping to ameliorate the awful health problems associated with a very unhealthy and exploitative trade. Or they are cashing in and profiting from a dreadful social problem.

When we move further down the hierarchy of the sex trade from the criminal organisations and the web of powerful interests that protect and profit from it, we come to the people who are visible within the trade: the merchants and the brokers and the managers. These are the people who run the industry on a day-to-day basis.

It is almost invariably a woman who deals with the women, with the clients and who is the intermediary between the sex workers and the senior, frequently male management. It is also not uncommon to find female brothel owners, who are usually former sex workers who have had ambitions. The female managers have a variety of names. Among the most familiar are *mama san*, *malkin* and *gharwali*. These women have a mixed reputation. Most are in their forties, fifties and early sixties. They know the trade inside and out; they know what the clients want because they have serviced so many themselves. Despite the constraints imposed by the nature of the *mama-sans'* work, some sex workers speak of their managers with affection – referring to them as 'auntie' or as someone who watches out for them. Clearly, there are good *mama-sans* and bad ones too. A few will try to ease girls into prostitution gently and some with violence. Some treat the girls with callous ruthlessness and others with care. I have met some *mama-sans* who have done the best for their girls within the milieu of a brutal trade. All these female brothel managers have a quick and clever mind. They are shrewd negotiators and, as I discovered many times and often to my disadvantage, they can assess people and their agendas with ease. I have yet to meet a stupid *mama-san*. It is a pity that the sex trade is the only avenue for their talents.

As in any business there are those who are good managers and those who are plain dictatorial. Unfortunately most managers in the sex trade are infinitely more concerned with making a profit than with promoting good human resource management. And because so much of the business of selling sex is the product of direct and indirect coercion, few *mama-sans* have to be concerned with creating a good environment for industrial relations. It simply does not matter.

The Pakistani pattern of brothel management is different from that of the rest of South Asia. Although there are female procurers and managers, particularly in the traditional and elite sectors of the sex industry, low-class brothels are often family businesses run by men. Abdul Sattar Edhi is a philanthropist who runs a Karachi-based charity helping the poor and destitute. His organisation operates homes throughout Pakistan that provide a place where women can seek refuge. Over a period of thirty years he has acquired an extensive knowledge of prostitution and its organisation within Pakistan. From his experience he concludes that much prostitution is small-scale, centred upon families and often inseparable from drug addiction. Women, according to his viewpoint, are forced into prostitution in order to feed the drug addiction of their husband or father.

The 'family' nature of prostitution in Pakistan is corroborated by Iqbal Hussain, a professor at the National College of Art in Lahore. He has lived for decades in Heera Mandi, the ancient red light district of Lahore, and knows the area well. Perhaps more than anyone else in Pakistan, Iqbal has an understanding of the industry and an emotional connection with the women working in it. He maintains that most of the new recruits to prostitution are born into the trade or brought into the brothels as brides. Usually the brides come from remote parts of Pakistan. Their husbands then act as their pimps. The women have to comply because they have absolutely no option. Once they are married they cannot return to their families, who believe that they have discharged their responsibility to their daughters. And they cannot leave their abusive husbands because they cannot support themselves either economically or socially as independent women unless they stay in sex work or join the elite group of highly educated women in professional jobs. Only the first option is within their reach.

The brothel hierarchy in Calcutta bears resemblance to that found in many red light areas in less-developed Asia. This hierarchy is strictly enforced. The community has its own subculture with its own standards and codes of conduct. Baitali Gangulay of Jabala, an NGO working with the children of sex workers in the Bowbazar brothel, describes how the value system of the red light areas makes a non-issue of abuses such as trafficking and debt bondage. 'Trafficking isn't considered bad by the boys and men from this community. It is just part of their job. They think nothing of trafficking children and women from Calcutta to Mumbai because they don't think they are doing anything wrong.'

A case that underlines the strength of this subculture and the difficulty of breaking away from its embrace is described by the staff of the Committed Communities Development Trust. This NGO operates a health clinic for the sex workers of Kamatipura in Mumbai. It also runs a day-care centre for the children of the women. One child had been in regular attendance at the centre for many years and the staff had watched her grow up into a teenager. This girl's mother was very concerned about her daughter and wished to protect her from the worst effects of life in a red light area and to avoid the almost inevitable certainty that she too would be a prostitute. She wanted something better for her daughter and that is why she had sent the girl to the centre. One day the mother arrived at the clinic in a distraught state. Her daughter, she said, had started her first period, and if the *gharwali* should discover this then the girl would be initiated into prostitution without any delay. Despite her mother's best intentions there was no escaping the all-seeing eye of the *gharwali*. There was no hope of resisting the pressures of life in an area in which a woman's only purpose is to provide sex to men and to earn money from its sale. A year later the girl, then fifteen, was being treated for gonorrhoea in the centre's own health clinic.

Sonagachi, Calcutta's largest red light area, has a complicated hierarchy. Houses are owned by individuals who rent out rooms. These are often sublet to *malkins* and independent sex workers who pay a daily rent each morning. The *malkins* have a great deal of power over the women they manage. Lower in the hierarchy are the pimps known as *dada*. Each brothel has its own pimps and the pimps are in competition with each other to bring clients to their respective brothels. The pimps are men, sometimes sons of sex workers but, even more often, they are from impoverished parts of the countryside around Calcutta.[12] Then there are the sex workers themselves and at the bottom of the heap are the domestic servants who work for the women. Many of these are men and, again, they are from desperately poor regions.

Other people operate within Sonagachi but their place within the hierarchy is not so clear. In particular, there are the *babus*, who are a combination of regular clients and partners for the sex workers. Some of these men are very powerful. They form relationships with women, visit them regularly, sometimes stay for periods with them, and live off their earnings. Frequently, *babus* form new relationships when their women begin to age and their earning capacity falls. The older women are then discarded. For many prostitutes the cultivation of a relationship with a *babu* is the closest they will come to forming a stable permanent relationship with an adult male and many say that their most cherished dream is to find a good *babu*.

Local youths in Calcutta's red light areas form clubs that are often based loosely around political parties. In practice, these clubs are responsible for law and order in their respective areas. They monitor what is going on and hand out punishment when the community's codes are breached or when individuals challenge established hierarchies. Like other brothel areas, Sonagachi is a haven for thugs and criminals, who use it as a base and as a place in which they can hide, sometimes for months. It is common practice for these men to marry the daughter of a prostitute. They then live within the protection of the community for a few months before abandoning the new wife once it is safe and convenient to leave. Unsurprisingly, the rejected bride then becomes a prostitute herself.

Women who have been sold and tricked into prostitution tell familiar stories about the management techniques of the brothel operators. This was how a Cambodian woman described the *mama-san* of the brothel to which she was sold by a friend:

> The brothel was owned by a man and a woman. They were married and about forty years old. The *mama-san* was nice to me. She was the one who looked after us girls. She gave me food and drink and said that everything would be fine if I did what I was told. When I refused to entertain the customers the man got two men to beat me so that my arms bled. After that the woman was nice to me again and she put some bandages on me. She said she would ask her husband to be kind to me if I went with the customers. They were always getting a gang to torture us and then the *mama-san* would promise to help us if we did as we were told.

Women in brothels that are run by men complained that they were repeatedly raped. In brothels that are managed by women some said that the *mama-san* had been fair, or that she was pleasant once the girl had been seasoned and no longer provided any trouble. A few spoke of terrible cruelty and, undoubtedly, some *mama-sans* perpetrate even greater evils than male customers upon the girls in their care. One young woman explained how the *gharwali* in Mumbai had treated her during her years of captivity.

> She liked to torture me. I don't know why she wanted to do

that. She used to cut me with a little knife when the customers complained that I didn't give good service. And often she wouldn't give me food so that I was always hungry.

Violence of this kind rarely has to be inflicted upon seasoned sex workers but it is common until a woman is conditioned. Control is the key to understanding the management style of most brothel *mama-sans*. This applies to fresh recruits whose will to resist needs to be broken and also to seasoned women who require a more sophisticated method of management. One of the principal means of doing this is to ensure that the women do not begin to establish relationships with people outside the brothel. In Mumbai, for instance, brothel managers will ensure that clients do not visit the same debt-bonded girl on a regular basis. This forestalls the development of any personal attachment between the prostitute and the customer, and which can sometimes lead to customers facilitating a girl's escape. This was how a young Mumbai prostitute described her relationship with one of her customers and how it was ended by the *gharwali*.

I didn't have any friends in the brothel. Most of the time I stayed in a little room. One customer felt sorry for me. He was a young man and he used to come and talk to me and bring me food. The *gharwali* was very angry about this and said that she would get some men to kill him. I don't know if he was killed but he never came back. I was sad when this happened because he was nice to me and I liked him.

The experience of two Cambodian sisters who were sold to a brothel by a couple they had met tells a familiar story of how women's existing relationships and emotional bonds are broken down by the brothel management. One of the sisters described what happened to them.

Right from the start the *mama-san* kept us apart. I never saw
my sister except when I went to the bathroom I would sometimes see her in another room. I wanted to go to her and talk
but it was forbidden. After a while we were both sold to new
brothels and I never saw her again.

The most efficient *mama-sans* exercise the strictest control over
the women in their charge. The debt bondage system is manipulated
in order to maximise leverage over women. In Delhi, women's debt
to the brothel owners has been reported to be subject to rates of up
to 300% a year.[13] When these rates are applied to a large initial debt
it can take many years to pay it off. A sex worker in Calcutta in her
late twenties explained how the debt was used to control her.

I worked in the *chukri* [bonded labour] system for twelve
years because my debt was big and it never went down and I
could not pay it off. Most of the clients were good but it was
difficult to refuse them because the brothel owner decided
who we would accept and how much it cost. She said I had to
entertain them because otherwise I would never be free. I
wasn't paid any money for twelve years. I only got tips.

A Cambodian girl explained how the regime operated in her
brothel.

The *mama-san* was very clever and very cruel. She chose my
clients and told me to entertain them. I couldn't say no. And I
never got any money. The *mama-san* would even check my
body after a customer had been and she would take away any
tips.

Women are made to feel isolated and disoriented in order to
increase the degree of control exercised over them. In countries like

Japan and Cambodia, girls are moved from sex establishment to sex establishment partly in order to cater to customer demand for new women and also to increase the women's sense of vulnerability and lack of control over their lives. In Cambodia, girls are moved on when brothel owners realise that a family is trying to trace its daughter. A similar practice is encountered in Thailand. Even women who manage to escape live in fear of recapture. The homes that shelter young women who have managed to flee from brothels in Phnom Penh are difficult to find. Purposely so. Some are also fortified because armed men from the brothels are anxious to reclaim the women by force so that they can recoup their investment.

Reselling a woman to another brothel has considerable advantages because it also condemns the woman to a new period of debt bondage. Because she is sold to a new owner she then has to repay yet another debt. It is not uncommon for brothel owners to resell girls who are approaching the point at which their debt will be cleared. They are thus locked into sexual slavery again. Similar manipulation of women's debt is found all over Asia. In Cambodia, for example, brothel owners arrange with the police for a prostituted woman to be arrested when she is nearing the end of her period of bonded labour. The kindly brothel owner pays the police to release her and will then tell the woman that she must pay a highly inflated price to cover the cost of this release. This sum is added to her debt. Another favourite trick is to arrange for the woman to be beaten and to need medical treatment. Again the brothel owner will step in to help with the cost of the medical expenses – thus increasing the woman's debt.

Effective brothel management requires good security. This is especially true in countries in which prostitution is technically illegal or in which a large number of women have to be physically coerced into the trade. A raid on a Malaysian brothel in July 1997 illustrated the lengths to which brothel owners will go in order to ensure secrecy and security. The 'Max 29' brothel was the largest ever raided in the country. Thirty-seven women were rescued from a prison-like brothel that resembled a fortress. It was situated on the second and third floors of a building, and the only means of access was through a heavily guarded triple-layer steel door. Within the brothel there were hiding places for the women and lots of small cubicles in which they serviced up to twelve clients a day. Virtually all the money from sex work went directly to the brothel owner, and the women were not allowed out. The young Thai women who were incarcerated there had gone to Malaysia after being promised jobs, primarily as domestic helps, and they had managed to alert the outside world to their plight only after one of the women had gained access to a client's mobile telephone and had called home.[14]

The discovery of the 'Max 29' brothel and the revelations about the conditions under which the women were kept corroborates allegations that Thai sex workers have made against Malaysian brothels. Brothel-keeping in Malaysia seems to be a more risky business than in Thailand and many Malaysian men travel to Thailand to buy sex. Thai women who have worked in Malaysia report extremely sophisticated methods of control and subterfuge, with brothels possessing secret rooms and passages in which to hide women in the event of a raid. Significantly there are few active organisations working on sex workers' rights and the trafficking of women in Malaysia. We should not assume therefore that the problems of prostitution do not exist in Malaysia. In fact, the reverse may even be true.

The power and control of the management is undiminished even in those areas in which the sex industry is diversifying and moving away from the traditional brothel sector. Because these newer parts of the industry are more sophisticated, the levers of controls are less overt. They may, however, be even more powerful. Parts of the sex industry in Japan are becoming almost invisible and impossible to monitor. In some instances trafficked girls do not have a base. They do not live or work in a brothel but are driven around in cars while waiting for a mobile phone call from their boss who will then direct the driver to a particular hotel for an appointment with a client. These girls claim that they do not know who they work for and that they have never met their bosses. They live in small hotels or apartments and are collected for work by drivers who also may not know who employs them.[15]

Asia's recent economic crisis was bad news for Asia's prostitutes. This was not because it cut down client demand – and in the brothel sector this was only a minimal reduction – but because it gave the brothel and club owners a further excuse to tighten control over women. In Bangkok, even those sex workers who are ostensibly the most empowered, and who do not work in systems of sexual slavery, reported that owners were placing new demands upon them. Girls working in Patpong clubs were not allowed out and were required to sleep on couches so that they could be available twenty-four hours a day to service men in the back rooms.[16]

In the more developed parts of the region a favoured management technique is to keep trafficked women dependent upon the brothel owners and managers. Confiscating a woman's passport is an effective means of doing this because it deprives the woman of mobility and strips her of her legal status. In Taiwan employers of migrant women sex workers and those who have been trafficked confiscate the women's passports. As many of these women do not possess work contracts they are rendered terribly vulnerable and, ironically, many come to believe that their manipulative boss is the only person who can protect them from the police. Exactly the same thing happens in Japan. The study of one hundred Filipina women who were trafficked to Japan found that eighty-four of the women had their passports confiscated on their arrival.[17] They were returned to them only when the women were on the point of leaving the country.

The shape of the sex industry is changing in Asia, as it is in the rest of the world. But the old patterns of power and control are identical.

In the more developed parts of the region the industry seems different because it is more sophisticated. However, the stories told by women who became prostitutes half a century ago are remarkably similar to the stories told today. Only the physical surroundings are different. In affluent Asia, sex workers may have better food, work in establishments with air-conditioning and be contacted by cellular phones, but the power structure that created their place in the world is exactly the same. We can guarantee that in another fifty years the basic structure of prostitution will be similar, but that the business will be made more acceptable by raised living standards, improving technology and the thorough commercialisation of sexual desire.

In poverty-stricken Asia the parallels with fifty years ago are very close because the quality of life within these countries has improved only marginally. A retired sex worker and brothel manager, who is in her late sixties and still lives in the red light area of Kirdipur in Calcutta, explained how the sex industry has changed shape over the years while retaining all of its old forms.

> I have been here for about fifty years. I was trafficked from Bangladesh. Many girls still come from the area around my own village, so things are the same now as then. The trafficking was the same. But some things are different. Conditions are much worse these days. Before, there wasn't so much competition. We could make a better living and live quite well. Now all the girls are poorer. There are so many poor girls and they compete against each other and drive down the price. And there are always new girls so the older ones get paid less if they want customers. It was much better when I was young.

An elderly prostitute in Pakistan related a very similar experience of life in the sex trade around forty years ago.

I came from a village in India. My family was quite well-to-do and I went to school. One day when I was on my way to school some men kidnapped me and took me to a place a long way from my home. I was about twelve years old and I was married to a man who was middle-aged. He had a cart and carried goods for people. He also sold me to lots of men. For a long time I was locked in a room and tied with a chain so that I wouldn't run away. After a while I didn't want to run away and I stayed with the man. He had another wife who was older. After about ten years he divorced me and I married another man. I did the same kind of work and entertained men who came to the house. After that husband I had two others. I never had children. I don't know why. I would have liked to have some children but God did not bless me with any.

Even if impoverished Asia was to suddenly switch into the fast track of economic development we can guarantee that the sex industry would accommodate the new circumstances. It is already accomplishing this feat in affluent societies. It might become a more professional and glamorised industry but its management structure will remain the same. Workers may be empowered *within* the industry but the industry itself will remain the product of men. Whatever the short-term benefits it may grant to successful female prostitutes and to those women who make it into the management division, the sex industry works to the benefit of *most* men and to the detriment of *most* women. That is exactly why it is so successful.

Chapter Seven

THE LAW

The only law that matters in a brothel is the law that grants men the right to buy sex. International declarations and national legal codes that attempt to outlaw prostitution or contain its excesses are little more than well-meaning but empty gestures. They are a kind of window-dressing to appeal to moral sensitivities. In reality, what is written in the statute books often bears little resemblance to the way laws are applied. Even when laws on prostitution are enforced they are interpreted in such a way that women are cast in the role of villains. At worst, men are seen as the weak victims of immoral women. Laws are routinely ignored or manipulated by clients, brothel owners and the very people who are supposed to enforce them. All these participants in the sex industry pay homage to an older and higher authority. This authority is not explicitly acknowledged in any legal code, although its logic underpins and gives shape to many – especially in Asia. In practice the fount of this authority is respected in all societies. It is called the law of the penis.

Red light areas have their own codes of conduct and their own morality. In places where the sex industry is especially lucrative and extensive, the laws of the state simply do not apply because the state's writ cannot compete with the finance or the organisational sophistication of the sex industry. In Patpong in Bangkok, in Kabukicho in Tokyo and Kamatipura in Mumbai the sex business *is* the law.

The sex industry flourishes in so many parts of Asia because it has protection from important quarters. It has protection from virtually all men. Even men who do not use prostitutes may still think of the institution as a 'necessary evil'. Those who are hostile to the purchase of sex will lay the blame upon the conduct of morally degraded women. Very rarely is any responsibility laid at the feet of a patriarchal society and men's sexual behaviour. As the sex business is an intrinsic part of the power structure it is supported by those in positions of power. Corrupt police, politicians and bureaucrats give the industry their unofficial blessing and protection. In return they receive bribes, political support and sexual favours. Some of these leading figures short-circuit this process and have found a better way to combine social power, sexual indulgence and financial gain: they own the brothels themselves. In a number of places the police do not tackle the traffickers and the brothel owners because they *are* the traffickers and the brothel owners.

A host of international conventions and declarations relate to prostitution, trafficking and sexual slavery. The relevant documents make edifying reading. The 1948 Universal Declaration of Human Rights contains articles prohibiting slavery and cruel and degrading treatment. A 1949 UN Convention on the Suppression of the Traffic in Persons and of the Prostitution of Others, although not well subscribed to by the international community, does make a commitment to halt trafficking in women. CEDAW (the Convention on the Elimination of All Forms of Discrimination Against Women), which was ratified in 1981, seeks, among other things, to suppress all forms of traffic in women and their exploitation in prostitution. This convention has been ratified by a large number of nations – even by those whose treatment of women should immediately disqualify them from claiming any measure of adherence to its provisions. The UN Convention on the Rights of the Child is widely accepted, and is also immensely relevant to the issue of child prostitution. In the last decade, the Platform for Action outlined at the 1995 Beijing Women's Conference identified forced prostitution as a serious form of violence against women and pledged to eliminate it. Similarly, the horrors of child prostitution were addressed at the 1996 Conference on the Commercial Sexual Exploitation of Children in Stockholm.

And now back to the real world. On paper these conventions are inspiring. But they are not universally ratified and they are not binding. For all the impact they have upon a girl incarcerated in a brothel they might as well not exist. Even Pakistan – of all places – has ratified CEDAW. It is a joke. Just as it is a joke to think that the national legal frameworks, and the authorities that enforce these laws in Asia, are anything but massively corrupted and complicit in the very activity they are supposed to regulate. Of course declarations of good intentions are necessary. But they are not enough. They provide the map for the route ahead. The problem is making sure that people – and by this I mean men – travel down the correct road and arrive at the destination rather than just talking about the journey or sometimes assuming that they have nearly arrived.

Societies manage prostitution in different ways. In some countries it is legal and in others it is illegal. But whatever the legal system, there are two threads common to all major societies: there are *always* girls and women in sexual slavery and there are *always* men ready to buy them.

Legal codes adopt four main approaches to the management of prostitution. Where prostitution is legalised, as in Nevada in the United States, the sale of sexual labour is recognised as work, and full legal rights are given to sex workers. Prohibition is the exact reverse. All prostitution is outlawed. This system is theoretically in operation in most of the Islamic world, in Sri Lanka, China, Vietnam, Burma, the Philippines, Nepal, and in Japan. Someone should inform them.

A tolerationist system criminalises the organisers of the sex industry but does not necessarily criminalise the act of selling sex providing that it is done discreetly and within certain guidelines. Malaysia and India are good examples of this tolerationist approach in Asia. Finally, a regulationist approach legalises prostitution, but only in specific zones.

Anyone passing through the red light areas of Asia's cities will be hard pressed to guess which legal system is in force. Lots of women are selling sex and lots of men are buying. It does not seem to matter which approach is theoretically followed. All legal codes nevertheless prohibit the 'forced' prostitution that produces Asia's sex slaves. Sometimes this is explicitly stated and, at other times, this crime falls under other rubrics, such as anti-slavery provisions. These legal niceties, however, are totally meaningless when a potent mixture of culture and poverty blend to produce a supply of prostitutes, a market full of clients and societies that look the other way.

The law in relation to prostitution as it is written, interpreted and practised throughout the world reflects the stigmatised role of the sex worker in societies run by and for the benefit of men. There is little mystery in this. Of course women are seen as criminals. To brand men as the culprits would cause the entire logic of the system to come crashing down. So when the authorities take action on prostitution they do not target the clients, nor the brothel owners, nor the pimps, nor the corrupt police and politicians. They select the women. They choose the most powerless people for punishment. They do this because it is easy and because the women are vilified targets. The women are simultaneously essential but peripheral to the trade. As a group they are essential but as individuals they are of no consequence because they are just bodies that can be so easily replaced. The women cannot speak out against unfair treatment because they are socially stigmatised people and from despised communities. Few decent citizens from the influential classes have the stomach to listen to a whore talking about her rights. Arresting a few prostitutes will not upset important figures and men of wealth and power. And, as well as all these other advantages, punishing prostitutes can win the authorities a veritable incandescence for their fight against vice.

Occasionally action is taken against traffickers but, unsurprisingly, it is always the small fry that are targeted. Big-time traffickers are protected. At the time of writing there has been no successful prosecution of a major trafficker in the whole of Asia. The ones who are charged and convicted are of virtually no significance. Often they are the first link in the chain of supply, which links the brothels to the homes of their victims.

India practises toleration of prostitution. Selling sex is legal providing the girl is sixteen or above and is working independently. Prostitutes must not solicit or practise their trade near a public place. However, try finding anywhere in an Indian village, town or city that is *not* near a public place and you will have an idea of the difficulty in adhering to these restrictions. A large proportion – perhaps even a majority of girls – begin prostitution when they are under sixteen. A lot of the business is conducted in brothels and is conspicuously public. Trafficking of women and girls is also an offence. Despite the official toleration of sex work, most prostitution in India is therefore illegal.

Like many other countries Nepal has a blind spot when it comes to the trafficking of its females. Propriety demands that the government, and even many voluntary organisations, maintain a fiction that girls are not sold into prostitution. Instead it is believed that a majority are duped. It does not reflect well on a society, whatever its travails of poverty, to admit that its families are selling the bodies of their young daughters, especially to foreigners. The government is therefore reluctant to admit the extent of the problem. As with all other difficulties encountered by Nepal, trafficking is blamed upon the twin evils of poverty and India. Trafficking is now illegal, as is prostitution, but little has been achieved in the war against the traffickers and not much can be expected. Nepali legislation has a tendency to languish, unheeded and unimplemented on the statute books. Certainly, those organisations dealing with the repatriation of Nepali girls from Indian brothels have received scant support from successive governments. It is little wonder: it would demand an uncharacteristic degree of efficiency on the part of the Nepali administration.

A social worker in Calcutta described the following case as an example of the bureaucratic delays in repatriating girls.

> We had a girl about three years ago who was tricked and came from Nepal when she was thirteen. She managed to get a customer to send a message to her family, and her father contacted the consulate and the police. But when the police arrived at the brothel they couldn't find her. She had been locked in a room, gagged and her feet and hands tied. Fortunately, someone heard a noise and she was discovered. I want to know how the brothel owner knew that the police were coming for her. She was taken to the government home and the papers took so long that she never did manage to get back to Nepal. She died in the home of tuberculosis when she was fifteen.

Women in Pakistan are woefully discriminated against by increasingly Islamised legal codes. Prostitutes, inevitably, are the most victimised women. Despite the claims of apologists, the Sharia – the Muslim legal code – is an exercise in misogyny. Muslim family laws provide an answer to the basic assumption that men's sexual desires are infinite and that some way must be found to manage these and to prevent fornication. The laws give men access to physical pleasure within a legitimate setting.[1] Men can have up to four wives at any one time and these can also be changed through repudiation. Women do not have these options. Although most Muslim men do not avail themselves of this opportunity with abandon, the fact that it is possible underlines and perpetuates the minimal respect given to female sexuality and to women as individuals.

In the 1970s the Pakistani President, Zia ul-Haq, mobilised support for his repressive regime by playing the card of religious conservatism. The Hudood Ordinances promulgated in 1979 and enforced in 1980 were a direct product of the manipulation of religious sentiments for political gain. These ordinances were designed to give constitutional sanction to Islamic orthodoxy. Of particular relevance to prostitution was the Zina Ordinance that followed the Sharia by punishing extramarital sexual relations. Severe punishments, with a maximum penalty of death by stoning, were fixed for adultery. But even unmarried people were prohibited from having sexual relations with one another. The punishment for this heinous crime could be a lengthy prison sentence and a brutal whipping.

The dreadful Zina Ordinance has been applied most harshly and consistently to women. And it has generated some terrible injustices. In line with Islamic law, four pious men are needed as witnesses to prove a crime of rape. It is therefore incredibly hard to prove a case of rape. Instead rape is conflated with female promiscuity. In a travesty of justice, there have been incidents of rape victims being charged under the Zina Ordinance on the grounds that they had been fornicating.[2]

A visit to the Central Jail in Karachi is a salutary experience. A high proportion of female inmates at any one time will be charged under the Zina Ordinance. In other words, women are incarcerated for having sex with a man who is not their husband. Many of the women I spoke to were prostitutes. But this was a fact they flatly denied. The women commonly described their alleged customers as being a 'friend' of their 'husband' who had come to the house to do some 'painting'. Either there are a lot of keen decorators in Karachi or the women need to think up more varied and convincing alibis. Two crucial points need to be made in relation to this. First, if women cannot admit they are prostitutes then they also cannot seek help when dreadful abuses are perpetrated upon them. Even a sex slave cannot easily seek help because she risks being charged with Zina. Second, lots of prostitutes are arrested, charged and convicted while, at the same time, the men who buy them are either not arrested, fail to be charged or receive less severe punishments. We should expect nothing else: sexually wayward men in Pakistan are not to be condemned. They are the otherwise pious victims of women's deadly sexuality.

The unfortunate women who are trafficked to Pakistan for prostitution are doubly burdened. The Bangladeshi women who were sold into sexual slavery in the 1980s and 1990s found themselves to be criminals worthy of prison rather than victims in need of help. They were arrested under the Foreigners Act prohibiting illegal entry to the country. And to increase the injustice they could also be charged under the Zina section of the Hudood Ordinance. Zia Awan is a prominent Pakistani human rights lawyer who has been closely involved in the cases of over two hundred Bangladeshi victims of trafficking and prostitution. He believes that the government and law enforcement agencies give a low priority to the problems of trafficking and prostitution because they involve women – and women in general are given a low priority in Pakistan. Prostitutes – both 'voluntary' and 'forced' – languish in Pakistani jails today for having had sex. Their customers do not. And it should go without saying that brothel owners and traffickers are conspicuous by their absence in the men's prisons.

Although Bangladesh is also a Muslim country, its relatively open and tolerant Bengali heritage has helped to spare it from some of the political and religious excesses that have had such a negative effect on many women in Pakistan. Bangladesh, however, suffers from the same schizophrenia as other Islamic countries when it comes to sex. Prostitution in Bangladesh is a legal confusion. Even senior decision-makers and academics do not seem to be totally conversant with the legislation. It does not inspire confidence to find that this uncertainty also afflicts police officers.

Prostitution is permitted in Bangladesh providing a woman is eighteen or above, is of sound mind and has chosen her profession. In order to prove that they are of an eligible age, prostitutes have an affidavit confirming their date of birth and signed by a notary public or a magistrate. The affidavit is sometimes referred to as a licence and the women are described as 'registered prostitutes'. In fact neither is true. And neither is the age commonly ascribed to the women. Brothel owners manipulate the provision of affidavits and will extort money from the women. Brothel owners then keep the affidavits so that they can increase their leverage over the prostitutes while they undergo their period of 'apprenticeship'. A woman can be charged anything from 2,000 to 5,000 taka (£24–£60) for an affidavit. This is a fortune for a poor Bangladeshi prostitute and she will have to service many, many clients in order to repay its cost.

The legal profession runs a profitable trade in affidavits. The profession does have a difficult job on its hands because establishing anyone's age in Bangladesh is a monumental task. The country's documentation system is virtually non-existent. There is no national system of birth registration and there are no reliable data on marriages and divorces. Women might not even know how old they are. But that does not mean that members of the legal profession cannot see the difference between a child and a woman. Girls of ten, eleven or perhaps twelve years old proudly showed me their affadavits certifying that they were adults. Their saris, however, did little else but reveal that these prostitutes were small, thin children wrapped in women's clothes. The law, however, tells men that these children are old enough to be bought for sex. There are papers to prove it.

Bangladesh instituted new legislation on trafficking and forced prostitution in 1995. It imposed severe punishments for the sale of children, including the death penalty. Accomplices to the crime of trafficking are also to be subject to the same penalties. Although the 1995 Act has some drawbacks – particularly because it lacks an adequate definition of trafficking – the real weakness of the legislation lies in the fact that it is unlikely to be implemented.

Thailand has been active in forming task forces, commissions and overhauls of the law relating to trafficking and prostitution. A new law in 1996 concentrated on punishing the procurers, the brothel owners and even the families who sold their children into prostitution. Closed brothels were targeted for closure. This was all very encouraging. And lots of the brothels did close. But then they reopened in a more sophisticated form as karaoke bars, massage parlours and restaurants. Others simply went underground.

The 1996 legislation prevented girls from living on the premises of Thai brothels. So instead the same old forms of control operated in two settings: the place in which the girl sold sex and the place in which she lived. Violence and debt bondage within the Thai sex industry still exist despite the legislation. The response of the sex industry to the new laws has been to 'clean up' the most visible parts of the trade. This, however, would almost certainly have happened as a natural phase in the development of the industry; the enactment of the new legislation simply accelerated the process.

Prostitution is illegal in Japan. We are supposed to believe that thousands of 'snacks' and clubs are providing entertainment to men but that this entertainment stops short of offering sex. It is incredible that a fiction can be maintained on such a scale. Women trafficked to Japan without legal visas are therefore breaking Japan's very restrictive Immigration and Nationality Law and also the laws on prostitution. Even women who are forced into prostitution in Japan feel unable to approach the police for help because they fear being branded as a criminal. Ironically, the law serves, in this instance, to trap migrants in exploitative situations. This phenomenon is not exclusive to Japan. Illegal migrants all over Asia find it very difficult to approach the authorities for help. A survey of NGOs working with illegal migrant prostitutes listed the most common barriers that dissuaded women from seeking help. They feared deportation; they had difficulty communicating in a foreign language; they lacked knowledge about their rights and the legal system; they had no access to legal assistance and no confidence in either the legal system or the law enforcers.[3] While there is so much fear and uncertainty in these women's minds they are unlikely to have the confidence to tackle their traffickers and to make an escape from situations of sexual slavery. To instil fear into women, snack owners and managers in Japan use threats of arrest, detention and deportation. These threats are effective and there is plenty of evidence to prove that the women's worries are not groundless.

In 1992 six Thai women in Japan were arrested for the murder of the brutal Taiwanese *mama-san* who operated them. The Shinkoiwa Case, and others like it, brought a spotlight to bear on the lives of trafficked women and illustrated the kind of treatment they could expect from the Japanese authorities. The case was investigated without the women being able to see a lawyer. As a result they were unaware of their rights under Japanese law. The women were detained in a Tokyo detention centre and were not allowed to speak Thai when meeting visitors. One of the women, who had sustained a leg injury, also received inadequate medical treatment. Despite their pleas that they were trying to escape inhuman conditions of sexual slavery and had been driven to murder by desperation, the women were convicted and imprisoned.

Around 3,000 women escape from brothels each year in Japan and flee to the Thai Embassy in Tokyo.[4] They do not flock to the

Japanese police for help. And they cannot expect a sympathetic response from the public. Although there was a series of shock revelations about trafficking and the sex industry in the 1980s and 1990s the public remains largely apathetic about the fate of foreign prostitutes in Japan. And this applies whether they were voluntary recruits to the industry or whether they were trafficked and coerced into prostitution. Intense and abiding racism contributes significantly to this lack of concern.[5]

The Philippines has a startlingly two-faced official attitude to prostitution. The sale of sex is illegal. Yet, at the same time, there is also an official licensing procedure for sex workers. Women have to submit themselves to regular medical examinations and are given cards guaranteeing that they are not infected with sexually transmitted diseases. These are shown to reassure clients, and a woman is prohibited from selling sex without one. According to the law, however, she should not be selling sex in the first place. Maybe the health check procedure is a sensible precaution taken by a responsible government, and can be justified on the dubious grounds that it helps to contain STDs and to keep the women safe for use by the clients, but it also makes a mockery of the law.

Labour export has been a major plank in the Philippines' development strategy. Filipinos are employed overseas, in the process decreasing pressure upon scarce jobs at home. The overseas workers also remit a large proportion of their money home. In theory this keeps poor families afloat and keeps the treasury filled with foreign exchange. But, for all too many Filipina women migrants, labour export has meant the export and sale of their sexuality. The government has made some efforts to prevent the sexual exploitation of migrant women. It has, for instance, worked with non-governmental organisations to raise awareness and it has deployed social workers at Ninoy Aquino International Airport to monitor the travel of minors abroad.[6] Initiatives like this, however, are largely fruitless when conditions of poverty and the cultural devaluation of women consistently produce a stream of girls who leave their homes in search of work both in the Philippines and abroad.

Although the legal frameworks governing or prohibiting prostitution vary from country to country in Asia, we can identify some patterns that are common throughout the region. The first is that the law has less to do with the reality of the sex industry and far more to do with political considerations and the image a society wishes to project of itself. The law is usually an irrelevance for the sex industry although in some instances the law may even be a boon for the business because it deprives women of even more control over their lives. Trafficked women in Japan and prostitutes in Pakistan receive dismal justice at the hands of legal systems that are respectively racist and deeply sexist.

In the past few years some countries in the region have enacted new legislation on the trafficking of women and children for prostitution. Many other countries plan an overhaul and improvement of current legislation. It is hoped that international co-operation, particularly in the Mekong Basin and to a lesser extent in South Asia, will curtail the incidence of trafficking and lead to the development of integrated regional legal frameworks. In April 2000 a conference in Manila attended by sixteen Asian and Pacific countries, the European Union, Russia, United Nations agencies and NGOs adopted a non-binding action plan to prevent trafficking.[7] Central to the plan was increased exchange of information and more severe punishment for traffickers. Initiatives such as these are encouraging because they mean that the issue, at least of international trafficking (if not sexual slavery and domestic trafficking) is at last receiving the attention it warrants. However, I believe that the problem is not one of poor legal frameworks and a lack of well-intentioned plans. The problem is one of implementation. Many countries already have flawed but adequate laws to deal with trafficking and sexual slavery. Creating new legislation will improve definitions and make the frameworks more comprehensive, but even strong and well-drafted laws need will and commitment to enforce them.

It is very difficult to gather sufficient evidence to charge traffickers. Women may be rescued years after they were trafficked. In South Asia some girls cannot even remember their native languages because they were incarcerated when they were children. They cannot remember the route they travelled to the brothel and the mechanics of the trafficking procedure. They do not remember the names or the faces of the traffickers. In some instances when the traffickers were their own family members they do remember but have adopted an understandable amnesia. Trying to secure a conviction is almost impossible when crucial witnesses are confused, forgetful or plainly traumatised by their experiences.

Significant pressures are brought to bear upon women who have been trafficked and/or forced into sexual slavery. Most important is the heavy weight of psychological conditioning. Many women believe that they have in some way deserved their fate and that there is no point in making a fuss because they are locked into a life of prostitution irrespective of any criminal conviction that can be brought against their traffickers or the brothel owners. In essence, it will not make a difference. In societies in which there is a premium placed upon virginity and where women's sexuality is tightly controlled, rape can effectively strip a woman of self-esteem and can prepare her for prostitution. War Against Rape is a Pakistani NGO working to help the victims of sexual abuse and to assist them in returning to normal life.[8] The organisation's task is monumental because the victims are seen by large sections of society as having been shamed and as having incited the rapist by being available to be raped. This even applies to the child victims of sexual abuse. To compound the problem, a raped woman is marked out as a certain candidate for further sexual assault. She becomes public property and, as no one would want to marry her, raped girls frequently find themselves drawn into prostitution. Disabled by mental frameworks like these it is not surprising that women in sexual slavery in Pakistan fail to speak out against the men who trafficked them or forced them into prostitution.

An entire religious, social and cultural matrix discourages women from pressing charges. Many parents would prefer to hush up a daughter's involvement in prostitution rather than to take action against those who coerced or encouraged her into the business. They do this for their own benefit and for that of their daughter. Many women feel shamed by sex work. They do not want to talk about their shame while standing in courts full of men who will treat them with contempt. Many women are also fearful. Throughout Asia, trafficked women and those forced into sexual slavery are afraid that speaking out will endanger their own lives or the lives of their families. During my last visit to Japan in August 1999 the staff of an NGO that deals with women's issues spoke of their anger and sadness at a recent and suspicious tragedy. One of the Thai victims of trafficking and sexual abuse in Japan had taken the incredibly brave step of providing evidence against her captors. The woman had returned to Thailand pending the court case. This fearless woman was killed in a road traffic accident before she could give evidence.

In areas where trafficking for prostitution is a local speciality there is intense social pressure for girls to keep quiet and to keep the system going by their silence. To provide evidence against recruiters, agents and brothel owners in this instance would be tantamount to treason and to an attack upon their own families and the entire community. Girls could expect severe recriminations. To add to this, there is also political pressure and the pressure of the wallet. Nepali women, for instance, are intimidated and offered bribes to drop cases.[9] Traffickers are also released on the orders of Nepali politicians,[10] and cases are abandoned because of a sudden and suspicious lack of evidence.

One school of thought argues that many abuses in the sex industry would be eradicated if prostitution was legalised. This argument completely bypasses the issue of the greatest importance. The greatest abuse is that sex can be bought and that people – specifically women and children, but also men – are valued for their bodies and their sexual functions. But even if we dismiss this basic point, the thesis that legalisation will curtail terrible abuses is difficult to apply, especially in the context of Asian societies. Lalitha Nayak of India's Joint Women's Programme is an activist working on trafficking and prostitution in India. Her view on the legalisation of prostitution is very clear, very hostile, and also very representative of the approach taken by a large proportion of women activists in South Asia. Legalisation, she argues, will make matters worse because it will give families and men the licence to legally exploit and abuse females. Removing the restriction on prostitution in a society in which women are devalued will not actually halt abuses. Instead it will only serve to encourage them. The present laws may not be good but they form a minimum line of defence against even greater abuses.

There is another approach to prostitution, and one that finds particular favour in Thailand. This view accepts prostitution as a form of work and advocates that the industry should be decriminalised, regularised and for it to be subject to the same kind of regulations and safeguards as other industries. A 1998 report by the International Labour Organisation on the sex sector in four countries of South-East Asia drew attention to the size of the industry, as if this was a reason that it should be legitimised.[11] Acknowledging the importance of the sex business and bringing it within the purview of the law would be good for the economic profiles of these countries. Statistics on the turnover of the sex trade would add to the figures on Gross Domestic Product and the lucrative industry could be taxed. The state, rather than just corrupt individuals within it, could profit handsomely from an expanding business.

The Global Alliance Against the Traffic in Women (GAATW) is an international NGO and is based in Bangkok. It works to end the abuses in the industry and simultaneously to promote the concept of prostitution as a viable career option. Siriporn Skrobanek, the chair of GAATW, explains that we cannot deprive poor women of the right to earn a living. She insists, 'Women should have the right to choose to become a sex worker if they wish. The important thing is that this should not be their only option.' This approach is rooted in a well-meaning desire to help women in prostitution. But it is also profoundly negative because it respects the foundations of the sex industry and not just the women who participate in it. If this approach is adopted prostitution would be decriminalised and the sale of women would be legitimised in law. The purchase of sexuality would be sanctioned by the state and would be regulated by market mechanisms. However, I would argue that there has to be some limit to the logic of the free market because the free market is only really free for the very luckiest. Poor women and girls are not lucky. Their luck is as rare as their vulnerability is abundant. There are far, far too many people who profit from their vulnerability to change this in any meaningful way.

Police forces give their blessing to prostitution. Some participate directly in the trade as clients and as the recipients of bribes and protection money. Some officers even own parts of the business. In northern Thailand police officers own brothels and they trade in girls. They do not take action against traffickers because they themselves form the largest single group of traffickers. In Cambodia a survey by the International Organisation for Migration revealed that many female brothel owners were married to policemen, and to military or border officials, or that they had very close contacts with them.[12] Direct police involvement in the management and ownership of the sex industry appears to be more serious in mainland South-East Asia than anywhere else in the region, but the patterns, if not necessarily the scale, are common everywhere.

The police and the legal profession take a big cut from the selling of sex. Traffickers, brothel owners and sex workers pay protection money. There are no exceptions to this. Inevitably, the pay-offs to the police are greatest in those countries where prostitution is illegal. Many brothels set aside a significant proportion of their income to pay off the police. Indian police take their regular *hafta*. A survey undertaken in Delhi on behalf of the Indian National Commission for Women found that the police took around 20% of the fee that customers paid to the brothel owners for each sex act.[13]

Pakistani prostitutes pay their weekly *bhatta* to the police to avoid arrest. And there are other charges too. The women who work in the traditional red light area of Naipier Road in Karachi pay a tax to the police every time they travel from their homes. This was how an elderly brothel manager explained the arrangement:

> The police know who the girls are. We cannot go out of the road without them watching us. They make us pay 500 rupees (£6) every time we leave. So we have to pay or the girls get arrested. It's worse now than it was because now the girls have to go out to entertain clients at parties and we have to pay more to the police. Business is bad these days.

When a new girl arrives at a Calcutta brothel, the police are informed and a payment is made. Very little goes on in the brothels without the police having knowledge of it. Likewise very little goes on in police headquarters without brothel owners knowing all about it. If a raid is planned, police officers will tip off the brothels and receive a payment for their information. This is common practice throughout Asia. In Thailand the amount of bribe a police officer receives depends upon his rank – that is how much he is risking by protecting the brothel – and also on the number of girls in the brothel and the number of laws being broken. A large number of foreign, and hence doubly illegal, child prostitutes, for example, will reap large dividends for the local police. At the time of writing brothels in Mae Sai were paying the police 2,600 baht (£43) per month for each girl on their premises. This is equivalent to the cost of around fifteen purchased sex acts with a Burmese prostitute. In other words, the police receive a substantial portion of the income generated by the selling of sex in Mae Sai.

A posting as a border guard in a prime trafficking area, or as a police officer in a red light area, can be very profitable. There is therefore competition to secure coveted posts. In many instances bribes are paid to secure lucrative postings. Thai officers compete to land jobs in Hat Yai police station so that they can take a cut in the lucrative sex trade generated by Malaysian men's sex trips to southern Thai brothels.

The Burmese prostitutes working in Thailand are defined as illegal migrants by the Thai authorities. In an effort to control migration from neighbouring countries there are numerous checkpoints on roads from the Burmese and Cambodian borders. Transporting foreign prostitutes around the country therefore becomes problematic, as the women are relatively easy to identify. The sex business found an ideal solution to this problem: in many instances police escort the women. The young women who move from Mae Sai to the brothels of Chiang Mai are taken there by police at a cost of 2,000 baht (£33) or about four times the price of the same journey in an air-conditioned luxury car. Significantly, no Thai police or border patrols have ever been punished for complicity in the trafficking of women.

It is a similar situation in Bangladesh where there is stiff competition, and bribery is practised in order to land a posting with the Bangladesh Rifles on the crossing points on the Indo–Bangladeshi border.[14] Official complicity in the trafficking process is incredibly blatant in these areas with border patrols implementing passage rates and even collecting fees on the buses.

The sex industry could not operate without police protection and connivance. In red light areas brothel owners work hand in hand with corrupt police officers. For example, Indian brothel owners arrange for the police to arrest women who are making demands and who they want to intimidate. When there is a crackdown on a brothel it is very often motivated by financial factors: the brothel has not paid sufficient protection money to the local police.

Sexual favours as well as bribes are given to police and border forces. The police are some of the principal clients of sex workers throughout the region. A survey by the Marie Stopes Clinic of 3,000 'floating' or street prostitutes in Bangladesh revealed that the police constituted their main client group.[15] Sex workers consistently mentioned that the police were regular clients. A Thai prostitute in Bangkok described the complex relationship with the police in this way:

> We know all the police in this area. They come to the brothel
> in their uniforms and sometimes say they will arrest us. Then
> they come back later as customers. And they want to be
> entertained for free or at special rates.

A similar phenomenon is found in northern Thailand. An official working for an organisation that assists sex workers in the region explained the delicacy – and the hypocrisy – of the situation that they had to encounter on a regular basis. The organisation sends teams to visit the brothels and to distribute information on HIV awareness to the sex workers and their clients. This becomes an exercise in dissembling when the clients enjoying themselves with the women are found to be senior and high-profile police officers. Both the members of the team and the police then go through a charade in which both pretend that the brothel is not a brothel and that the men are not there either to buy sex or to enjoy it as a perk of the job. This allows everyone to save face, and for the team to continue their work without subsequent police interference.

Sex workers in Nepal report that police officers demand sex

without payment in return for their non-interference in the women's work.[16] Those women who had been prostitutes in India stated that the Nepali police were worse than those they had encountered in India. Judging by the experiences of prostitutes in India this must mean that the Nepali police are outstandingly dreadful. A Nepali girl who was forced into prostitution in Mumbai painted a depressing but wholly typical picture of police manipulation and abuse:

The police came into the building. There were about five or six of them and they talked to the *gharwali* and they started to look around the brothel. They made two of us stand up and turn around and they said we looked very young. We said we were twenty-five, like the *gharwali* had told us to say, although we were really fifteen. Then the police went away but three of them came back later and we had to entertain them. The *gharwali* said it was a favour for them.

Abuse of trafficked women and prostitutes is not confined to the brothels. It takes place in police stations too. A child who was trafficked from Bangladesh to Delhi for sexual abuse was rescued from her traffickers only to find herself in an even more terrible situation and abused by the very people who were supposed to protect her.

Some of the people in the neighbourhood realised what was happening to me because they could hear me crying. So they helped me to escape and they found one of my aunts who was also living in Delhi. I was taken to the police so that they could help me and punish the trafficker but instead they arrested me because I didn't have a passport. In the *thanna* [police station] I was locked in a room. It was like at the trafficker's house because five policemen raped me.

The police officers involved in this crime were convicted and imprisoned for child rape. This is unusual and, unfortunately, there are many other similar cases that never come to light, never mind to trial. Often terrible abuses of this nature are not even considered to be a crime because the rape of a prostitute – however young she may be – is considered to be a contradiction in terms. Prostitutes are not raped. They work.

An Asia Watch Report in 1991 stated that over 70% of women in police custody in Pakistan were subject to sexual or physical abuse.[17] Because these women were not in the protection of their families they were considered to be 'fair game' by police officers. The treatment of prostituted women was inevitably the most dreadful of all. In response, the Pakistani government instituted a directive in 1996 that prohibited women from being kept overnight in police custody. Women's police stations were established and were staffed by female officers. However, the directive remained largely ignored. Reports from Lahore-based newspapers in the first six months of 1997 documented 52 cases in which violence was perpetrated upon women in police custody.[18] We can assume that the actual incidence of abuse is far higher than these figures indicate. What is more, the police effectively evade the directive by holding women in non-notified detention centres.[19] This means that they can still be abused – but in the safety of unofficial police custody.

Sex workers consistently complain that the police refuse to help them and that they cannot expect justice at the hands of the legal system. Like lots of women this experienced prostitute from Sonagachi in Calcutta had only negative things to say about the police:

> There are lots of problems being a sex worker. The worst are
> the police and the hoodlums and the fact that the rest of
> society looks down on us. The police want money from us
> and so do the hoodlums. They are always asking for dona-
> tions for festivals – big donations that we cannot afford but if

we don't pay they make problems for us. But then we can't go to the police because they ignore us because we are sex workers. Even when the customers are bad and violent with the women the police don't do anything because they think we deserve it. They don't help us.

Women from the Durbar Mahila Samanwaya Committee, a sex workers' organisation in Calcutta, are insistent that the existing laws covering prostitution in India make their lives more difficult. The law grants the police a licence to extort money from the women and to abuse their positions of power. Sadhana Mukherjee, a charismatic leading figure in the organisation, is candid about the difficulties imposed by the police. 'With knowledge we can help to prevent Aids,' she says, 'but there is nothing we can do about the police.'

It is impossible to involve local police forces in genuine crackdowns on red light areas and rescues of imprisoned girls without courting the danger of the whole operation being undermined by inside information leaking out to the brothels. A Bangladeshi street prostitute remembering her teenage years spent in a closed brothel in Calcutta related a familiar story.

We always knew when there was going to be a police raid – even though that wasn't very often. The owner would hide the youngest girls and the older ones wouldn't serve any customers until she knew that the police wouldn't come back. The *malkin* said she had some good friends in the police and that if we ran away they would put us in prison.

Voluntary groups in Thailand report a similar situation. An organisation that is concerned about child prostitution in northern Thailand and occasionally takes action to secure the release of children in brothels explains that it is impossible to work with the local police. It is not, they explained, because all the police are corrupt. The trouble is that no one is able to identify the incorruptible officers with any degree of certainty. If action needs to be taken in response to a case of sexual slavery, particularly of children, then the Crime Suppression Unit from Bangkok has to be called in. Working through the local police force guarantees that on the night assigned for the raid absolutely no one is to be found selling sex in Chiang Mai.

Of course there are honest police officers. But it takes only a minority of corrupt ones to destroy the reputation and the effectiveness of an entire force. Amod Kant is the Deputy Commissioner for Police in Delhi. He has taken a great interest in the trafficking of women and the issue of sexual slavery in the city, and has launched a large-scale, if intensely controversial, round-up of suspected child prostitutes. He outlines the difficulty in monitoring and controlling a situation in which the police have to cope with a sophisticated, quickly adapting industry that has the money to buy a minority of his officers. Senior police officers, he maintains, are committed to tackling the sex trade but they are hampered because they cannot always be confident of the sincerity of a very few junior officers.

I suspect that more than a 'few' officers are corrupt. This corruption extends far beyond the police's involvement in the sex industry. It is endemic. Part of the problem lies in the poor pay given to the police in many developing countries. Taking bribes is sometimes the only way that officers can feed their families. Protection money and sexual favours are rather like a perk in an otherwise rather unattractive job. It does not justify corruption but it goes a long way to explain it.

Gauri Pradhan is the director of the Child Workers in Nepal NGO, based in Kathmandu. He has in-depth experience of working with trafficked children and those who have returned from Indian brothels, and he is convinced of the necessity of working with the police in order to stem the trade. As a result he is anxious not to demoralise honest police officers by damning the whole institution with constant talk about universal corruption. He has a point. Programmes have therefore been instituted among police officers to train them to spot and deal with traffickers. But this is just the easy bit. Devising a training programme to tackle a whole culture of corruption and gender bias is a much more complex task.

Laws prohibit slavery and in many countries in Asia they also outlaw human trafficking. The sexual exploitation of women in prostitution continues, however, because it is acceptable in cultural codes that are constructed upon two fundamental premises: the first is that females can be bought and sold, and the second is that men have the right to buy sex. These are the laws that matter. Terrible poverty and acute disparities in wealth encourage these laws to be implemented with savagery.

It takes more than legislation to get rid of deep-seated cultural practices. It takes a seismic shift in attitudes. None of the women I met and who had been trafficked or sold into sexual slavery ever questioned the *right* of their families, or the agents, to sell them. Almost all said that what had happened was unfair and they bemoaned their fate, but no one ever expressed their grief or anger in terms of the infringement of their rights. I believe that many women do not express their anger at being sold because they do not believe that they possess some of the most fundamental of human rights. These same women failed to express any faith in the legal systems of their own countries, or of the countries to which they were trafficked. They are sceptical about the police and the sincerity of the authorities in tackling traffickers and ending systems of sexual slavery. And it is only natural that they should feel this way. The law, the police and the lawyers are, with only minor exceptions, part of the very same power structure that incarcerated them in a brothel and put them up for sale.

Chapter Eight

LIFE AND DEATH

Successful careers in prostitution rarely last long. Unfortunately, neither do many of the young women who provide sexual services. HIV/Aids is taking a terrible toll of sex workers in areas like northern Thailand, Cambodia and parts of India. Here, the majority of a whole generation of prostitutes is being wiped out by disease. Even those women who chose to sell sex never imagined that the decision to join the business would be tantamount to a death sentence. Ironically, those girls who were lured and forced into the trade because customers demanded young, 'clean' and disease-free prostitutes have some of the highest rates of HIV. Many of these victims of disease, and of the sex trade, were recruited in their mid-teens. They will be discarded by the consumers and the brothel owners when they are in their early twenties and they will die before they are thirty.

Brothels are the place to buy very young girls and women. Although a few physically attractive and highly skilled women continue to sell sex in brothels into their thirties, most brothels place an emphasis on youth. Cheap youth. Women therefore rarely work in brothels for more than a few years before they move on to other sectors of the sex industry. Their time in the brothel is marked by two stages: seasoning and acclimatisation. Once they have been initiated into the trade they condition themselves to life in the brothels. This is not because most like the work, but because they have no other option.

Prostitution is not 'easy' work for most brothel-based women. For a start they have to be available to service men almost constantly. The Thai women involved in the Shimodate Case in Japan (which was another instance of a *mama-san* who was killed by debt-bonded sex workers) explained that they had to work in the nightclub every day of the year except New Year's Eve. They were not even given time off during their periods. In Cambodia, most of the girls who worked in brothels reported that their brothels were open twenty-four hours a day during holidays. Women working in brothels on the Thai–Cambodian border shared similar experiences and were expected to work twenty-four hours a day, seven days a week.[1]

Girls in the *casas* of the Philippines have no regular working hours. They have to be on twenty-four-hour call and must service any customers the *mama-san* sends them. They have no control over the number of men they have to service. Ninety-five per cent of these girls work a seven-day week.[2] The Centre for the Protection of Children's Rights in Bangkok estimates that Thailand's child prostitutes work for between ten and fourteen hours every day. Usually they service seven clients on weekdays and twice as many at weekends.[3] The concept of holidays and time off is unknown for women and girls in Indian brothels, until they can be trusted not to run away. In practice, this may mean that young prostitutes have no freedom for years. Then, once they do have a degree of liberty, they will be allowed only a couple of days off each month. Long-serving ones will be granted a holiday to return to their village to recruit new girls for the industry. This is based on the belief that they cannot escape to begin a new life and will probably make excellent recruiters.

Women are not busy all the time they are on call. A large proportion of the day and night is spent waiting around for clients. This time was often described as being 'boring'. Girls said that the routine of life in the brothel was the same every day. They are not allowed out and, apart from the clients, they see the same people every day. Only a relatively small percentage of the women's time is spent servicing the customers. The number of clients a girl receives is dependent upon the brothel and the country in which it is situated. Those in more developed countries, and more prosperous cities, generally service fewer men. In contrast, girls in cheap brothels in poor countries operate on a kind of production line. They may serve ten customers a day, and more on holidays. It is not uncommon in places like Phnom Penh or Mumbai to meet young women who claim to have serviced twenty men every day.

A sex worker in Bangladesh described the situation for new, young girls in the brothel in which she worked.

The girls who were pretty got paid more and also got more clients. The price was usually 100–200 taka (£1.20–£2.40) and the men used to take five or ten minutes. I am not so pretty so I cost 75 taka (90p) and I usually had about ten to twelve clients a day.

A *mama-san* from the Philippines explained that the pretty teenagers found themselves in a difficult situation because there was so much demand for their services. Ironically, there is most demand for a prostitute in the period in which she is new and has yet to acclimatise herself to selling sex. By the time she has been both physically and emotionally conditioned she will be less attractive to the clients, will command less money and will service fewer men.

Because brothel-based prostitution is cheap it also rarely offers much in the way of frills. In order to be economical the whole process is over very quickly so that the girl and/or the bed can be ready for the next customer. Girls reported that the brothel owners pressured them into making the customers stay for as short a time as possible. A young woman who had worked in a Cambodian brothel described how the brothel owner would begin to knock on the door of the cubicles if girls were taking too long to service the clients. The demands to hurry up would begin after ten minutes. If the girls took more than fifteen minutes, they would be beaten for providing 'unprofessional' service.

The same woman commented that this did not happen with the majority of clients but that she always experienced problems with men who had been drinking.

> The worst ones were the ones who were really drunk so that they took so long and it was very painful. Usually it took only a few minutes but the drunk ones took over half an hour and they would smell so bad and a few were sick on me.

Not only do young women have more clients but they are also in a weak position when it comes to refusing clients or having any say in what is done to them. Because they are under the control of the brothel owner they cannot choose their clients. And because the all-powerful client has paid for her body, he believes that it is his right to be serviced as he sees fit. Vulnerable and intimidated new recruits to sex work often have little knowledge about health risks. More to the point, girls are unable to negotiate the basic terms of the sex act, even if they know about the principles of safe sex, because they are in a position of acute powerlessness. In particular, they are unable to demand that the client uses a condom. Sex workers who are insistent upon condom use are seen as demanding and unappealing women among a customer base that places a premium on youthful submissiveness. Young powerless brothel girls rarely demand condom use. They demand nothing. That is why they are there. Over 70% of Nepali sex workers in India interviewed in a UNICEF study said that they had rarely or never refused to have sex.[4] Although around 86% of their clients used condoms, this still leaves a sizeable proportion of sex acts that are unprotected.[5] A Calcutta prostitute said this about safe sex practices:

> Some of the clients use condoms but many don't. The *malkins* tell us not to use condoms because the customers don't like it and they will not earn so much money. It is very difficult. We can't make the customers use condoms. If they don't want to, and we try to make them, they just go to another woman and we have lost business.

The physical surroundings of prostituted women vary enormously but there are the constant themes of surveillance and lack of control. In India, a woman might queue for a bed upon which to service her customers while, in Japan, the client might take her to a luxurious hotel. Both women, however, can be locked into exactly the same system of debt bondage and sexual slavery. Thai women in Japan who were long past the point of successful seasoning and were unlikely to make a bid for freedom reported that they were kept under surveillance by local tough guys and by closed-circuit television. Many Cambodian women are not allowed to leave the brothel without an escort. Some cannot leave at all. If they need to buy goods the brothel owner will do this for them and will add the cost to their debt – usually at high rates of interest.

Irregular eating, monotonous food, inadequate sleep and cramped and overcrowded living spaces were common complaints of women in the brothel sector right across the region. A Filipina woman, who is currently working in a bar in Manila and who was trafficked to Japan and forced into prostitution, claimed that she had spent six months in a club somewhere in Tokyo and that she had never left the building during the entire time except in the company of a guard or trusted customer of the club. She worked, ate and slept in the same place. Eight women – all Filipina – slept together on the floor of a small room at the top of the building, monitored, again, by closed-circuit television. This room together with a bathroom and a small kitchen constituted the only living space for these trafficked women.

Complaints about poor food were frequent but not universal. A child prostitute in Bangladesh explained her perspective on prostitution in a disturbingly pointed manner.

> I never got any money but the pimp promised that if I
> worked hard I would get some. He paid for my food and
> bought me two nice dresses and some makeup. The food he
> gave me was really good. I ate twice a day and wasn't hungry.

For this child, the indignities and terrors of prostitution took second place to destitution and starvation in the pantheon of horrors and injustices.

Even well-seasoned women do not always make compliant prostitutes. Many women accept prostitution as their work but it does not mean they enjoy it. Drug use and dependency is a way that many women overcome their fears and unhappiness over what they do to earn a living. Alcohol is a cheap and, in the short-term, easy palliative to the rigours and emotional damage of prostitution for those women who never manage to acclimatise themselves. Excessive drug use is not very common among young brothel-based prostitutes because they do not have the money to afford such dubious luxuries, but the early foundations of addiction are often laid down during the trauma of seasoning and the early years of sex work. Young prostitutes are provided with alcohol to suppress their inhibitions. Women who had worked in *casas* in the Philippines described drinking cough medicine to help them cope. Some used a favourite drug of older sex workers called 'shabu'. In Thailand, prostitutes are encouraged by brothel owners to take drugs. Supplying amphetamines to sex workers has a double advantage: the brothel owners make money out of women's addiction and women on a drug-induced high are more productive because they can service a greater number of customers with a greater degree of enthusiasm.

A succession of clients for the prostitutes is invariably accompanied by a succession of sexually transmitted diseases. Women live with STDs and wage a constant battle against them. Ultimately, it is a battle that some will lose. A Bangladeshi prostitute talked about her health in this way:

> We got good food in the brothel but I kept losing weight because I always had sexual diseases. I felt sick and could not eat. Someone would bring us lots of different medicines because we could not go out and see a doctor. Sometimes a government person would come and tell us about condoms and give us some.

Women in Mumbai, Dhaka and Phnom Penh report that they take antibiotics on a regular basis. Some do so continuously. Cambodians are particularly fond of taking even simple medication by injection. This practice has been linked to the spread of HIV because the fondness for needles is rarely complemented by an insistence on the fact that they are also sterile. Dhaka street prostitutes claim that they spend the most significant part of their income on medication for STDs. Although the clients of brothel-based prostitutes are just as likely to be infectious as the clients of other sex workers, brothel girls do not have the same kind of access to drugs. Although it is in the interest of brothel owners to maintain the girls in reasonable physical shape, this is not essential. A diseased girl can always be replaced.

Experienced women take care to avoid STDs. Indian sex workers explained how they rub lime or lemon juice onto their palms before massaging the client's penis. If he winces they can deduce that he is suffering from some form of STD. In Thailand and Japan women said that they included an inspection of the man genitals as part of the sexual servicing. The pre-sex bath and massage gives them a good opportunity to check out his sexual health. For brothel-based girls who are sent clients by the management and who are required to provide fast service, this kind of inspection is impossible. Besides, they are not able to refuse the client even if they suspect that he is infected with STDs.

Brothel owners sometimes take care to ensure that their girls do not become pregnant. Contraceptive pills are given to girls in the better brothels. It is common in big and well-organised Indian brothels for a doctor to pay a regular visit to give girls contraceptive injections – sometimes all with the same needle. In this context the common claim that it is easier for prostitutes to acquire HIV/Aids than to get pregnant is probably vindicated. Even so, many of the new recruits to the industry find that they become pregnant within a short time. Few of these girls will give birth to their children. It would be very bad for business. Women who have had children are not in such great demand and are paid less because customers prefer childless women who have tighter vaginas.

Abortions are very common. The method of abortion varies from country to country and brothel to brothel. In the Philippines prostitutes said that a woman had visited the brothel and had massaged their stomach vigorously in order to dislodge the foetus. Sometimes they had to endure this procedure on numerous occasions. In India and Cambodia women said that they had been given medication that had made them ill. Many also had surgical terminations. Despite the pain and the emotional trauma that they had suffered, women reported that they were forced back into work very quickly. Many were given only a few days off. This Cambodian girl's story is typical.

The *mama-san* was so angry when she found I was pregnant. She gave me some medicine and it made me vomit a lot but the baby didn't come out. She tried this three times. Then when my stomach got so big that the customers started to talk about it she took me to a doctor and I had an abortion. The baby had been in my stomach for about five months. I went back to the brothel the same day and after four days I started entertaining the clients.

Teenage girls may become pregnant several times in their early sex work career but many older women find it difficult to become pregnant when they wish to. Repeated abortions and a succession of STDs leave many women infertile or sub-fertile. This is a tragedy for most women and especially for sex workers. Even in South Asia where the average woman usually has around four children, very few sex workers have more than two children. Sometimes this is because they know that having children is bad news for their career and sometimes it is because they are unable to have more. Among South Asian sex workers in particular, children provide many women with the only true and honest relationships they will have in their adult lives. A large number of well-meaning NGOs try to help sex workers by taking their children into care and hence into a safer environment. In some cases this is appropriate and in the best interests of the children. Often it is what the women themselves wish for their children. However, it is rarely in the best interests of their stigmatised and socially isolated mothers.

HIV/Aids has given sex work a whole new dimension. It has elevated prostitution from a grubby little problem hidden in societies' dark corners to an issue of international concern. Without HIV/Aids we can be sure that the issues of prostitution and trafficking would still be lost in those dark corners. Prostitution has become a subject worthy of study because the service that prostitutes offer to clients is seen as a medium through which HIV/Aids is spread through society in general. The missionary-style health care activity in red light areas is rarely motivated by a government's or a medical establishment's sudden urge to help a despised community of women. Quite the reverse: they want to save the rest of society from the despised women.

Governments, public health institutions and medics have rushed to slow the spread of the disease. Some have blamed prostitutes for spreading Aids and have adjudged it a righteous curse for their immorality. They have not made it clear, however, if the invisible clients who buy the prostitutes should be equally cursed. The more enlightened have sought to control HIV/Aids by encouraging safer sex practices. To this end HIV/Aids programmes are disseminating information on how HIV is spread. Condom use is promoted among sex workers and the programmes, in many cases, cultivate good relations with brothel owners on the grounds that they can then get their message through to girls and women who are confined within the brothels. If only it was that easy. Protecting oneself from infection is not only about receiving and understanding a message. The girls and women who sell sex, and those who are sold for sex, are not stupid. They understand the message if they are given the chance to hear it. But the important point is whether the women have the power to act upon this message. The poorest and youngest and most vulnerable do not. That is exactly why they are in such demand.

Combating HIV/Aids is not just about making people aware of safe sex. It is also about ensuring equality of power within relationships – whether those relationships do not involve a financial transaction, or whether they are purchased in cash or in kind. Some of the best HIV intervention programmes address this problem by trying to encourage a sense of empowerment among sex workers and to demand sex workers' rights. The STD/HIV Intervention Programme in Calcutta is one of the best examples of this strategy. Its approach grew from the realisation that women could not insist upon a client's condom use if they did not have the ability to determine their conditions of work and if they did not possess self-esteem and a sense of pride in themselves as women who sell sex. A strong link has therefore developed between Aids control and the need to eradicate the stigma associated with prositution. This has found practical application in a powerful and persuasive alliance between those who advocate sex work as a legitimate and ethically desirable form of employment and a medical establishment that seeks to slow the spread of HIV/Aids by empowering prostitutes and encouraging them to demand safe sex.

HIV/Aids prevention campaigns have tended to concentrate upon modifying behaviour rather than changing it. Safe sex is encouraged – and that is all to the good. But campaigns have not encouraged men to question their prostitute use. The purchase of sex is taken as absolute and unchangeable. For example, Aids has been a national issue in Japan since the early 1990s but it has had minimal effect upon men's practice of buying sex. In 1991 a controversial poster published by the Ministry of Health and Welfare showed a man hiding his face with a passport. The accompanying slogan read, 'Have a nice trip but be careful of Aids.'[6] Perhaps the mysterious man was on his way to Mae Sai to purchase a Burmese virgin. In which case *he* was not the person who had to worry about HIV/Aids.

Although prostitution is illegal in the Philippines the government tries to make the women safe for the clients by insisting that 'entertainers' have weekly health checks. Strangely, this requirement does not apply to the customers who are freed from any obligation to prove their own sexual health credentials. Presumably they play no part in the transmission process and are thought to be free of infection until they come into contact with diseased women. Such illogical apportioning of blame for HIV/Aids and STDs cannot help in their control. Prostitutes are no more conduits of infection than the men they service.

The Philippines' health check is a confidential service, but women who fail the examination are refused a card guaranteeing their clean bill of health. A large proportion of girls who work in *casas* are unregistered and therefore do not carry a health card because they are children. Despite their youth, *casa* owners often take girls to be given the medical. They either lie about their age and/or they pay a suitable bribe. Some have private doctors who visit the brothels in order to carry out the weekly examinations in a secure setting. Such concern for the girls' health has little to do with the well-being of the young prostitutes and far more to do with securing the confidence of the brothels' customers.

Medics are placed in a difficult ethical position when they treat child prostitutes and women held in sexual slavery. Some doctors could not care less about the principles of their profession, or the fate of the girls they treat, as long as they earn a good living from it. Others, however, are caught in a horrible dilemma. If they report the abuse to the police, they run the risk of being exposed as informants by corrupt police officers. The medics will then lose the confidence of brothel owners and they will not be able to treat those girls and women who so desperately need their help. On the other hand, their silence also amounts to a form of complicity because treating the victims of sexual slavery prepares the victims for yet more abuse. It is a no-win situation.

The women who are in the direst need of help are rarely those who receive it. Trafficked women are unlikely to be let loose to consult a local doctor. HIV/Aids intervention programmes rarely reach these women. They are held in captivity and frequently speak a foreign language. They are the women for whom the safe sex message is just about as redundant as it can get. If they cannot negotiate their basic human rights and their right to freedom they are hardly in a position to demand that the man who has purchased their body also wears a condom.

Even girls and women who have received the safe sex message –

and, more importantly, are able to do something about it – will not always insist upon condom use. Clients sometimes refuse to use one. Women from Kamatipura in Mumbai claimed that customers would say something along the lines of, 'Why should I use one when I am paying for pleasure?' The women said that he was then likely to leave and go to the next sex worker who would offer him condom-free sex. Rules about refusing customers who will not use condoms are therefore only practical when all women agree to abide by the rules. However, older women who can no longer trade on their youth and looks will often compete with younger girls by offering unsafe sex. Brothel owners therefore encourage their girls to offer the same kind of service on the grounds that they might otherwise lose trade. This is the real face of sex work.

There is another complicating factor in the safe sex debate: some sex workers who possess the power to demand condom use will not always require clients to use them. Women in brothels sometimes have special clients – namely ones that they like: ones that they say are kind to them. These men are special because they are people with whom the women share some kind of emotional bond. The way that the women show their special favour to these men is to do away with condoms. It is a gesture of affection, and of trust. Sadly, it is also a gesture that may kill them.

Other sex workers fail to insist upon condom use. This is especially true of young and experienced girls who do not always like customers to use condoms. Recent recruits who are forced to take numerous clients complain of the intense pain of condom friction. Not only does it hurt, but it also takes longer for the customer to be serviced. In these circumstances girls may not put up much resistance to unsafe sex and, at times, it may even be a temporary relief.

Despite all the publicity about Aids, the prevalence of HIV among sex workers in red light areas in Asia is awesome. The ASHA project in Kamatipura in Mumbai estimates from sample surveys that about 60% of sex workers in the area are HIV positive. Around 40% of

men living in the area are also affected. These men are not sex workers themselves but they may buy sex and they may be partners of sex
workers.[7] These prevalence rates are representative of many red light
areas throughout the region. In 1997 the Cambodian Ministry of
Health's National Aids Control and Prevention Programme estimated that HIV prevalence among sex workers in Phnom Penh
stood at 42%. In Batambang the rate was 58% and in Sihanoukville
it was 52%. It is therefore with absolute justification that in 1996
UNICEF wrote, 'Without significant behavioural change the personal, social and economic cost [of HIV/Aids] to Cambodia will be
unbearable in the next century.'[8]

In theory the infection rates in the HIV hot-spot of Thailand
have plateaued. Perhaps this might be true among middle- and
high-class sex workers and their customers. However, it is a different
story for the lower class brothel women and especially the cheapest
prostitutes who are from Burma. Jackie Pollock, a member of an
organisation known as EMPOWER, which assists sex workers in
Chiang Mai in northern Thailand, believes that infection rates
among Burmese brothel-based prostitutes are every bit as high as
the early 1990s when a majority of sex workers were supposedly
infected. These girls are the most powerless of Thailand's sex workers and their clients are the most callous. Many of these men have
bought sex for years and did so in the years when safe sex was not
high on the agenda. Some of these men know that they are now HIV
positive but they have not adjusted their behaviour accordingly.
They continue to purchase sex and to have multiple sexual partners
and, because they themselves are already infected, they do not feel
any obligation or moral imperative to use condoms when they buy
women. They do not care. When I heard this it came as a shock but,
on reflection, this piece of news shouldn't have been a surprise.

The international NGO World Vision has run an HIV/Aids intervention programme in Mae Sai on the Thai–Burmese border since
the early 1990s. According to its sample surveys around 20% of sex

workers in the town are HIV positive.[9] When we analyse figures like this we have to remember that these girls arrive as virgins and stay in the town for only a few months before they move on to brothels further south. As HIV cannot be detected immediately it is contracted, the enormity of what happens to girls in Mae Sai and the impact upon their lives and, just as accurately, their deaths is obvious. EMPOWER's representatives in Mae Sai claim that most girls leave the town with HIV. These girls pay a terrible price to escape from the poverty of their Burmese homes.

One of the greatest ironies of the sex industry is that the people who are supposed to be the freest from disease are probably actually the sickest. Men buy child prostitutes because they are thought to be 'clean'. But even the first sexual act puts the child at physical risk because clients pay for the privilege of condom-free sex, safe in the knowledge that the girl's health is guaranteed. Young girls, however, are not designed for sex – and especially not with adult men. Their vaginal secretions do not act as an effective barrier to infection and their physical size makes them subject to vaginal abrasions that facilitate the transmission of HIV. Almost 70% of those girls and young women I interviewed who were, or had been, child prostitutes were HIV positive. Rates were especially high among Nepali and Cambodian girls. Although this sample is biased, and is not representative of sex workers as a whole, it does indicate the dangers posed to the most vulnerable people involved in the sex industry and especially to its youngest victims who may not live long enough to graduate into survivors.

The understandable preoccupation with Aids has sidelined the other health issues faced by sex workers. Gynaecological problems are among the most serious complaints of prostitutes, but there is little interest in them as they are not problems that affect the women's male clients. In the less-developed parts of the region prostitutes share many of the diseases of other poor people. And once a woman becomes ill her descent is rapid. Unhealthy-looking sex workers do not attract many clients. That means they do not earn much money. And if they do not earn much money they cannot eat properly or afford decent accommodation. Their health therefore deteriorates further. It is a vicious circle from which it is very hard to escape. Sick girls will be expelled from captivity in a brothel without much delay. Many brothel owners with a reputation to preserve will test for HIV on a regular basis and dispose of infected women. Others with persistent health problems receive the same treatment. Thin and ailing prostitutes are a bad advertisement for the brothel. Poor diets, lack of exercise and cramped living conditions combine to age sex workers in the poorer parts of the region at an accelerated rate. In these areas tuberculosis, a disease of poverty and over-crowding, probably kills as many sex workers as Aids. In fact it is TB that finishes off many women and girls living with Aids. Maiti Nepal, which runs a shelter home in Kathmandu for Nepali girls returned from Indian brothels, is overflowing with girls afflicted with both HIV and tuberculosis.

The physical damage of prostitution is easy to see. You cannot ignore the signs of Aids or tuberculosis. You can see the results of savage beatings and doctors occasionally have the difficult task of repairing the internal damage done to girls who are not old enough – or willing enough – to have their bodies sold to men. Psychological damage on the other hand is more insidious because it is also invisible. Some sex workers I have met during the course of this research have been confident and assertive women. I cannot therefore claim that all sex workers are one undifferentiated and subjugated mass. But there are many others who are haunted by their memories and crippled by a lack of self-esteem. Their psychological problems manifest themselves in different forms ranging from self-mutilation to drug abuse to the tolerance of grossly abusive relationships. Those young girls who are penned into Indian brothels as children will be scarred by the experience for their entire lives. By the time they are old enough to leave the brothel, many do not wish to go. The brothel is their whole world. Paradoxically, it is the only place they feel safe.

This Nepali girl, who was a teenage prostitute in Mumbai, described her life in the brothel in sad and bitter tones:

> I was in that place for three years and for two of them I never saw the sun. They never let me out. I was in a little room with two other girls and there was no window. It was always dark and there was only one light that was on almost all the time. Often we would talk to each other and imagine what it would be like to be outside and in the sunshine. I thought about my home but it just made me upset.

Women adopt survival strategies in order to help them cope. This applies to those who are new recruits and to those who have already been seasoned. Distancing techniques are a common method of insulating the women from further psychological harm. Girls who live and service men in the same tiny cubicle say that they use a separate blanket on the mattress when they entertain clients or that they rearrange their possessions before and after the client's visit. Some have clothes that they never wear while they are entertaining the clients. These little rituals help to separate the women as individuals from the functions that their bodies are compelled to perform. They help them to maintain their integrity and sense of self. A Thai woman who was trafficked to Japan and who was given a Japanese name said that she did not mind the new name, 'because it helped me. I said that the men were buying the woman with the other name and not me. It happened to someone else.'

Almost all girls and women report feeling homesick, especially in the early years. Even when they have fled from a bad home life, there is often someone – their mother or a little brother or sister – that they miss acutely. Developing relationships with other prostitutes and the brothel management is one way the women attempt to fill the emotional void. Perhaps strangely, *mama-sans* can act as substitute mothers or female relations to hard-working girls. And, in time the brothels become their home. Brothels have their own culture and behavioural codes and, eventually, girls will accept these because they have to. Women who have been forced or tricked into prostitution may then say with total honesty that they choose to sell their bodies. In this sense, the insistence upon their agency and choice in the matter is a survival strategy too. It gives them dignity.

Baitali Gangulay, who runs an NGO to help the children of sex workers in Calcutta's Bowbazar red light area, has some unconventional views on sex workers' attitudes to their occupation. Based on her experience of work in the brothels, she believes that girls may be initially trafficked and forced into prostitution but that after seasoning they become conditioned to the life and to the apparent power that sex work gives them. Usually, these girls are from impoverished families in which they have been a burden and considered of little value. Then they come into sex work and men desire them and some even appear to care for them. For a short while they can exercise a degree of power that would otherwise be unavailable to them. The realisation of this power helps in the conditioning process and may reconcile some women to the profession. However, this cannot be true of the newest girls. In order for them to enjoy the precarious short-term benefits bestowed by the exercise of this power, they have to undergo a physically painful and emotionally wrenching initiation. I cannot imagine that a young woman held within a system of sexual slavery has a highly developed sense of her own power. It is her very lack of power that has led to her captivity in the first place.

Brothel communities have a cohesiveness in South Asia's large traditional red light areas. Women can find an identity and a place in this community even when they are rejected by the outside world. Paradoxically, women who are outcastes from society see the brothel community as their only safety net in a hostile environment. In smaller red light areas, and particularly in the newer brothels that are dispersed throughout Asian cities, women are more isolated. They do not have the comfort of bonds created by the sheer number of women in traditional red light areas. I do not, however, want to overplay the strength and warmth of these bonds. Life in brothels is vicious – especially if you are old or ailing. There is competition between brothels and between women within those brothels. In Mumbai, for instance, Nepali women and those from different Indian regions staff separate brothels and there is little social inter-action between them. In Japan there is fierce competition between clubs that offer the services of a particular nationality. Sisterhood and the bonds created by the shared experience of prostitution are undermined by the economics of selling sex.

Prostitutes form friendships in the brothel. But they can just as easily form enmities. Seasoned girls compete for customers because their freedom from debt bondage depends upon it. A Nepali sex worker in India described the tensions this competition can create in the closed environment of the brothel.

A girl who is very young and pretty gets lots of clients. This can be a problem for her because the others get jealous because they can't earn as much money. They can be cruel and make life difficult for her. They tell stories about her and take her things and sometimes they pull her hair and pinch her.

Brothel owners play women off against each other on the grounds that business is easier to manage by divide and rule techniques. Sometimes one of the older women is given some extra money and presents or she is given better treatment. In return she is expected to act as an informant and to keep the younger inmates in line. Encouraging a sense of insecurity is a common way to keep sea-soned women under control. Denying them any control over their lives and the services they provide is an effective way of disabling a potential mutiny among the ranks of prostitutes.

Fledgling friendships are often undermined by rotating girls from brothel to brothel. This has the three-fold advantage of stymieing potential alliances, keeping girls in a state of insecurity and also providing the 'fresh' prostitutes that novelty-seeking customers demand. Women in Japan report being passed on from one club to another. Similar reports are heard from Cambodia and Thailand. One Burmese girl said she had been in five brothels in the preceding twelve months.

For every brothel manager who acts as a substitute mother to her girls, there are many more who are tyrants. A Dhaka prostitute painted this picture of life in her brothel:

> Madam was ferocious. All the girls were frightened of her. Whenever she would do her rounds in the morning the girls would rush to put on some more makeup and to brush their hair. Every morning we had to prepare ourselves carefully and to go and sit in the reception and wait for the clients. Madam checked us carefully because she said that we had to look pretty for the customers.

Prostitution has a career ladder. Mass-market prostitutes in the less-developed parts of the region tend to start on the middle rungs of the ladder and literally work their way down. The harder they work, the faster is their descent. There is a little more flexibility in the more developed markets and amongst higher class sex workers. In Thailand a skilled ethnic Thai sex worker can graduate from massage parlours to clubs and the call girl sector. For the majority the high point in their career is to go to Japan. Within Thailand the highest status is given to those girls who work in places like Thaniya Road in Bangkok and service wealthy Japanese tourists and businessmen. But careers are short even for these women. They may have the income to pay for the high-cost maintenance of their looks but money cannot postpone age and redundancy indefinitely. Women in the lower echelons of the industry cannot afford the luxury of intensive maintenance regimes. In places like Bangladesh they can barely afford a nutritious diet. And it shows. By the time they are twenty-five most poor sex workers in Dhaka look worn out because they *are* worn out. By the time they are thirty most cannot make a living from selling sex because they look like very old women.

Ageing prostitutes are not wanted in the brothels because they do not bring in the clients. Women are therefore freed from the brothels not only because they have worked off their debt but also because it is more profitable for the owner to acquire new girls. Under the *chukri* system in Calcutta, a girl will have repaid her debt at least two times over by the time she is released from her bond. Typically she will then join the *adhiya* system, whereby she works as an independent who pays half her earnings to a *mashi* who operates the brothel. A woman in her mid-twenties who has moved on from being debt bonded under the *chukri* system described her move in positive terms:

> Now I am in the *adhiya* system it is much better. But sometimes when there are only a few clients we have to accept clients who don't use condoms or who want oral and anal sex. We have to do this to earn some money. Most of the clients want to buy younger women so it is harder for us who have been doing this work for a long time.

Living in a brothel is the least favourable option for Cambodian sex workers. They are forced to work longer hours, have less freedom, service more clients and earn less money.[10] Women and girls have to endure these conditions because they are younger than prostitutes working in other sectors and so they have less knowledge of how to work the system. Many of them will have been forced or tricked into sex work. The sex industry and the clients then benefit from the girls' youth and from their lack of experience.

Sex workers are believed to earn substantial sums once they have completed their period of debt bondage. For most prostitutes this is a myth. Elite prostitutes can make substantial sums of money if they work independently and manage their business well. And the average income even for mass-market sex workers is commonly above the average income of other women workers who have comparable educational levels. A UNICEF study estimates that around 70% of Cambodian sex workers who had paid off their debt could earn around $100 per month.[11] This compares with the salary of approximately $40 that a woman can earn in a garment factory. Estimates for the income of sex workers in India varies. The National Commission for Women suggests that the mean income is around 1,000 rupees (£14.20) per month[12] whereas UNICEF suggests that most women earn 500–1,000 rupees per week.[13] The UNICEF figures, however, may be misleading because they refer to Nepali women in Indian cities who may be able to command a higher price than the average Indian prostitute. Uneducated women with minimal skills would find it difficult to earn a comparable amount in any other occupation.

The crucial point, however, is that sex workers cannot earn a living for very long. Women in sexual slavery receive nothing, or, at best, a pitiful fraction of the income that the brothel owners collect from the sale of their sexual labour. Some women will earn nothing but an early death and the condemnation of society. For a short while, most prostitutes are highly paid relative to women in their own social classes because their work is both hazardous and stigmatised. The women who manage to survive and who learn to prosper from sex work will gain confidence and knowledge. Their relationship with the management of the sex industry will change because they understand how the system works. They learn how to negotiate and they learn about power. But they also become older and their accumulated knowledge is a threat to the industry. Ironically, but inevitably, once they are in a position to work the system, there is no longer any demand for them. Mature and empowered sex workers – especially in an Asian setting – are the ones with flagging careers. They have traded their social acceptability and their sexuality in exchange for the economic benefits of selling sex. Some women believe the trade-off to be worthwhile but many others are never given the liberty and the economic freedom to allow them to weigh the costs and benefits of the exchange. They do not possess the power to define the terms of the contract that binds them into the sex industry. These young women are the goods and not the merchants.

Chapter Nine

THE SHAME

It is always easy to begin sex work. The trouble is that in many societies – and especially in Asian societies – it is also almost impossible to leave it. This is because in large parts of the region women are still defined by their relationships with men. They are mothers, wives, daughters, or they are public women. Females who choose, or who are forced into, sex work will acquire an identity that will remain with them for the rest of their lives. They can escape physically from prostitution but they cannot escape from being branded a whore in the eyes of society. Women are permanently shamed by their experiences and find it difficult to speak about their lives, even if there is a sympathetic audience willing to listen. Their silence and shame are built upon sexual trauma and are compounded by public opinion that characterises prostitutes as morally degraded criminals rather than as the victims and survivors of unjust social systems and perverse sexual codes.

Where do all the women go when they are no longer wanted as sex slaves and brothel prostitutes? This is one of the most difficult questions to answer. Sadly, ageing prostitutes often die before they ever enter into old age. HIV/Aids is a messy but convenient way of getting rid of sex workers made useless by creeping middle age and declining sexual utility. Drug addiction, alcoholism and diseases of poverty also help in reducing the numbers of redundant old women.

In communities where sex work is becoming a career option for girls, retired prostitutes might return home as prodigal daughters after a decade or so selling sex. The girls who left their homes in parts of northern Thailand and Nepal at thirteen may return in their early to mid-twenties. They will bring home their savings and some will also bring HIV. Over 40% of the female sex workers who return to northern Thailand are thought to carry the disease.[1] In general only successful girls will return. This is because the stigma associated with prostitution has not been totally eradicated. It can be erased providing the girl has amassed enough money; her relative wealth in the midst of a poor community will buy her social status. The successful women purchase respect through conspicuous consumption and they flaunt their wealth earned through sex work by upgrading the houses of their families and purchasing showy consumers goods.[2] A girl who returns from the brothels without money cannot buy the status to compensate for the social stigma of selling sex and therefore she 'loses face'. In parts of northern Thailand a poor prostitute is scorned because she is both poor and has failed as a sex worker.

This pattern is increasingly common throughout the Mekong Basin. Social attitudes towards prostitution are being altered in disadvantaged communities because the financial rewards of successful returning prostitutes are being paraded before poor families. The relative prosperity of returning prostitutes makes them exciting role models for poorly educated girls who have ambitions but no other opportunities to lift themselves out of lives of poverty and toil in the fields or in factories. Returnees open small businesses such as grocery stores and beauty salons with their savings.[3] Others are able to marry because their wealth makes them attractive brides to financially insecure bridegrooms.

Burmese sex workers returning home from Thailand also open businesses. The most ambitious open brothels and utilise the management skills they have acquired in Thailand. Tachilek on the Thai–Burmese frontier has brothels run by former sex workers. Although they are a little rougher and cheaper than their Thai equivalent, they bear striking resemblance to the brothels in Mae Sai on the opposite side of the border.

Women who return to those communities in the Nepali hills where prostitution is accepted as a survival strategy are also welcomed back home – providing they have contributed to the family's fortunes. Successful sex workers are respected in an environment in which prostitution brings more money into a family's coffers than farming minute plots of land or the unskilled wage labour its men can perform. Again the importance of role models is crucial. This was how a Nepali woman described her initial decision to travel to India to become a sex worker:

> My family were poor and we didn't have enough land. Sometimes my father worked as a porter and my brothers and I looked after animals but there were lots of children so we never got enough to eat. I was always hungry. There was a woman in the village who worked in India and she used to send money to her family so they had good food with rice and meat. She left her work in India and she came home with lots of money and nice things. She had nice clothes and gold jewellery and bangles and she had different colours of paint for her nails. I wanted to be like her so I said I would go back to India with her and do the same kind of work.

Some of these returning Nepali women will marry because they can afford to provide themselves with a dowry that is substantial enough to make an impoverished man forget his qualms about his wife's former occupation. Some of these women, like their Thai equivalents, settle down to a happy married life with their new partner. They have children and live contentedly. And some do not. Many of the marriages contracted by former Nepali sex workers last only as long as their money. What is more, many women who return from the brothels are either fertile or sub-fertile as a result of years of sexually transmitted diseases. In the context of a highly traditional society where a woman is valued for her reproductive capacities, the inability to bear children brands them as failed women. They have failed to fulfil the two most basic functions of decent women: to be chaste and fertile. In this case they are despised for being both whores and, what is more, barren whores.

Tales of sex workers who return to their place of origin as confident women with stashes of riches are true. But they do not tell the whole story. In fact they tell a frighteningly one-sided story. The distorted interpretation of prostitution that poor rural communities receive only serves to supply yet more girls to the sex industry and to portray the entire sad, and often violent, business as a kind of development project aiding poor girls from disadvantaged villages.

Rich prostitutes in struggling villages give the impression that it is easy to make money from selling sex. Thai agents, for example, will introduce families with teenage daughters to those women who are prostitution's success stories. Understandably, the women who did not manage to make it as prostitutes are never used as an advertisement for a career in sex work. Moreover, few returnees will complain about the conditions they faced. Some want to spare their families from the pain of really knowing what they went through in order to help feed and educate their siblings or to pay for the construction of a new storey on the family home. Women do not want others in the community to know what they endured. They will not tell of the incessant client demands and their inability to say no. They will not talk of powerlessness and fear. Public confessions of shame and pain will cause them to lose face. Instead they remain silent about abuse and concentrate on how successful they have been in earning money. And because no one speaks out about the fact that sex work was really a horrible ordeal, women often think that their experience was unique – that it was not the same for other women and that, perhaps, they were unlucky or maybe that they did something to deserve it. When they believe that their own unhappiness was not shared by other women they are even less likely to speak out and bring shame upon themselves and their families.

Communities in which sex work is accepted as normal are still in a minority. In most parts of Asia prostitution is stigmatised work. This, however, does not stop families sanctioning their daughters' migration to the cities, or to another country, in search of work – work that often turns out to be prostitution. When these girls return home they do not talk about their experiences because it is in everyone's interest to maintain the fiction that she really did do respectable work as a domestic help in a rich person's house or as a waitress in a restaurant. The family benefits because it does not have to accept the shame of sending a child into prostitution and enjoying the fruits of her labour; a girl benefits because she is not publicly embarrassed; and the sex industry benefits because yet another one of its victims is too shamed and her voice is too isolated to challenge its power.

In other communities the stigma of prostitution is ineradicable – or at least it is at the moment. We can safely assume, however, that this will change when the profession can be proved to pay well enough for people to forget how the money was earned. Sex workers returning to Yunnan in southern China report that social stigma from local people is the biggest burden that they have to face in reintegrating themselves into the community.[4] Prostitution – for women – is a sin from which there is no absolution and no return in large parts of Asia. This applies whether a woman chose to sell sex, whether she was forced by economic circumstance, or whether she was physically coerced. A married woman who has sex with anyone but her husband, or an unmarried woman who has sex with any man, is a whore no matter what the circumstances may be.

Vietnamese women who have been trafficked to Cambodia or who have chosen to migrate there to work as prostitutes suffer serious discrimination if they are 'rescued' or arrested. They can expect little help even if they are the victims of sexual slavery. Repatriated women who have been held in sexual slavery are still thought to be morally suspect – and all prostitutes are considered to be in need of rehabilitation. They are heavily stigmatised and are forced to live under a regime that bears marked similarities to the kind of incarceration they had recently escaped. They take part in re-education programmes and are taught how to earn a decent living. To add to the injustice, women are labelled as illegal migrants and are held up for public condemnation. In some instances this enables them to be victimised by the agents who trafficked them in the first instance. It is no wonder therefore that few Vietnamese victims of sexual slavery and abuse break the silence that surrounds the industry, the men that exploit them and the hypocrisy of a society that sanctions the injustice by ignoring it.

The saddest stories are told by those girls who are born into societies in which a prostitute can never be 'rehabilitated'. These stories are especially common in South Asia. Nepali girls from non-traditional prostitute-recruiting grounds face terrible discrimination if they ever return home from the brothels. How the girls entered prostitution in the first place makes absolutely no difference to how she is welcomed back into the family and the village. Returning Nepali girls speak of being ostracised by other villagers and some describe being rejected by the families who sent them to India when they were children. This was how a woman returning to Nepal from eight years in Mumbai described her experience of village life:

It is very hard because I am not used to life in the village.

There is no electricity and the food is not good. But the worst
thing is how people treat me. They think I am not a proper
person and that I don't have feelings. When I walk down the
road people avoid me and no one wants to talk to me. When
I go to the shop the women who are there talking just leave.
The men talk about me and sometimes they make rude comments and call me a prostitute. The young boys throw things
at me and the other people in the village don't let me take
water from the well. They say it is because I am bad and that
I will do something to the water. I want to tell them that I am
just like everyone else but no one wants to listen to me.

The Bangladesh National Women Lawyers' Association is the
leading Bangladeshi organisation working on the issue of trafficking
and child prostitution. Its president, Salma Ali, has encountered
enormous difficulties in reuniting prostituted and trafficked girls
with their families. She cites an example that is not untypical of the
cases with which she has to deal. A teenage girl was given to an
agent by her much-married father, who had many children by different wives. She was not sold for cash because her father thought it
enough simply to get the girl off his hands and to entertain the pos-
sibility that her labour would one day result in money being sent
home. The girl was prostituted in India and then, after a number of
years, was repatriated to Bangladesh with the aid of NGOs. This
girl is still a child and wants to return home to her family. Her father,
however, has other ideas and refuses to accept her back. She is, as he
explained to Ms Ali, a disgrace to his family and it would be an
embarrassment to have her living in his house. There is nothing
that he or anyone else can do to help her. She is a prostitute and
therefore she is finished.

Prostituted girls are not always sent into sex work by avaricious
families. It is impossible to estimate how many families knowingly
send their daughters to brothels. But it is a lot easier to say that

there are many families who are desperate about the fate of their girls and that they are overjoyed when they are safely returned. Chanthol Oung, the director of the Cambodian Women's Crisis Centre, has overseen the reunion of dozens of girls and their families. She told me that witnessing these reunions can be an immensely moving experience. Clearly, not all girls are sent by their families into a life of prostitution, and their return from a brothel is often a cause for celebration rather than shame. If only that was always the case.

The Nepali women who were returned from their brothels in Mumbai in 1996 were not welcomed back home. The government did not want them and, true to form, it failed to make arrangements for their repatriation. Instead, a handful of ill-equipped NGOs tried to deal with the women among a barrage of press criticism and public condemnation that vilified the girls as the carriers of Aids. Like so many Asian countries, Nepal takes very poor care of its daughters. Former sex workers are pariahs in Nepali society. Women with Aids are classified as carriers of the 'whores' disease', and returning prostitutes are publicly shamed by having their photographs reprinted in the papers along with salacious descriptions of their work.

The most damaged women never make it home. They die. Or they are so emotionally battered that they cannot face the prospect of reintegration into the communities of their birth. This applies especially to women in less-developed parts of Asia. Some may not want to return to the homes they left as children. Like other migrants, they see themselves as being split between two worlds. They have built a life in the city or in a foreign country. For some this may be a good life but, for most, it will be the only kind of life they can envisage and, for some, the only kind of life they can really remember.

Some brothel workers eventually climb into management positions. These women are good at selling sex and they are shrewd businesswomen. Ironically, even girls who were initially trafficked and forced into prostitution may become the very women who help to keep the system running. These women are the ultimate survivors of the industry because, in order to survive, they have absorbed its values and made them their own. Such heights within the industry are reserved for a tiny minority of women. A small number will become *mama-sans* and will rise into this position over a number of years of managing girls within a brothel setting. An even smaller number will become brothel owners.

A larger proportion will enter the management structure at a lower level and will become procurers. With the process of seasoning long past them and with the amnesia created by time and imminent poverty, ageing sex workers become the vehicle for the perpetuation of the industry. In order to survive they earn money in the only way they know how: they recruit young girls from the countryside and from poor communities in the towns and then they put them to work as prostitutes. Twenty years before, they themselves had been brought into prostitution in exactly the same way. And so the cycle continues.

Women who do not make it onto the management track and who do not operate as procurers can often find a little niche within the industry as domestic helps for working prostitutes. They may work as baby-sitters or as cooks and cleaners. In the less-developed parts of Asia, women who cannot find work within the industry will disappear into the informal sector. They will become street vendors, cleaners and beggars. Women who are approaching middle age and who are no longer desirable commodities within the sex market may be lucky enough to secure a job as a peer educator in an HIV/Aids education project. This is because they have lots of experience of the industry and also because their lack of clients means they have time to devote to the project and enough financial need to make it necessary. The luxury of a job in such a project, however, is open only to very, very few.

Other former brothel-based women stay in sex work but do so

under the most demeaning conditions. Forced to compete against younger women, they lower their price and expand their repertoire in line with their increasing age. Sex workers who would not have considered offering oral sex as young women (except under conditions of debt bondage) will then offer it as middle age approaches. As old age beckons, anal sex is one of the only ways to make money. These least fortunate women are on an ever downward career escalator. They become street prostitutes or the cheapest kind of prostituted women working on the fringes of the brothel sector. In time they can be found selling sex for the price of a bowl of rice or a bucket of water. In India and Bangladesh I have met older women who service men all day and night just to earn the few rupees or taka it takes to pay for a single meal. And some people will tell you that prostitution pays well.

The difficulties faced by women in sexual slavery do not vanish once they have been rescued or have escaped from captivity. Some escape by running away. I met one Nepali girl who had broken her leg by leaping from an upper storey of her brothel. A girl in the Philippines had escaped by removing the air-conditioning unit and climbing in through the hole that was left in the wall. Other women plot with sympathetic clients who agree to help them. Yet, for some, rescue might not be as welcome as we might have predicted. In some cases rescued girls escape one form of abuse for another. Although there are a number of excellent NGOs offering shelter to child prostitutes there are also others that function as a kind of brothel in which the former sex workers and child prostitutes can be abused within a legitimate setting. In Calcutta I met indignant women who claimed that they had been 'rehabilitated' and placed in homes where they were taught new skills. They said that the male instructors involved in these programmes had sexually abused them repeatedly and that, unlike their earlier customers, these men did not pay. Unsurprisingly these young women returned to prostitution once they had completed their 'rehabilitation'.

The physical conditions of many shelters and women's refuges in poor parts of the region are abysmal and are worse than the brothels from which the women and girls have been saved. India's government homes are notoriously bad. Women and girls are kept in overcrowded conditions with inadequate sanitation. A similar scenario is found in Pakistan where the Dar-ul Aman (government homes) are feared and where a leading charity, the Edhi Foundation, runs shelters which are well managed but which verge on the draconian.

Only a small proportion of the victims of trafficking and sexual slavery are ever rescued. Even so there are never adequate facilities to assist the small number who manage to escape and who require help. There is rarely even enough sympathy. I met a delightful teenage girl in Calcutta who was suffering from Aids after being compelled to sell sex since she was a small child. The NGO that was caring for her told me that it had been difficult to find any doctor willing to treat her and that she had been taken to a string of hospitals in which she had been shunned and turned away by the medical staff.

This kind of attitude is typical of rich as well as poor societies. In Japan I met a Vietnamese woman who had worked in Thailand and who had then been trafficked to Japan and forced to provide sexual services. Eventually she was ejected from her 'snack' because she had contracted HIV either in Japan or perhaps before her arrival in the country. However, because she was an illegal migrant and had no proof of her nationality the Vietnamese government refused to repatriate her. Thailand accepted no responsibility for her and the Japanese refused to pay for her medical treatment on the grounds that she was not Japanese. As I write this she is living and dying in limbo – a stateless person and a victim of trafficking.

Some of the worst shelters are a kind of reform school. The best are places that allow the grief and sorrow of the girls and women to be expressed and their worth as human beings to be affirmed. They provide the women with the psychological support that helps them to readjust. Sanlaap, an NGO working with child prostitutes in Calcutta, is a positive example for other shelters. It provides counselling to the girls it cares for. The youngest are educated and the older girls are given vocational training in semi-skilled work. Wherever possible the girls are returned to their homes and, when it is not possible, they stay at the shelter until they are adults.

The rescue of girls and young women may be difficult but it is far easier than deciding what to do with them once they have been rescued. Many are suffering from psychological problems and staff at some shelters talk candidly about the difficulties in caring for child prostitutes. The girls have been accustomed to an irregular schedule and to wearing fashionable clothes and jewellery. In a shelter they may have to follow a fairly strict routine and to abandon their fine clothes. They have also been accustomed to constant sexual attention. The consequent behavioural problems include disruptive behaviour, lack of concentration, aggression and conflict between the girls and the members of staff, episodes of violence, self-mutilation and long periods of deep depression. Suicide is not uncommon.

Reintegrating girls and women into mainstream society poses even greater difficulties. The skills that former sex workers are taught after leaving prostitution are rarely sufficient to secure them a living wage. In less-developed Asia, the girls and women who are the victims of trafficking and sexual slavery are very poorly educated. That is why they found themselves in prostitution in the first instance and why they find it difficult to escape from it. Skills such as block-printing, mat-weaving and candle-making that are taught to former sex workers might give the women a pride in their ability to create but, unfortunately, they rarely give them an income that is adequate to live on. Women who have been rescued and taught a more 'worthy' way of earning a living often end up right back in the brothels from which they escaped. In South Asia, in particular, there is no road back from prostitution. It is virtually impossible for them to be reintegrated into society and for them to marry. For most, prostitution is their only option.

In 1996 the police authorities in Mumbai decided to round up prostitutes in one of its periodic purges of vice. Ostensibly this action was a crackdown on child prostitution. In fact it was nothing of the sort. Rumours, based upon hard facts, were circulating that the HIV prevalence rate in the city's red light areas was around 60%. Action was therefore necessary to clean up the industry, to get the diseased women out and, presumably, to get new and clean ones in. Over two hundred Nepali women and girls were 'rescued' in this operation. A significant proportion of these women did not want to be 'rescued'. In a survey of the rescued women, 56% of those who responded stated that they did not want to return to the brothel. Of the 44% who did, 29% said that they were happy to be sex workers while the rest cited other reasons. The most common were that they had no other skills, that they could not return to society, that they had dependent families to support and that they would otherwise be destitute.[5]

Sex workers in South Asia repeat similar stories about their acceptance of prostitution. A woman in Lahore described her enmeshment in the industry in this way

> I don't like this work but there is nothing else that I can do, I
> haven't got a good husband and family. I haven't got an edu-
> cation. I am an ignorant woman. This thing – entertaining
> men – is the only thing I can do.

In mainstream society these women are shunned as social out-castes. In the brothel they are accepted. They are vulnerable to physical and sexual abuse but, when they are among other women like themselves, they have protection from society's scorn. They are buffered from contempt. Prostitutes from Bangladesh's Goalunda brothel are ostracised from the society of respectable people. They are not allowed to wear shoes in public places and they are not allowed to bury or cremate their dead. Instead their bodies are thrown into the river. Yet within the brothel community the women find acceptance. Where on earth would they find the courage to leave the only people who treat them as human?

Social contempt and a sense of being shamed locks women in the countries of South Asia into brothels. The internalisation of the bad woman image is one of the most effective chains tying women into sex work. These women and girls carry the heaviest burden of the sexual double standard. A Khmer proverb 'Men are gold, women are cloth' encapsulates the mentality that pervades most Asian societies – just as it did Western societies until very recently. A young Cambodian woman explained the proverb in a 1993 study:

> The men look like gold. When it drops in mud we can clean
> it, but the women look like white clothes; when it drops in
> mud we cannot clean it to be white again.[6]

There can be fewer greater injustices than the stigmatisation of prostitutes in societies in which many – and sometimes most –men buy sex. Men have created this skewed and horrible sexual system and individual women are blamed for it. But acknowledging that the stigmatisation of prostitution is wrong should not lead us to the conclusion that prostitution is acceptable. I cannot believe that prostitutes, as individuals, should be held in contempt. It is the institution of prostitution, the people who profit from it, and the men who enjoy it who deserve our unreserved condemnation.

On one occasion a young Cambodian man who worked for an NGO grew agitated when I asked him about the Vietnamese prostitutes in Phnom Penh. 'Some people,' he insisted, 'say that they are immoral women . . . but they have so much honour. They choose to come here because their families are so poor and there is nothing for them in Vietnam.' I knew exactly what he meant. Many of the women

I have met in the course of the research for this book have been anything but immoral. They have survived abuse and exploitation and
have sought to live with as much dignity as their occupation allows
them. They are mothers who have sold sex in order for their children
to eat, they are poor girls escaping impoverished homes and they are
young women who are sold for sex so that their brothers and sisters
can have a better chance in life than they themselves were offered.
Prostitution, in these instances, is a human rights abuse. And so is the
poverty and the limited life chances that force or encourage many
women to sell their bodies in the first case.

Prostitution is not always about violence but it is always about
power. It is about the power to buy intimacy and the power to establish a relationship of domination. The apparently civilised
transaction between elite prostitutes and their clients in luxury
hotels is underpinned by the same logic that underpins the forcible
sale of girls in a Bangladeshi brothel. This logic is premised on a
value system that grades girls and women – and sometimes men and
boys – according to their sexual value. This logic is sustained by the
emptiness of those men who buy sex and by the commercialisation
of life that makes prostitution increasingly possible.

Objections to prostitution are not simply based on the importance
of aesthetics and the importance of preserving sex as a celebration of
life rather than as a mechanical and commercial engagement. Neither
is it a matter of religious puritanism. Prostitution should be condemned because it encapsulates the very worst of human failings: the
exploitation of the weakest; the power of money; the superficiality of
appearance; men's abuse of power; and the categorisation of women
according to their sexual utility and their relationship to men.

This book has focused upon the brothel sector of mass-market
prostitution and upon some of the most exploited people within the
sex industry. The scale of the abuse that these girls and women have
suffered tends to be diluted the further we ascend in the prostitution
hierarchy. Righteous crusades against prostitution have tended to

fasten upon atrocities within the industry in order to discredit it and to whip up moral indignation. These sorts of crusades feed on rumours and they work upon fears and anxieties.

Societies undergoing periods of change and crisis are likely scenes for panics related to prostitution and its evils. England during the 'White Slavery' Campaign of the 1880s was bombarded with horror stories of child prostitution and 'Five Pound Virgins' that actually turned out to be the product of journalists' imagination.[7] Reports of the abduction and trafficking of women in early twentieth-century China are now considered to have been exaggerated and to have been stoked by alarm over the perceived breakdown of Chinese society.[8] New York in the late 1970s was incorrectly portrayed as host to child prostitutes who came in a 'pipeline' from Minnesota.[9] If fabrications or elaborations like this have happened in the past can we then assume that the same kind of hysteria is being applied to the issue of trafficking and sexual slavery in Asia today? I fear not. I have only one answer to those who express their scepticism: meet the children and the women who are sold into this trade and then go home, and from somewhere in your conscience try to muster the conviction to write about prostitution as if it is an intellectual exercise.

If there are elements of exaggeration in the analysis of prostitution in contemporary Asia they lie in two main areas. First, not all sex workers are victims. At least they are no more victims than many other people who sell their labour under exploitative conditions. And a tiny minority of women do make a substantial living from selling sex. The proportion of girls and women who enter the sex industry and who are totally 'innocent' is almost certainly exaggerated. I use the term 'innocent' warily. Sadly, women who have chosen to become prostitutes but who are then subject to horrendous forms of abuse are often denied the support they need on the grounds that they were guilty and 'asking for it'. In intensely patriarchal societies women who have lost their claim to innocence by consenting to sex outside marriage are treated as if they have also lost all their claim to justice. I suspect that the emphasis upon 'innocence' is something of a public relations exercise utilised by groups who want to highlight the real and grave abuses within the sex industry in societies in which prostitutes are heavily stigmatised. It is comparatively easy to generate public concern for child prostitutes and for the 'innocent' victims of the sex trade. Generating sympathy for whores in difficulty, on the other hand, is a fruitless exercise.

The other area in which there is exaggeration is in the line pushed by the pro-prostitution lobby. Despite its claims, I seriously doubt how far it is possible to 'clean up' the sex industry. And I doubt that the stigma can be removed from prostitution. Besides, in most Asian societies the institution of prostitution is not stigmatised, even though official pronouncements sometimes give this impression. Buying sex is fine because it is something that men do. It is the women who sell it who are stigmatised.

Perhaps the greatest distortion of all is the argument over who should be considered a victim. According to pro-prostitution groups, labelling sex workers as victims infantilises them and makes them appear as helpless and naive and in need of rescue. But, they argue, these women are not often victims but are in fact active and entrepreneurial women who are trying to make their own way in the world. This is a very dangerous but appealing argument. It is appealing because it is seen to endow stigmatised women with a degree of control over their lives and because it recognises, quite correctly, that many of the new entrants to prostitution are girls and women who have left their homes in search of a better life. However, it is dangerous because we must never forget that a very large proportion óf the girls and women at the sharp end of prostitution really are victims of many types of injustice. To understand prostitution we have to recognise the power dynamics of the industry and the power dynamics of the transactions that take place within it. We have to recognise vulnerability. So, if something is to be done to improve the lives of women in prostitution – if we wish to stop the worst exploitation and if we wish to help those who survive it – then we also have to recognise that many prostitutes were victims long before they ever became survivors.

Pro-prostitution groups will tell you that dwelling upon victimhood, and the tendency for do-gooder outsiders to interfere in the lives of sex workers, is misplaced. Sex workers themselves can articulate their own problems and determine their own solutions. I am sure they can, but I would also question how representative the voice of some of the more vocal sex workers actually is. The most outspoken are often experienced women who have been in the trade for years and who have been successful at their work. Often they work in the better parts of the industry and many are in its management structure. They are the natural spokeswomen for the industry because they are the ones who have survived it. I am not confident that they speak for the young, coerced girls and women who have yet to be seasoned, or for those women who never acclimatise themselves to their work.

By way of contrast, the reflections of trafficked girls and those held in systems of sexual slavery would make a dreadful advertisement for prostitution. It is difficult to make a case for the sex industry when you have seen the psychological and emotional harm that prostitutes have suffered. Many of the youngest girls have lost their faith in people. They do not trust anyone. And you can hardly blame them. On four separate occasions I met girls who had left prostitution by a variety of routes and who were extremely wary of me. They said that they did not know why they should trust me because I might be a trafficker. I abandoned an interview with one frightened girl who sobbed, 'How do I know you won't sell me?'

Very few young women and girls feel confident about their ability to analyse why they were trafficked or why they were forced into prostitution. The vast majority repeat the same explanation. They say that it was their 'fate'. Many, especially in the poorer parts of the region, believe that it was something from which they could never have escaped. A young Cambodian woman asked me, 'What did I do in my past life to have made this one so bad?' I was not able to suggest any answers that could console her.

Many women cited poverty as the reason that they were forced into prostitution. Poverty and fate, it seems, are a fatal combination. Very few ever said that they were angry with the men who had bought them. Men seemed to be excused on the grounds that they were men and that having sex and buying women was just one of those things that men did. Anger was saved for those who had *allowed* the men to buy them. It was saved, in particular, for traffickers and for the people who had sold them into prostitution. A Cambodian prostitute described her confusion, 'Sometimes I am angry, but I don't know who to be angry with. Perhaps it is my destiny.'

Young girls rescued from brothels in Calcutta expressed anger against the families who had sold them but they were placed in the difficult position of having to rationalise and control their anger because there was no alternative to returning home. A child prostitute in Mumbai who had fled from sexual abuse at home said that she thought with longing of the brothers and sisters whom she had not seen for five years. 'My dream,' she explained, 'is that I can go back to my home and see my mother.' She will never fulfil this dream because she died of tuberculosis and Aids shortly after telling me her story. She was sixteen.

Women internalise the social attitudes that blame 'fallen' women for prostitution. Another child prostitute, this time from Dhaka, described her feelings.

I am angry at my fate. If my mother was well she would have arranged a good marriage for me and I would not have to suffer this shame. My life is ruined. I want to learn a skill so that I can earn money and look after my mother. No one will want to marry me because of what has happened to me. I won't live long and before I die I will pray five times a day to God to apologise for what has happened.

Many of the women feel unsure of where they really belong. Their sense of identity has been shaken by their experiences of prostitution. Some find a kind of peace in embracing the world of the sex industry while others try to return to the world outside. Neither option is easy.

Strength is the abiding image that I have of many of these women. For them to have suffered so much, and at such a young age, and for them to then carry on with their lives is a testimony to the resilience of women and to the strength that lies behind the overworked image of the meek Asian woman. In Phnom Penh I visited the home of a nineteen-year-old who had been rescued from a brothel. Now she has a job in a garment factory and earns £25 a month. She rents a room in a wooden shack and she shares this room with another teenager. This young woman manages to save a little money and she proudly told me that she sends it to her mother to help feed her family. She lives with HIV and yet she looks to the time when her wages will be sufficient to pay for her sister to be educated. She cried when she spoke of her illness and she said that fate had been so bad to her. The memory of this HIV-infected girl, sitting in her home surrounded by her few possessions, and the knowledge that she is working to make the best of the rest of her life, is one of the most poignant and powerful images I carry with me. It illustrates both the unforgivable brutality of prostitution and the capacity of those women caught within it to be bigger and stronger than the men who had bought them.

The debate on trafficking and sexual slavery is fixed very firmly upon why, and how, women enter the industry. This is essential information but it is also highly predictable. It would be a surprise if the sex industry's mass market was not staffed by poor, badly educated women from troubled families. Analysis of the industry's clients would yield far more interesting answers. To date, however, this essential factor in the sex-for-sale exchange has been largely ignored. It is almost as if the industry exists independently from the customers. The Asian buyers of commercial sex possess the miraculous qualities of being simultaneously ubiquitous and yet invisible. During informal conversations, dozens of men told me, in the utmost confidence, that all their friends and acquaintances buy sex and that it is acceptable behaviour providing it is a hidden activity. Needless to say, not one of these men had ever bought a woman himself.

Asia's sexual codes are built on the subjugation of women and the exploitation of the vulnerable. In this sense Asia is just like anywhere else. But in Asia the level of hypocrisy is greater. More accurately it is staggering. In official discourse and in everyday life the subject is wrapped in silence although, among men at least, it is a badly kept secret. To raise the issue of prostitution is not considered polite and, in most quarters, its very existence would be denied – with the exception, of course, of the depredations of Western sex tourists. Yet although it is shrouded in a silence that is either conspiratorial or based upon wilfully massive ignorance, the sexual behaviour of Asian men is not a private act. It may be hidden, but it is also very public. Prostitution occurs on such a scale that individual, purchased sex acts cannot be anything other than an intrinsic part of society and a reflection of its social and economic structure.

Poverty, inequitable economic systems, skewed sexual codes and discrimination against females are terrible burdens for many women throughout the world. In Asia these burdens are especially heavy. The most vulnerable women find themselves caught in a trap from which they cannot escape. Whenever I interviewed girls and women in the course of my research I explained that I was writing a book to tell people in my home what trafficking was and what it was like to be a sex worker in their country. This explanation elicited a number

of responses that varied from the pleased, to the indifferent, to the
overtly cynical. One seasoned woman smiled politely and asked very
pointedly, 'And how will that help us?' I was lost for words because
I simply did not have any answer. Others were more enthusiastic
about the project. A Filipina woman expressed a sentiment that was
common among many women when she said:

> I am happy that people in your country will know what life is
> like for us and what happened to us. Perhaps if I tell my story
> to other people then the bad things that happened to me will
> not happen to other girls.

The Cambodian woman who now works in a garment factory
thought along similar lines.

> I want the whole world to know about the things that are
> done here. I want all this to stop and I don't want what hap-
> pened to me to happen to my little sisters.

Evils like this, however, do not stop. They are deeply and indelibly
carved into a society's cultural and political makeup. One of the
most gut-wrenching episodes I encountered took place in a narrow,
dirt road in Bangladesh. It was so shocking because it made me
appreciate the powerlessness of individuals to affect a vast trade. I
had stopped to talk to street-based sex workers. They were extremely
poor and haggard women who had been child prostitutes in closed
brothels but who had long since been expelled when they had
approached their early twenties. A ragged woman and a thin girl of
about nine held onto my *shalwar kameez* as I left. The woman
pushed her daughter forward and I could see the desperation in the
girl's eyes. The mother said very quietly, 'Please help us or my own
girl will become like me. Ask people in your country to help us.
Will your book help me? What can you do to help my girl?' I did not

have the courage to say that there was nothing I could do to help. Her daughter is doomed to a life of prostitution.

Sadly, this book will have absolutely no impact upon the life of this Bangladeshi child and her mother, or upon the lives of the other women that I met. It will not affect the poverty that forces an impoverished girl to sell sex in order to survive and it will not hinder men from buying frightened children and those young women who do not possess the power to choose to sell their bodies. My hope is that, in some small way, it will help the many, many prostitutes who are already in the making. If the stories that are told in these pages can begin to shake some shibboleths and to break some silences then they will have accomplished something. Prostitution has to be damned for the dehumanising, woman-hating activity that it is. And the sanctimonious moral high ground occupied by Asia's prostitute users cannot be left unchallenged. Sex and slavery are natural partners in a manmade world. In Asia they are absolutely inseparable. Sex slaves are an intrinsic product of male-dominated Asian societies. They are part of a vicious game that men play with women. They are the abused, stigmatised and bitterest sum of Asian values. And they cannot, forever, continue to live and die in silence.

NOTES

Chapter One: The Market

1 The best account of this dismal episode is George Hicks, *The Comfort Women: Japan's Brutal Regime of Enforced Prostitution in the Second World War* (New York: W.W. Norton, 1995). For disturbing first-hand accounts by the women themselves see Keith Howard (ed), *True Stories of the Korean Comfort Women* (New York: Cassell, 1995).

2 A number of excellent books have been written on military prostitution in Asia. Among the best and most easily available are Saundra Pollock Sturdevant and Brenda Stoltzfus, *Let the Good Times Roll: Prostitution and the US Military in Asia* (New York: The New Press, 1992), and Katharine H.S. Moon, *Sex Among Allies: Military Prostitution in US–Korea Relations* (New York: Columbia University Press, 1997).

3 Numerous and often indistinguishable articles have been written on the sex tourist trade. Among the best and most important books are Thanh-Dam Truong, *Sex, Money and Morality: Prostitution and Tourism in South-East Asia* (London: Zed Books, 1990), Ryan Bishop and Lillian S. Robinson, *Night Market: Sexual Cultures and the Thai Economic Miracle* (London: Routledge, 1998) and Jeremy Seabrook, *Travels in the Skin Trade: Tourism and the Sex Industry* (London: Pluto Press, 1996).

4 I am indebted to Yayori Matsui, Director of the Asia–Japan Women's

Resource Centre, Tokyo, and to Rutsuko Shoji, Director of the HELP Asian Women's Shelter, Tokyo, for providing me with much of the detail on this phenomenon.

5 National Commission for Child Welfare and Development, Ministry of Women, *Combatting Child Trafficking, Sexual Exploitation and Involvement of Children in Intolerable Forms of Child Labour: Country Report on Pakistan* (Islamabad: Government of Pakistan, 1998).

6 My definitions are taken from Marjan Wijers and Lin Lap-Chew, *Trafficking in Women, Forced Labour and Slavery-like Practices in Marriage, Domestic Labour and Prostitution* (Utrecht: Foundation Against Trafficking in Women, 1997), pp. 36–8.

7 There is no consensus on the numbers of women involved. I have therefore taken 'average' figures based on the most authoritative studies.

8 Based on interviews with Aida Santos and the staff of WEDPRO, Manila.

9 The best book on prostitution written from the perspective of pro-sex work groups and individuals is Kamala Kempadoo and Jo Doezema, *Global Sex Workers: Rights, Resistance, and Redefinition* (London: Routledge, 1998).

Chapter Two: The Commodity

1 John Frederick, 'Reconstructing Gita', *Himal*, Vol 11, No 10, October 1998.

2 Sarah C. White, *Arguing With the Crocodile: Gender and Class in Bangladesh* (Dhaka: University Press, 1992), pp. 102–7.

3 Khawar Mumtaz and Farida Shaheed, *Women of Pakistan: Two Steps Forward, One Step Back* (London: Zed Press, 1987), p. 27.

4 Mahbub ul Haq, *Human Development in South Asia 1997* (Oxford: Oxford University Press, 1997), p. 23.

5 China Data Center, University of Michigan, 1998. Figures are taken from China's National Bureau of Statistics.

6 Haq, *Human Development in South Asia 1997*, pp. 20–4.

7 Haq, *Human Development in South Asia 1997*, pp. 21–2, 40–41.

8 Haq, *Human Development in South Asia 1997*, p. 20.

9 Marjery Wolf, *Women and the Family in Rural Taiwan* (Stanford, California: Stanford University Press, 1972), p. 14.

10 Wolf, *Women and the Family*, pp. 207–8.

11 Cited in Moon, *Sex Among Allies*, p. 40.

12 Government of Pakistan, *Report of the Commission of Inquiry for Women* (Islamabad, August 1997), p. 88.

13 Jean D'Cunha, *The Legalisation of Prostitution: A Sociological Enquiry into the Laws in Relation to Prostitution in India and the West* (Bangalore: Wordmakers, 1991), pp. 31–2.

14 Dina M. Siddiqi, 'Taslima Nasreen and Others: The Contest over Gender in Bangladesh', in Herbert L. Bodman and Heyereh Tohidi (eds), *Women in Muslim Societies: Diversity Within Unity* (Boulder, Colorado: Lynne Rienner, 1998), pp. 208–9. Santi Rosario in *Purity and Communal Boundaries: Women and Social Change in a Bangladeshi Village* (Sydney: Allen and Unwin, 1992), pp. 104–5 quotes figures of 200,000–400,000 rapes.

15 Bangladesh National Women Lawyers' Association, *Survey in the Area of Child and Woman Trafficking* (Dhaka, 1997), pp. 36–7.

16 Bangladesh National Women Lawyers' Association, *Survey in the Area of Child and Woman Trafficking*, p. 33.

17 Marjorie Muecke, 'Mother Sold Food, Daughter Sells Her Body: The Cultural Continuity of Prostitution', *Social Science and Medicine*, Vol 35, 1992, pp. 891–6.

18 Joint Women's Programme, *Banhi: Prostitution with Religious Sanction. The Devadasi Problem, Venkatasani/Jogini and the Basavi Cult*, Third edition (Delhi, 1988). I am also indebted to Prithi Patak of Prerana, Mumbai, for her detailed explanation of the *devadasi* system and its impact upon prostitution in Kamatipura.

19 Thomas Cox, *The Badi: Prostitution as a Social Norm Among an Untouchable Caste of West Nepal* (unpublished manuscript, undated).

20 I am indebted for these insights to discussions with Emma Porio of Ateneo de Manila University and Amparita S. Sta. Maria of the Ateneo Human Rights Centre, Manila.

21 Arno Schmitt and Jehoeda Sofer (eds), *Sexuality and Eroticism Among Males in Moslem Societies* (New York: Haworth Press, 1992), p. 3.

22 Afiya Shehrbano Zia, *Sex Crime in the Islamic Context: Rape, Class and Gender in Pakistan* (Lahore: ASR Publications, 1994), p. 15.

23 Fatima Mernissi, *Beyond the Veil: Male–Female Dynamics in a Modern Muslim Society* (New York: John Wiley, 1975), p. 14.

24 For fascinating analysis of this, see Maria Jaschok and Suzanne Miers (eds), *Women and Chinese Patriarchy: Submission, Servitude and Escape* (London: Zed Press, 1994), and Maria Jaschok, *Concubines and Bondservants: The Social History of a Chinese Custom* (London: Zed Press, 1988).

25 Gail Hershatter, *Dangerous Pleasures: Prostitution and Modernity in Twentieth-Century Shanghai* (Berkeley: University of California Press, 1997), pp. 196–7.

26 Xia Peijun, 'Country Report on China'. Paper presented at the Regional Meeting of the Coalition Against Trafficking in Women, Dhaka, Bangladesh, June 1998.

27 Lin Lean Lim (ed), *The Sex Sector: The Economic and Social Bases of Prostitution in Southeast Asia* (Geneva: International Labour Organisation, 1998), p. 29.

28 Annuska Derks, *Trafficking of Vietnamese Women and Children to Cambodia* (Geneva: International Organisation for Migration, 1998), p. 9.

29 National Commission for Women, *The Velvet Blouse* (New Delhi: Government of India, 1997), p. 9.

30 Siriporn Skrobanek, *Traffic in Women: Human Realities of the International Sex Trade* (London: Zed Books, 1997), p. 34.

31 National Commission for Women, *Societal Violence on Women and Children in Prostitution* (New Delhi: Government of India, 1996), p. 12.

32 UNICEF, *A Situation Analysis of Sex Work and Trafficking in Nepal With Reference to Children* (Kathmandu, June 1998), pp. 19–20, 36.

33 UNICEF, *A Situation Analysis*, pp. 51, 56.

34 UNICEF, *A Situation Analysis*, p. 59.

35 UNICEF, *Children and Women of Nepal: A Situation Analysis 1992* (Kathmandu: UNICEF, National Planning Commission, Government of Nepal, 1992), p. 64

36 Interview with Jackie Pollock, EMPOWER, Chiang Mai, Thailand.

37 Kritaya Archavanitkul, *Trafficking in Children for Labour Exploitation including Child Prostitution in the Mekong Delta* (Bangkok: Institute for Population and Social Research, Mahidol University, ILO-IPEC, July 1998), p. 34.

38 Mr He Zhixiong, Yunnan Academy of Social Sciences, speaking at a seminar in Mae Sai, Thailand, November 1997.

39 Archavanitkul, *Trafficking in Children*, p. 28.

40 Archavanitkul, *Trafficking in Children*, p. 3.

41 International Movement Against All Forms of Discrimination and Racism, *Trafficking in Women in Asia: A Reference Manual for Public Officials and Private Citizens* (Tokyo, undated), p. 12.

42 Skrobanek, *Traffic in Women*, p. 74.

43 Than-Dam Truong, *Sex, Money and Morality*, p. 74.

44 I am indebted to Sompop Jantraka of the Daughters' Education Programme Mae Sai for his observations on these points.

45 *Girl Trafficking in Sindhupalchowk: A Situation Analysis Report on Mahankal and Inchowk Village Development Committee* (ABC Nepal, undated), p. 6.

46 Child Workers in Nepal (CWIN), 'The Road to Bombay', in *Voices of Child Workers* (Kathmandu, December 1992), p. 52.

47 Ecumenical Council on Third World Tourism, *Caught in Modern Slavery: Tourism and Child Prostitution in Asia* (Bangkok, 1992), p. 41.

48 Warunee Fongkaew, 'Sexuality and Gender Norms Among Thai Teenagers', Paper presented at the Regional Workshop on the Social Sciences and Reproductive Health, Karnchanaburi, Thailand, July 1996 pp. 3–4.

49 Archavanitkul, *Trafficking in Children*, p. 69.

50 Lin Lean Lim, *The Sex Sector*, p. 39.

51 In conversation with Salma Ali, Director of the Bangladesh National Women Lawyers' Association, Dhaka, Bangladesh.

52 Lin Lean Lim, *The Sex Sector*, p. 3.

53 UNICEF, *A Situation Analysis*, p. 91.

54 Department of Epidemiology, All India Institute of Hygiene and Public Health, 'Assessment of the Sex Trade in Calcutta and Howrah', undated, p. 52.

55 I am grateful for discussions with Indrani Sinha and the staff of Sanlaap, Calcutta, for this information.

56 S.D. Punekar and Kamala Rao, *A Study of Prostitution in Bombay: With Reference to Family Background* (Mumbai: Lalvani Publishing House, 1962).

57 Gracy Fernandes, 'Report on the Rescue of Commercial Sex Workers', paper presented at the Regional Meeting on the Trafficking in Women, Forced Labour and Slavery-Like Practices in Asia and the Pacific, Bangkok, February 1997. Organised by the Global Alliance Against the Traffic in Women.

58 Lin Lean Lim, *The Sex Sector* , pp. 147–9.

59 *Far Eastern Economic Review*, 29 April 1999.

Chapter Three: The Agents

1 National Commission for Women, *The Velvet Blouse*, p. 3.

2 Rita Rozario, *Trafficking in Women and Children in India* (New Delhi: Uppal Publishing House, 1986), p. 117.

3 UNICEF, *A Situation Analysis*, p. 68.

4 UNICEF, *A Situation Analysis*, p. 86.

5 UNICEF, *A Situation Analysis*, p. 87.

6 I am indebted for these observations to Sr Fernandes of St Catherine's Home, Mumbai, which operates a shelter for girls in distress and those escaping prostitution.

7 Committed Communities Development Trust, Mumbai. Draft report on the development of brothel-based sex work in Mumbai, 1999.

8 In conversation with I.A. Rehman, Chairman of the Pakistan Commission for Human Rights, Lahore.

9 Skrobanek, *Traffic in Women*, p. 30.

10 Archavanitkul, *Trafficking in Children*, pp. 46–67.

11 Foundation for Women, *Our Lives Our Stories* (Bangkok, 1995), pp. 71–3.

12 In conversation with the staff of EMPOWER, Chiang Mai and Mae Sai.

13 I am indebted to the staff of the World Vision STD/HIV intervention programme in Mae Sai for this information.

14 Archavanitkul, *Trafficking in Children*, p. iii.

15 In conversation with Chanthol Oung, Director, Cambodian Women's Crisis Centre.

16 Cambodian Women's Crisis Centre, *Annual Report 1997–1998*, Phnom Penh, p. 22.

17 International Organisation for Migration and the Global Alliance Against the Traffic in Women, *Qualitative Survey of Brothels on the Thai–Cambodian Border*, 1998.

18 In conversation with the staff and women of HELP Asian Women's Shelter, Tokyo, Japan.

Chapter Four: Seasoning

1 Information from the staff of Prerana, Mumbai.

2 Information from the staff of the Joint Women's Programme, Delhi.

3 Interviews with the staff of the World Vision HIV/Aids intervention programme, Mae Sai, Thailand.

4 This is an unlikely price for one girl but may have been the cost of two. Even so, it is unusually high.

5 Archavanitkul, *Trafficking in Children*, p. 44.

 6 Archavanitkul, *Trafficking in Children*, p. 48.

 7 M.N. Islam and H.K.M. Yusuf, 'Fertility and Reproductive Health Status of Married Adolescents in Rural Bangladesh', unpublished paper, 1990.

 8 National Commission for Women, *The Velvet Blouse*, p. 23.

 9 K.K. Mukherjee *et al.*, *Child Prostitution in Rajasthan* (New Delhi: National Commission for Women, Government of India, 1997).

10 Salma Ali, 'Children in Prostitution/ Children of Prostituted Women'. Paper presented at the regional meeting of the Coalition Against the Traffic in Women. Dhaka, Bangladesh, 25–9 January 1999, p. 8.

11 Estimates based on interviews with Chanthol Oung, Executive Director of the Cambodian Women's Crisis Center, Men Sedtharoat, Director, Agir pour les Femmes en Situation Précaire, Phnom Penh, and Yim Po, Director, Cambodian Center for the Protection of Children's Rights.

12 Lin Lean Lim, *The Sex Sector*, p. 89.

13 UNICEF, *A Situation Analysis*, p. xiv.

14 UNICEF, *A Situation Analysis*, p. xv.

15 Lin Lean Lim, *The Sex Sector*, p. 43.

16 Lin Lean Lim, *The Sex Sector*, p. 144.

17 Department of Epidemiology, 'Assessment of the Sex Trade in Calcutta and Howrah', p. 11.

18 Department of Epidemiology, 'Assessment of the Sex Trade in Calcutta and Howrah', p. 52.

Chapter Five: The Customers

 1 The best books on the subject are Indrani Sinha and Carolyn Sleightholme, *Guilty Without Trial: Women in the Sex Trade in Calcutta* (New Brunswick, New Jersey: Rutgers University Press, 1996), Siriporn Skrobanek, *Traffic in Women: Human Realities of the International Sex Trade* (London: Zed Books, 1997), Rita Rozario, *Trafficking in Women and Children in India* (New Delhi: Uppal Publishing House, 1984), Ryan Bishop and Lillian S. Robinson, *Night Market: Sexual Cultures and the Thais Economic Miracle* (London: Routledge, 1998), Jeremy Seabrook, *Travels in the Skin Trade: Tourism and the Sex Industry* (London: Pluto Press, 1996). On Japan, two excellent books related to the sex industry are Anne Allison, *Nightwork: Sexuality, Pleasure and Corporate Masculinity in a Tokyo Hostess Club* (University of Chicago Press, 1994) and Anne

Allison, *Permitted and Prohibited Desires: Mothers, Comics and Censorship in Japan* (Boulder, Colorado: Westview Press, 1996).

2 Duang Pratheep Foundation, 'Klong Toey Aids Control Project', Bangkok, 1998, p. 14.

3 Hanna Phan and Lorraine Patterson, *Men are Gold, Women are Cloth* (Phnom Penh: CARE Inernational, 1994).

4 Archavanitkul, *Trafficking in Children*, p. 59.

5 Reay Tannahill, *Sex in History* (New York: Stein & Day, 1992), p. 357.

6 Alfred C. Kinsey *et. al.*, *Sexual Behaviour in the Human Male* (London: W.B. Saunders, 1948).

7 Samuel S. Janus and Cynthia L. Janus, *The Janus Report on Sexual Behaviour* (New York: John Wiley, 1993), p. 348.

8 *Guardian*, 26 September 1997.

9 Sinha and Sleightholme, *Guilty Without Trial*, p. 10.

10 Cited in Chris Beyrer, *War in the Blood: Sex, Politics and Aids in Southeast Asia* (London: Zed Books, 1998), p. 14.

11 World Health Organisation and Joint United Nations Programme on HIV/Aids, *Report on the Global HIV/AIDS Epidemic*, June 1998.

12 World Health Organisation and UNAIDS, *AIDS Epidemic Update*, December 1998.

13 World Health Organisation and UNAIDS, *India: Epidemiological Fact Sheet on HIV/AIDS and Sexually Transmitted Diseases*, June 1998.

14 Cynthia Enloe, 'It Takes Two', in Sturdevant and Stoltzfuz, *Let the Good Times Roll*, p. 25.

15 Sinha and Sleightholme, *Guilty Without Trial*, p. 113.

16 Phan and Patterson, *Men are Gold, Women are Cloth*.

17 Phan and Patterson, *Men are Gold, Women are Cloth*.

18 The best analysis is by Sudhir Kakar, *The Inner World: A Psycho-analytic Study of Childhood and Society in India* (Delhi: Oxford University Press, 1981). On Japan see an interesting and very readable treatment by Ian Buruma, *A Japanese Mirror: Heroes and Villains of Japanese Culture* (London: Cape, 1984).

19 Kakar, *The Inner World*, p . 87–9.

20 See Anne Allison, *Permitted and Prohibited Desires*, for an excellent analysis of the socialisation process on the construction of Japanese men's sexuality.

21 I am grateful to Dr Norihiko Kuwayama of the Department of Neuro-Psychiatry, Yamagata University, for sharing with me the benefit of his

experience in dealing with the psycho-sexual problems of Japanese marriages.

22 Peter N. Dale, *The Myth of Japanese Uniqueness* (Croom Helm, 1986), p. 160.

23 Allison, *Permitted and Prohibited Desires.*

24 Anne Allison, *Nightwork*, p. 175.

25 Schmitt and Sofer, *Sexuality and Eroticism Among Males in Moslem Societies*, p. 3.

Chapter Six: The Management

1 T. Yunomae, 'Commodified Sex: Japan's Pornographic Culture', AMPO, Vol 24-4–Vol 26-1:55-9, 1995, cited in Marjan Wijers and Lin Lap-Chew, *Trafficking in Women, Forced Labour and Slavery-like Practices in Marriage, Domestic Labour and Prostitution*, p. 55.

2 Pasuk Phongpaichit, Sungsidh Piriyarangsan and Nualnoi Treerat, *Guns, Girls, Gambling, Ganja: Thailand's Illegal Economy and Public Policy* (Chiang Mai: Silkworm Books, 1998), p. 8.

3 Indrani Sinha and Anindit Roy Chowdhury, 'Child Trafficking and Prostitution', unpublished paper.

4 Foundation for Women, *Our Lives, Our Stories* (Bangkok, 1995), pp. 29–31.

5 International Organisation for Migration, *Trafficking in Women to Japan for Sexual Exploitation: A Survey on the Case of Filipino Women* (Geneva, 1997), p. 37.

6 Based on a presentation by, and an interview with, Mumtaz Begum and the women of Kandupatti Council of Evicted Sex Workers, Dhaka, Bangladesh.

7 'Tanbazar Alert', report by the Network of Sex Work Projects, August 1999.

8 Cited in Jacqui Dunn and Tuol Kork Dike Clinic Staff, 'Demographics, Working Practices and AIDS Awareness of Commercial Sex Workers in Tuol Kork Dike Area', *Cambodia Disease Bulletin* No.6, May 1995, p. 17.

9 Ishrat Shamim and Farah Kabir, *Child Trafficking: The Underlying Dynamics* (Dhaka: Centre for Women and Children's Studies, 1998), p. 40.

10 In conversation with Professor Ishrat Shamim, University of Dhaka.

11 National Commission for Women, *Societal Violence*, p. 14.

12 I am indebted to Sadhana Mukherjee, Secretary of the Durbar Mahila

Samanwaya Samiti, Calcutta (a sex workers' organisation), for her description of brothel hierarchies in Sonagachi.

13 S.A. Lalitha and S.C.N. Shalini, *Women Soliciting Change* (New Delhi: India Social Institute and the Joint Women's Programme, 1996), p. 24.

14 'Thai Girls Rescued from a Kuala Lumpur Brothel', Global Alliance Against the Traffic in Women Newsletter, October–December 1997.

15 In conversation with the staff of HELP Asian Women's Shelter, Tokyo, Japan.

16 In conversation with Suryang Janyam, EMPOWER, Bangkok.

17 International Organisation for Migration, *Trafficking in Women to Japan for Sexual Exploitation*, p. 36.

Chapter Seven: The Law

1 Zia, *Sex Crime in the Islamic Context*, p. 15.

2 Government of Pakistan, *Report of the Commission for Inquiry for Women*, (Islamabad, August 1997), p. 72.

3 Marjan Wijers and Lin Lap-Chew, *Trafficking in Women, Forced Labour and Slavery-like Practices*, p. 103.

4 Yayori Matsui, *Women in the New Asia* (London: Zed Books, 1999), p. 18.

5 In conversation with Yayori Matsui, April 1998.

6 National Commission on the Role of Filipino Women, *Philippines Plan for Gender Responsive Development 1995–2025* (Manila: Government of the Philippines, 1995), p. 305.

7 *Financial Times*, 1–2 April 2000.

8 I am grateful to War Against Rape in Lahore, Pakistan, for information on its experience in working with the victims of rape.

9 Human Rights Watch/Asia, *Rape for Profit: Trafficking of Nepali Girls and Women to India's Brothels* (New York, 1996), p. 57.

10 Gauri Pradhan, 'The Road to Bombay: Forgotten Women' in ABC Nepal, *Red Light Traffic: The Trade in Nepali Girls* (Kathmandu, 1996), p. 38.

11 Lin Lean Lim, *The Sex Sector*.

12 Annuska Derks, *Trafficking of Vietnamese Women and Children to Cambodia* (Geneva: International Organisation for Migration, 1998), p. 35.

13 National Commission for Women, *Societal Violence*, p. 14.

14 Shamim and Kabir, *Child Trafficking: The Underlying Dynamics* (Dhaka: Centre for Women and Children's Studies, 1998), p. 27.

15 Centre for Women and Children's Studies, *Trafficking and Prostitution* (Dhaka, April 1997), p. 14.

16 UNICEF, *A Situation Analysis*, p. xi.

17 Asia Watch Report, *Double Jeopardy*, January 1991.

18 Government of Pakistan, *Report of the Commission of Inquiry for Women* (Islamabad, August 1997), p. 83.

19 Human Rights Commission of Pakistan, *State of Human Rights in 1997* (Lahore, 1998), p. 185.

Chapter Eight: Life and Death

1 Global Alliance Against the Traffic in Women, International Organisation for Migration and the Cambodian Women's Development Association, *Cambodian and Vietnamese Sex Workers Along the Thai–Cambodian Border*, March 1997, p. 12.

2 Virginia A. Miralo, Celia O. Carlos, Aida Fulleros Santos, *Women Entertainers in Angeles and Olongapo: A Survey Report* (Manila: WEDPRO, 1990), pp. 16–19.

3 Centre for the Protection of Children's Rights, *Preliminary Survey on Regional Child Trafficking for Prostitution in Thailand* (Bangkok, 1995), p. 47.

4 UNICEF, *A Situation Analysis*, p. 74.

5 UNICEF, *A Situation Analysis*, p. 75.

6 For an excellent discussion of Aids awareness campaigns in Japan and their impact upon the commercial sex industry see Sandra Buckley, 'The Foreign Devil Returns: Packaging Sexual Practice and Risk in Contemporary Japan', in Lenore Manderson and Margaret Jolly, *Sites of Desire, Economies of Pleasure: Sexualities in Asia and the Pacific* (University of Chicago Press, 1997).

7 I am indebted to the ASHA Project of Kamatipura, Mumbai for the opportunity to visit the project and for the details on HIV sample surveys.

8 UNICEF, *Towards a Better Future* (Phnom Penh, 1996), p. 92.

9 In conversation with the staff of the World Vision HIV/STD intervention programme, Mae Sai, Thailand.

10 Cambodian Women's Development Association, *Knowledge, Attitudes and Behaviour Among Commercial Sex Workers in Phnom Penh, Cambodia* (September–October 1995), p. 29.

11 UNICEF, *Towards a Better Future*, p. 148.

12 National Commission for Women, *Societal Violence*, p. 15.

13 UNICEF *A Situation Analysis*, p. 72.

Chapter Nine: The Shame

1 Beyrer, *War in the Blood*, p. 27.

2 Skrobanek, *Traffic in Women*, p. 92.

3 Archavanitkul, *Trafficking in Children*, p. 59.

4 Archavanitkul, *Trafficking in Children*, p. 57.

5 Gracy Fernandes, 'Report on the Rescue of Commercial Sex Workers', p. 15.

6 Phan and Patterson, *Men are Gold, Women are Cloth*, p. 19.

7 Judith R. Walkowitz, *Prostitution and Victorian Society* (Cambridge University Press, 1980), pp. 17, 247.

8 Hershatter, *Dangerous Pleasures*, p. 203.

9 Frederick K. Grittner, *White Slavery: Myth, Ideology and American Law* (London: Garland, 1990), pp. 168–70.

SELECT BIBLIOGRAPHY

Official Reports by Governments and International Agencies

Acharaya, Usha D. *Country Report on Trafficking in Children and Their Exploitation in Prostitution and Other Intolerable Forms of Labour in Nepal* (Kathmandu: International Labour Organisation, 1997).

Archavanitkul, Kritaya *Trafficking in Children for Labour Exploitation including Prostitution in the Mekong Delta* (Bangkok: Institute for Population and Social Research, Mahidol University/ILO-IPEC, July 1998).

Bangladesh National Women Lawyers' Association *Survey in the Area of Child and Woman Trafficking* (Dhaka, 1997)

Caouette, Therese M. *Needs Assessment on Cross-border Trafficking in Women and Children: The Mekong Sub-region* (Bangkok: UN Working Group on Trafficking in the Mekong Sub-region, 1998).

Derks, Annuska *Trafficking of Vietnamese Women and Children to Cambodia* (Geneva: International Organisation for Migration, 1998).

Government of Pakistan *Report of the Commission for Inquiry for Women* (Islamabad, August 1997).

Government of Pakistan *Combatting Child Trafficking, Sexual Exploitation and Involvement of Children in Intolerable Forms of Child Labour: Country Report on Pakistan* (Islamabad, 1998).

International Organisation for Migration, Global Alliance Against the Traffic in Women, and the Cambodian Women's Development Association *Cambodian and Vietnamese Sex Workers Along the Thai–Cambodian Border* (March 1997).

International Organisation for Migration *Trafficking in Women to Japan for Sexual Exploitation: A Survey on the Case of Filipino Women* (Geneva, 1997).

International Organisation for Migration and the Global Alliance Against Trafficking in Women *Qualitative Survey of Brothels on the Thai–Cambodian Border* (1998).

Lim, Lin Lean (ed) *The Sex Sector: The Economic and Social Bases of Prostitution in Southeast Asia* (Geneva: International Labour Organisation, 1998).

Mukherjee, K.K. *et al. Child Prostitution in Rajasthan* (New Delhi: National Commission for Women, Government of India, 1997).

National Commission for Women *Societal Violence on Women and Children in Prostitution* (New Delhi: Government of India, 1996).

National Commission for Women *The Velvet Blouse* (New Delhi: Government of India, 1997).

National Commission on the Role of Filipino Women *Philippines Plan for Gender-Responsive Development 1995–2025* (Manila: Government of the Philippines, 1995).

UNICEF *Children and Women of Nepal: A Situation Analysis* (Kathmandu: UNICEF and the National Planning Commission, His Majesty's Government of Nepal, 1992).

UNICEF *Towards a Better Future* (Phnom Penh, 1996).

UNICEF *A Situation Analysis of Sex Work and Trafficking in Nepal With Reference to Children* (Kathmandu, June 1998).

Reports by Non-Governmental Organisations

ABC Nepal *Girl Trafficking in Sindhupalchowk: A Situation Analysis Report on Mahankal and Inchowk Village Development Committee,* (Kathmandu, Undated).

Asia Watch Report *Double Jeopardy* (January 1991).

Cambodian Women's Crisis Centre *Annual Report 1997–1998* (Phnom Penh).

Cambodian Women's Development Association *Knowledge, Attitudes and Behaviour Among Commercial Sex Workers in Phnom Penh, Cambodia* (Phnom Penh, September–October 1995).

Cambodian Women's Development Association *'Selling Noodles', The Traffic in Women and Children and Cambodia* (Phnom Penh, 1996).

Centre for the Protection of Children's Rights *Preliminary Survey on Regional Child Trafficking for Prostitution in Thailand* (Bangkok, 1995).

Centre for Women and Children's Studies *Trafficking and Prostitution* (Dhaka, April,1997).

Child Workers in Nepal (CWIN) 'The Road to Bombay' in *Voices of Child Workers* (Kathmandu, December 1992).

Duang Pratheep Foundation, 'Klong Toey Aids Control Project' (Bangkok,1998).

Ecumenical Council on Third World Tourism *Caught in Modern Slavery: Tourism and Child Prostitution in Asia* (Bangkok, 1992).

Foundation for Women *Our Lives Our Stories* (Bangkok, 1995).

Gauri Pradhan 'The Road to Bombay: Forgotten Women' in ABC Nepal *Red Light Traffic: The Trade in Nepali Girls* (Kathmandu, 1996).

Global Alliance Against the Traffic in Women 'Thai Girls Rescued from a Kuala Lumpur Brothel', Newsletter, October–December 1997.

Human Rights Commission of Pakistan *State of Human Rights in 1997* (Lahore, 1998).

Human Rights Watch *The Human Rights Watch Global Report on Women's Human Rights* (New York, 1995).

Human Rights Watch/Asia *Rape for Profit: Trafficking of Nepali Girls and Women to India's Brothels* (New York, 1996).

International Movement Against All Forms of Discrimination and Racism (IMADR) *Trafficking in Women in Asia: A Reference Manual for Public Officials and Private Citizens* (Tokyo, Undated).

Joint Women's Programme *Banhi: Prostitution with Religious Sanction. The Devadasi Problem, Venkatasani/Jogini and the Basavi Cult* Third Edition (Delhi, 1988).

Lalitha, S.A. and S.C.N Shalini *Women Soliciting Change* (New Delhi: India Social Institute and the Joint Women's Programme, 1996).

Lawyers for Human Rights and Legal Aid *Trafficking of Women and Children in Pakistan: The Flesh Trade Report 1995–1996* (Karachi, 1996).

Miralo, Virginia A., Celia O. Carlos, and Aida Fulleros Santos *Women Entertainers in Angeles and Olongapo: A Survey Report* (Manila: WEDPRO, 1990).

Phan, Hanna and Lorraine Patterson *Men are Gold, Women are Cloth* (Phnom Penh: CARE International, 1993).

Physicians for Human Rights *Commercial Sexual Exploitation of Women and Children in Cambodia. Personal Narratives: A Psychological Perspective* (Boston, 1997).

Shamim, Ishrat and Farah Kabir *Child Trafficking: The Underlying Dynamics* (Dhaka: Centre for Women and Children's Studies, 1998).

World Vision *The Commercial Sexual Exploitation of Street Children* (Milton Keynes, undated).

Newspaper and Magazine Articles

Frederick, John 'Reconstructing Gita', *Himal*, Vol 11, No 10, October 1998.

Guardian 26 September 1997.
Financial Times 1–2 April 2000.

Journals, Conference Proceedings and Miscellaneous

Ali, Salma 'Children in Prostitution/Children of Prostituted Women'. Paper presented at the Regional Meeting of the Coalition Against the Trafficking of Women. Dhaka, Bangladesh, 25–9 January 1999.

Cox, Thomas *The Badi: Prostitution as a Social Norm Among an Untouchable Caste of West Nepal* (unpublished paper, undated).

Department of Epidemiology, All India Institute of Hygiene and Public Health, 'Assessment of the Sex Trade in Calcutta and Howrah', (Calcutta, undated).

Dunn, Jacqui and Toul Kork Dike Clinic Staff 'Demographics, Working Practices and AIDS Awareness of Commercial Sex Workers in Tuol Kork Dike Area', *Cambodia Disease Bulletin*. No 6, May 1995.

Fernandes, Gracy 'Report on the Rescue of Commercial Sex Workers'. Paper presented at the Regional Meeting on the Trafficking in Women, Forced Labour and Slavery-like Practices in Asia and the Pacific, Bangkok, February 1997. Organised by the Global Alliance Against the Traffic in Women.

Fongkaew, Warunee 'Sexuality and Gender Norms Among Thai Teenagers'. Paper presented at the Regional Workshop on the Social Sciences and Reproductive Health, Karnchanaburi, (Thailand, July 1996).

Islam, M.N. and H.K.M. Yusuf 'Fertility and Reproductive Health Status of Married Adolescents in Rural Bangladesh' (unpublished paper, 1990).

Muecke, Marjorie 'Mother Sold Food, Daughter Sells Her Body: The Cultural Continuity of Prostitution', *Social Science and Medicine*, Vol 35, 1992, pp. 891–6.

Sinha, Indrani and Anindit Roy Chowdhury 'Child Trafficking and Prostitution' (unpublished paper, undated).

Books (and chapters within books)

Allison, Anne *Nightwork: Sexuality, Pleasure and Corporate Masculinity in a Tokyo Hostess Club* (University of Chicago Press, 1994).

Allison, Anne *Permitted and Prohibited Desires: Mothers, Comics and Censorship in Japan* (Boulder, Colorado: Westview Press, 1996).

Altink, Sietske *Stolen Lives: Trading Women into Sex and Slavery* (London: Scarlet Press, 1995).

Barry, Kathleen *Female Sexual Slavery* (New York University Press, 1979).

Barry, Kathleen *The Prostitution of Sexuality* (New York University Press, 1995).

Beyrer, Chris *War in the Blood: Sex, Politics and Aids in Southeast Asia* (London: Zed Books, 1998).

Bishop, Ryan and Lillian S. Robinson *Night Market: Sexual Cultures and the Thai Economic Miracle* (London: Routledge, 1998).

Buckley, Sandra 'The Foreign Devil Returns: Packaging Sexual Practice and Risk in Contemporary Japan', in Lenore Manderson and Margaret Jolly *Sites of Desire, Economies of Pleasure: Sexualities in Asia and the Pacific* (University of Chicago Press, 1997).

Buruma, Ian *A Japanese Mirror: Heroes and Villains of Japanese Culture* (London: Cape, 1984).

Cook, Nerida 'Thailand: "Dutiful Daughters" and Estranged Sisters', in Krishna Sen and Maila Stivens *Gender and Power in Affluent Asia* (London: Routledge, 1998).

Dale, Peter N. *The Myth of Japanese Uniqueness* (Croom Helm, 1986).

D'Cunha, Jean *The Legalisation of Prostitution: A Sociological Enquiry into the Laws in Relation to Prostitution in India and the West* (Bangalore: Wordmakers, 1991).

Enloe, Cynthia 'It Takes Two', in Sandra Pollock Sturdevant and Brenda Stoltzfuz, *Let the Good Times Roll: Prostitution and the US Military in Asia* (New York: The New Press, 1992).

Evans, Harriet *Women and Sexuality in China: Dominant Discourses of Female Sexuality and Gender Since 1949* (Cambridge: Polity Press, 1997).

Grittner, Frederick K. *White Slavery: Myth, Ideology and American Law* (London: Garland, 1990).

Haq, Mahbub ul *Human Development in South Asia, 1997* (Oxford: Oxford University Press, 1997).

Hershatter, Gail *Dangerous Pleasures: Prostitution and Modernity in Twentieth-Century Shanghai* (Berkeley: University of California Press, 1997).

Hicks, George *The Comfort Women: Japan's Brutal Regime of Enforced Prostitution in the Second World War* (New York: W.W. Norton, 1995).

Howard, Keith (ed) *True Stories of the Korean Comfort Women* (New York: Cassell, 1995).

Janus, Samuel S. and Cynthia L. Janus *The Janus Report on Sexual Behaviour* (New York: John Wiley, 1993).

Jaschok, Maria *Concubines and Bondservants: The Social History of a Chinese Custom* (London: Zed Press, 1988).

Jaschok, Maria and Suzanne Miers (eds) *Women and Chinese Patriarchy: Submission, Servitude and Escape* (London: Zed Press, 1994).

Kakar, Sudhir *The Inner World: A Psycho-analytic Study of Childhood and Society in India* (Delhi: Oxford University Press, 1981).

Kempadoo, Kamala and Jo Doezema *Global Sex Workers: Rights, Resistance and Redefinition* (London: Routledge, 1998).

Kinsey, Alfred C. *et al. Sexual Behaviour in the Human Male* (London: W.B. Saunders, 1948).

Mandelbaum, David G. *Women's Seclusion and Men's Honor: Sex Roles in North India, Bangladesh and Pakistan* (Tucson: University of Arizona Press, 1988).

Manderson, Lenore and Margaret Jolly *Sites of Desire, Economies of Pleasure: Sexualities in Asia and the Pacific* (University of Chicago Press, 1997).

Matsui, Yayori *Women in the New Asia* (London: Zed Books, 1999).

Mernissi, Fatima *Beyond the Veil: Male-Female Dynamics in a Modern Muslim Society* (New York: John Wiley, 1975).

Moon, Katharine H.S. *Sex Among Allies: Military Prostitution in US–Korea Relations* (New York: Columbia University Press, 1997).

Mumtaz, Khawar and Farida Shaheed *Women of Pakistan: Two Steps Forward, One Step Back* (London: Zed Press, 1987).

Phongpaichit, Pasuk, Sungsidh Piriyarangsan and Nualnoi Treerat *Guns, Girls, Gambling, Ganja: Thailand's Illegal Economy and Public Policy* (Chiang Mai: Silkworm Books, 1998).

Punekar, S.D. and Kamala Rao *A Study of Prostitution in Bombay: With Reference to Family Background* (Mumbai: Lalvani Publishing House, 1962).

Rosario, Santi *Purity and Communal Boundaries : Women and Social Change in a Bangladeshi Village* (Allen and Unwin, Sydney, 1992).

Rozario, Rita *Trafficking in Women and Children in India* (New Delhi: Uppal Publishing House, 1986).

Scambler, Graham and Annette Scambler (eds) *Rethinking Prostitution: Purchasing Sex in the 1990s* (London: Routledge, 1997).

Schmitt, Arno and Jehoeda Sofer (eds) *Sexuality and Eroticism Among Males in Moslem Societies* (New York: Haworth Press, 1992).

Seabrook, Jeremy *Travels in the Skin Trade: Tourism and the Sex Industry* (London: Pluto Press, 1996).

Siddiqi, Dina M. 'Taslima Nasreen and Others: The Contest over Gender in Bangladesh', in Herbert L. Bodman and Heyereh Tohidi (eds) *Women in Muslim Societies: Diversity Within Unity* (Boulder, Colorado: Lynne Rienner, 1998).

Sinha, Indrani and Carolyn Sleightholme *Guilty Without Trial: Women in the Sex Trade in Calcutta* (New Brunswick, New Jersey: Rutgers University Press, 1996).

Skrobanek, Siriporn *Traffic in Women: Human Realities of the International Sex Trade* (London: Zed Books, 1997).

Sturdevant, Saundra Pollock and Brenda Stoltzfus *Let the Good Times Roll: Prostitution and the US Military in Asia* (New York: The New Press, 1992).

Tannahill, Reay *Sex in History* (New York: Stein & Day, 1992).

Truong, Thanh-Dam *Sex, Money and Morality: Prostitution and Tourism in South-East Asia* (London: Zed Books, 1990).

Walkowitz, Judith R. *Prostitution and Victorian Society* (Cambridge University Press, 1980).

White, Sarah C. *Arguing With the Crocodile: Gender and Class in Bangladesh* (Dhaka: University Press, 1992).

Wijers, Marjan and Lin Lap-Chew *Trafficking in Women, Forced Labour and Slavery-Like Practices in Marriage, Domestic Labour and Prostitution* (Utrecht: Foundation Against Trafficking in Women, 1997).

Wolf, Marjery *Women and the Family in Rural Taiwan* (Stanford, California: Stanford University Press, 1972).

Zia, Afiya Shehrbano *Sex Crime in the Islamic Context: Rape, Class and Gender in Pakistan* (Lahore: ASR Publications, 1994).